Mihir Desai was born in India and raised in Hong Kong and New Jersey. As a professor and award-winning teacher at Harvard Business School and Harvard Law School, Desai teaches finance, tax law and entrepreneurship and has recently developed an online finance course for the HBX platform. His scholarship on corporate finance, international finance and tax policy has prompted several invitations to testify before the US Congress and serves as the basis of his advisory role to leading global companies and organisations.

Praise for *The Wisdom of Finance*

"*The Wisdom of Finance* offers a thoughtful explanation of how money works that recognises how perverted the industry can be, but which also argues that 'there is great value—and there are great values—in finance' . . . This is a charming, provocative and readable book. For non-financiers, it can be a great teaching tool; for financiers, it is a badly needed rap on the knuckles, and perhaps an inspiration." *Financial Times*

"Those familiar with the world of finance will have their perspective shifted, and for the rest of us, Desai provides a welcome entry." *Boston Globe*

"Desai takes a real step towards creating a dialogue of disciplines . . . if only more people—whether financiers or academics—could combine with such finesse economic knowledge and an appreciation of the human condition." *Times Higher Education Supplement*

"This book is startling, a stunning, erudite, fascinating look at the world as we think we know it, but it's a world where all roads lead to finance, and in particular, insurance. Highly recommended." Seth Godin, author of *Purple Cow*

"A fascinating romp through history and Desai is to be commended for finding fresh examples away from the obvious reference points . . . highly original." *Money Week*

"Desai skilfully makes his subject accessible without dumbing it down." *Director* magazine

"For those of us who have long believed that the field of finance was more than a way to make a good living, Mihir Desai has written a liberating book. He shows us how an understanding of the humanities can increase our effectiveness as financial practitioners and add a dimension of joy to process." Byron R. Wien, Vice Chairman, Multi-Asset Investments, Blackstone Group

"Mihir Desai is a fortunate person: he is an expert economist who is also well-read. In this book he uses his skills to provide a fascinating new perspective on modern finance, showing how the main concepts have parallels in literature and the arts. Students of finance will learn literature, students of literature will learn finance, and everybody will learn something." Oliver Hart, 2016 Nobel Laureate in Economics

"The Wisdom of Finance is fascinating and delightful throughout. Desai explains the world of economics to those who love literature and the world of literature to those who are passionate about economics. And if you enjoy both—well, then you are in for an extra-special treat. I kept shouting aloud: 'I get it, I finally get it!' Here is a book that will make you richer in spirit—and maybe in money, too." Will Schwalbe, *New York Times* bestselling author of *The End of Your Life Book Club* and *Books for Living*

"*The Wisdom of Finance* is required reading for anyone interested in finance or in pursuing a career in the industry. Mihir eloquently traces the products, practices and services of our modern financial system to their roots while providing literary context and illustration. It's a refreshing approach to what can be a turgid topic, and it can provide practitioners with a new appreciation (and understanding) of their role in their companies, the industry, and in the broader economy." Vikram Pandit, Chairman and CEO of The Orogen Group and former CEO of Citigroup

"In *The Wisdom of Finance*, Mihir Desai masterfully achieves two goals—bringing great clarity to how finance works and why it is important, and shining a bright light on how the humanities help us to better understand our lives and world." Clayton Rose, President of Bowdoin College

"Mihir Desai brilliantly applies original lessons drawn from the world of finance to enable all of us to lead more secure, fulfilling and happy lives. Using myriad examples from historical sources and current experiences, Desai takes essential financial theories and translates them into easily understood ways to enrich and improve our lives." Bill George, former Chairman and CEO of Medtronic and author of *Discover Your True North*

"*The Wisdom of Finance* does for the global economy what Alain de Botton's *How Proust Can Change Your Life* did for French literature: it expands our idea of an obscure topic and illuminates its centrality to your everyday. This is a work of true philosophy and passion, incorporating thinkers and artists from E. O. Wilson to Jeff Koons elegantly into our understanding of how we make choices. In a chaotic world, everyone should read Mihir Desai's extraordinary debut." Lea Carpenter, author of *Eleven Days*

"*The Wisdom of Finance* is that rare book that manages to be both illuminating and truly fun to read. It puts in deeply human terms ideas that have so often become caricatured and one-dimensional. You will be glad you spent time with Mihir Desai, and you will think of several people to whom you will send this book once you've finished." Gayle Lemmon, author of *Ashley's War*

"Mihir Desai has written a thoughtful and remarkable book. It takes us not only on a functional journey about the role of finance in society, but also an ethical and social one." Rakesh Khurana, Dean of Harvard College

"A scholar who is equally at home with art, literature, contemporary culture and financial theory, Mihir Desai improbably brings these worlds together in an absorbing, personal narrative that has much to teach us about how they are deeply connected." Will Goetzmann, author of *Money Changes Everything*; Edwin J. Beinecke Professor of Finance and Management Studies; Director, International Center for Finance, Yale School of Management

"This slender but erudite treatise . . . does valuable work toward demystifying finance for laypeople and deepening the art for practitioners. Desai's approach will broaden and enrich any perspective." *Publishers Weekly*

"Mihir has written a remarkable book—he uses the humanities to demystify and humanize finance. It is a remarkable intellectual accomplishment that those within finance—and those curious about it— will enjoy deeply.' Deepak S. Parekh, Chairman, HDFC Ltd

"By linking to literature, history and philosophy, [Desai] tries to build deeper resonance. It is a daring, intriguing work, offbeat and fascinating, something both practitioners of finance and the general public can learn from." *Globe and Mail*

*The*

# WISDOM

*of*

# FINANCE

HOW *the* HUMANITIES CAN

ILLUMINATE *and* IMPROVE FINANCE

# MIHIR A. DESAI

## P
**PROFILE BOOKS**

This paperback edition published in 2018

First published in Great Britain in 2017 by
Profile Books Ltd
3 Holford Yard
Bevin Way
London
WC1X 9HD

*www.profilebooks.com*

First published in the United States of America by
Houghton Mifflin Harcourt Publishing Company
*www.hmhco.com*

3 5 7 9 10 8 6 4

Book design by Greta D. Sibley
Printed and bound in Great Britain by CPI Group (UK) Ltd, Croydon CR0 4YY

Illustration credits appear on p. 215
Excerpt from 'Two Tramps in Mud Time' from *The Poetry of Robert Frost*, edited
by Edward Conney Lathem. Copyright © 1969 by Henry Holt and Company,
copyright © 1936 by Robert Frost, copyright © 1964 by Lesley Frost Ballantine.
Used by permission of Henry Holt and Company, LLC. All rights reserved.

A CIP catalogue record for this book is available from the British Library.

ISBN 978 1 78816 005 6
eISBN 978 1 78283 422 9

*To*

TEENA, MIA, ILA,

*and*

PARVATI

Money is a kind of poetry.

    —Wallace Stevens, *Adagia* in *Opus Posthumous*

# CONTENTS

*Author's Note*   xi

*Introduction: Finance and the Good Life*   1

CHAPTER 1 The Wheel of Fortune   11

The Flitcraft Parable—The Quincunx—From Bottomry to Tontines—We Are All Insurance Companies—Wallace Stevens and *Ideas of Order*

CHAPTER 2 Risky Business   35

Lizzy Bennet as Risk Manager—If Isaac Newton Had Worked at Goldman Sachs—I Would Prefer Not To—Stephen Curry, Stringer Bell, and the Only Free Lunch in Finance—The Negative Betas of Your Life

CHAPTER 3 On Value   58

The Parable of the Talents—The Cruel Logic of Value Creation—Is Education Worth It?—Your Terminal Values—The Talents of Samuel Johnson and John Milton—Alpha-Beta Soup—Have You Financed?

CHAPTER 4 Becoming a Producer   75

Bialystock and Bloom on Corporate Governance—Apple and Tootsie Roll—A Daisy Chain of Principals and Agents—Vyse vs. Emerson—Mel Brooks on Freud—A Blank Sheet of Paper

CHAPTER 5 No Romance Without Finance 97

*Working Girl*—The Dowry Fund of Renaissance Italy—The
M&A Pages—A May-December Romance—Mergers and
Marriages Gone Wrong—General Motors and Fisher Body—
Romance Without Finance

CHAPTER 6 Living the Dream 120

Adam Smith vs. Jeremy Bentham on Leverage—The Hooks
of Gratitude and Obligation—Jeff Koons vs. George Orwell
on Leverage—Mr. Stevens and Debt Overhang—The Power of
Commitments—Popeye in Las Vegas

CHAPTER 7 Failing Forward 142

The Man Who Could Have Been on the $10 Bill—The
Bankruptcy Act of 1800—An Automatic Stay—A Strategic
Bankruptcy at American Airlines—Agamemnon, Arjuna,
Hecuba, and Bankruptcy

CHAPTER 8 Why Everyone Hates Finance 161

The Temptation of Pakhom—The Lobster and the Squid—More
and More Is Less and Less—The Asshole Theory of Finance—
Alexandra Bergson as Finance Hero

*Afterword* 175
*Acknowledgments* 179
*Notes* 182
*Illustration Credits* 215
*Index* 216

# AUTHOR'S NOTE

This book is not about the latest study that will help you make money in the stock market or that will nudge you into saving more. And it's not about the optimal allocation of your retirement assets.

This book is about humanizing finance by bridging the divide between finance and literature, history, philosophy, music, movies, and religion.

This book is about how the philosopher Charles Sanders Peirce and the poet Wallace Stevens are insightful guides to the ideas of risk and insurance, and how Lizzy Bennet of *Pride and Prejudice* and Violet Effingham of *Phineas Finn* are masterful risk managers. This book looks to the parable of the talents and John Milton for insight on value creation and valuation; to the financing of dowries in Renaissance Florence and the movie *Working Girl* for insight on mergers; to the epic downfall of the richest man in the American colonies and to the Greek tragedies for insight on bankruptcy and financial distress; and to Jeff Koons's career and Mr. Stevens of *Remains of the Day* for insight on the power and peril of leverage.

In short, this book is about how the humanities can illuminate the central ideas of finance. But this book is also about how the ideas of finance provide surprising insight on common aspects of our humanity.

So, this book is also about how understanding insurance can help us make sense of and confront the disorder of the world; how understanding the capital asset pricing model can allow us to realize the value of relationships and the nature of unconditional love; how understanding value creation can help us live a meaningful life; how understanding bankruptcy can help us react to failure; and how appreciating theories of leverage can teach us about the value of commitments.

For readers unfamiliar with, but curious about, finance, this book attempts to outline the main ideas of finance without a single equation or graph — and only with stories. I'm always struck by how intimidating finance is to many of my students. There's a reason for this — some people in finance want to intimidate other people. By attaching stories to the ideas of finance, previously intimidating material will hopefully become accessible and fun. For concerned citizens or aspiring professionals, finance has never been more important — and ignorance of it has never been more costly. At a minimum, when someone you know starts going on about options, leverage, or alpha generation, you'll know what they're talking about.

For students or practitioners of finance, this book allows them to revisit the big ideas of finance in a fresh, different way. Many practitioners of finance I see in my classroom were taught finance in a mechanistic way that has led to a fragile understanding of the fundamental ideas. When I probe them for the underlying intuitions, their understanding of the formulae helps little, and they can struggle to relay the conceptual underpinnings of what they do. By seeing these same ideas in a completely different way than you're used to, you will deepen your understanding and, most importantly, your intuitions.

For those readers engaged in finance deeply, the book holds one final promise. Your endeavors are routinely maligned today, and it can be difficult to make sense of one's life when your work is characterized in such a negative way. But there is great value — and there are great values — in finance. By reconnecting to that value — and those values — perhaps you can understand your life's work as a meaningful extension of the values you hold dear. At the end of his poem about a recreational woodchopper, "Two Tramps in Mud Time," Robert Frost captures vividly how important it is for us to understand our work and our lives as an integrated whole.

> My object in living is to unite
> My avocation and my vocation
> As my two eyes make one in sight.
> Only where love and need are one,
> And the work is play for mortal stakes,
> Is the deed ever really done
> For Heaven and the future's sakes.

Most ambitiously, this book endeavors to improve the practice of finance by rediscovering the humanity of the core ideas of finance. The demonization of finance is counterproductive, and regulation, while helpful, holds only limited promise for addressing the transformation of finance into an extractive, rather than a value-creating, industry. Perhaps we can all find our way back to a more noble profession by enlivening the ideas of finance through stories that illuminate our lives and our work.

*The*

# WISDOM

*of*

# FINANCE

# INTRODUCTION
## *Finance and the Good Life*

The "Wall Street vs. Main Street" rhetoric that has become so pervasive reflects a common view of finance as an industry that extracts more value from the economy than it creates. At the same time, there is a growing awareness of how central finance is to our economy and our lives. We see finance everywhere, from our retirement assets to our investments in housing and education. The combination of deep suspicion and curiosity is further complicated by the complexity in which finance shrouds itself—mind-numbing acronyms, formulae, and spreadsheets serve as barriers to understanding the world of finance.

For practitioners of finance, this creates several problems. They need to explain and justify what they do more clearly to win back confidence. They need to ensure that their activities are truly value creating. More personally, working in an industry that is perceived negatively can take its toll. With expectations so low, finance professionals have little to aspire to, which creates a downward spiral of low expectations and poor behavior.

How do we open up the ideas of finance to everyone so they can access them in an affirmative way? How do we recover a sense of the virtues of finance so that the practice of finance can be improved?

This book takes the unorthodox position that viewing finance through the prism of the humanities will help us restore humanity to finance. The problems that finance addresses, and the beauty of the approach it adopts, are most easily understood by attaching finance to the stories of our lives. More than regulation or outrage, fixing finance requires practitioners to return to the core ideas, and ideals, of finance—which can help them ensure that they are creating value and not extracting it. By linking those core ideas to literature, history, and philosophy, we give them deeper resonance and make them more resistant to corruption.

I stumbled upon the idea of linking finance to stories. In the spring of 2015, I found myself in a position I often do—struggling at the last minute to make good on a commitment. I had agreed to give one of the "last lectures" to the graduating MBA class of Harvard Business School. The so-called last lecture is a tradition that allows professors to offer students, on the eve of their graduation, words of wisdom. At its best, it returns the university to a bygone era. Rather than the production and dissemination of specialized knowledge, for a moment we would all return to an antiquated notion of a university that acknowledged that, as John Henry Newman put it more than 150 years ago, "the general principles of any study you may learn by books at home; but the detail, the color, the tone, the air, the life which makes it live in us, you must catch all these from those in whom it lives already."

Having procrastinated for a while, I initially retreated to familiar territory and decided to give a talk about recent financial developments in American corporations. It would be titled "The Slow-Motion LBO of America" and it would describe how the current share repurchase craze should be understood and reversed. I had something concrete to say, it would be provocative, and, to make myself feel even more superior, I rationalized that it was meatier than the puffery that is usually offered in these settings.

After I made this decision, I saw a dear friend and colleague. In the last year, he and I had engaged in a series of discussions about how to reinvent ourselves by forcing ourselves into new challenges. After I told him of my decision to talk about these developments, his reaction was muted. I had internalized his voice enough to hear him asking me: "Really? Do you think that's what they need as they graduate? And is that what you need?"

His silence was enough to make me realize that I was missing an opportunity. And his friendship gave me the courage to think about doing something that was a challenge to me—a social scientist weaned on statistics and economic models. Instead of a safe topic, I would try to talk about the good life. But what did I, a man in my middle years, know about the good life?

I had long been bothered by the common presumption that markets, and finance in particular, were a crass domain that we had to shelter ourselves from in order to live a good life. It has become common to denigrate finance and to assume that finance has little of value to offer the world, and certainly has no wisdom behind it. Executives who make ham-fisted comparisons between finance and God's work only make the case that finance has little wisdom in it.

But this common rejection of finance and markets is problematic. For starters, the rejection of markets and finance as a source of wisdom is deeply unhelpful. Many highly educated individuals are deeply engaged in markets and concern themselves with financial matters for most of their time on this earth. By suggesting that finance has no positive values embedded in it, we encourage these individuals to live a professional life without values and to separate their personal, moral selves from their work. That compartmentalization is difficult and often untenable. Can you engage in a life's work that is bereft of wisdom and values and hope to live a good life?

Aside from being highly impractical, this rejection seems plain wrong. Many of my friends and former students love finance, markets, and business and find them life-affirming. They understand that finance is far from God's work, but they derive real joy from what they do. Could something so crass and devoid of moral value yield such joy and professional satisfaction? If the common presumption is unhelpful and incorrect, what might the opposing view be?

As is typical, I committed to a title — "The Wisdom of Finance" — but remained unsure about what it meant. In the subsequent weeks, I was surprised by how easily I could connect the lessons of finance to life, and how rich those linkages were. After the lecture was delivered, I was overwhelmed by the reaction of the MBA students, who were clearly hungry for wisdom that was not distilled from on high but from their own worlds and their own work. Midcareer executives were even more appreciative, as they understood better so many of the challenges that life presents. And, as has happened before in my life, I unwittingly stumbled into a commitment that provided returns that far exceeded the investment I had made.

While the lecture was successful as a means of mapping the core ideas of finance to the questions of a meaningful life, writing a book created a new problem. The correspondence between finance and life's problems could be easily sustained for an hour amongst people who appreciated business. But could I sustain and enliven that correspondence over the course of a book for many different types of people? Did I have a talk or a book?

As I struggled with these questions, I recalled that the best description of finance I had ever found came not from a textbook or a CNBC special but from a parable told by a Sephardic Jew writing in Spanish in Amsterdam in 1688.

In *Confusion de Confusiones*, Joseph de la Vega provides a vivid description of the nascent financial markets that were mesmerizing many observers at the time. Those vibrant markets featured the stock of only one company, the Dutch East India Company, which today would be analogous in its reach and dominance to some combination of Google, Alibaba, and General Electric.

Some of de la Vega's commentary seems remote. He explains, for example, that the dividends of the Dutch East India Company "are sometimes paid in cloves . . . just as the directors see fit." Other parts of his story are remarkably current, as when he provides an explanation of how frothy markets are driven by excessively low interest rates and how a bankrupt company is restructured.

Rather than dryly articulating the nature of those markets, he told a story—a conversation between a merchant, a philosopher, and a shareholder. The merchant and the philosopher are archetypes of the doer and the thinker. Puzzled by how financial markets work, they consult the shareholder for insight.

When the philosopher explains how little he understands about financial markets, the shareholder responds with my favorite description of finance: "I really must say that you are an ignorant person, friend Greybeard, if you know nothing of this enigmatic business which is at once the fairest and most deceitful in Europe, the noblest and the most infamous in the world, the finest and the most vulgar on earth. It is a quintessence of academic learning and a paragon of fraudulence; it is a touchstone for the intelligent and a tombstone for the audacious, a treasury of usefulness and a source of disaster, and finally a counterpart of Sisyphus who never rests as also Ixion who is chained to a wheel that turns perpetually."

De la Vega captured the best and worst of finance by relaying a story — and that story led me to see finance in many stories. I had always enjoyed stories, but becoming an economist made me distrust them. Now, I would return to them.

Soon I began to find finance in literature, in philosophy, in history, and even in popular culture. Once I began seeing the parallels, I couldn't stop. And I began to understand why finance and these fields were deeply connected. Many distrust markets, particularly financial markets, because they are thought to be hostile to humanity — but perhaps that has things completely upside down. Perhaps finance is deeply connected to our humanity.

As one example of the alternative view, the philosopher Friedrich Nietzsche notes that the whole idea of duty and personal obligation is rooted in "the oldest and most primitive personal relationship there is, in the relationship between seller and buyer, creditor and debtor. Here for the first time one person moved up against another person, here an individual *measured himself* against another individual. We have found no civilization still at such a low level that something of this relationship is not already perceptible. To set prices, to measure values, to think up equivalencies, to exchange things — that preoccupied man's very first thinking to such a degree that in a certain sense it's what thinking *itself* is. Here the oldest form of astuteness was bred: . . . the human being describes himself as a being which assesses values, which values and measures, as the 'inherently calculating animal.' "

Released from the conventional wisdom of the opposition of finance and markets to humanity, I decided to write a book that tried to unify them. That unification is my effort to fix finance and to make it accessible.

The following chapters can be sampled in any order. But the book is organized purposefully. Ideally, the reader is unconsciously taking a course in finance and emerging with the intuitions of finance, but only by enjoying stories.

While many analogize finance to physics, the better analogy is to biology. There is a branch that, like molecular biology, precisely focuses on the most essential building blocks of life. That branch is called "asset pricing." And there is a branch called "corporate finance" that is akin to sociobiology, interested in all the contingencies and messiness of the world that we actually observe. The book follows a conceptual arc that is divided roughly between those two branches.

The first three chapters consider the foundational question of asset pricing—how does one deal with the omnipresence of risk in the world? As I conceived the book, I was reminded of how central insurance is to finance and to my way of understanding the world—so the first chapter lays down the foundations of risk and insurance, with the help of Francis Galton's quincunx, the author Dashiell Hammett, the philosopher Charles Sanders Peirce, and the poet Wallace Stevens.

The next chapter extends the logic of insurance to two key risk management strategies—options and diversification—that correspond to strategies for dealing with uncertainty. In this chapter, authors Jane Austen and Anthony Trollope as well as the Greek philosopher Thales do most of the work. With the foundations of risk and insurance well laid, the next chapter addresses how risk corresponds to return and how that relationship dictates the conditions for creating value in the world. Here, John Milton, Samuel Johnson, and the parable of the talents serve as our guides.

The asset pricing branch of finance tries to establish the value of assets by thinking hard about the risks they present and the returns we demand for bearing those risks. There are many who dismiss markets as mechanisms for establishing true values. This first part of the book suggests that the question of value—how it arises and how we should measure it—bridges finance to the humanities in rich ways.

Asset pricing provides a powerful perspective on risk and value —but does so by ignoring much of the messiness of life. Indeed, a founding myth of asset pricing is a story of individuals on islands who own trees that produce fruit and must exchange fruit with each other. Asset pricing focuses only on the relationship between owners and their disembodied assets, thereby shearing the world of complexities like companies, more complex individual motivations, and the uneven diffusion of resources and information. That messiness is what most of us experience every day, and that is the subject of corporate finance.

The next four chapters consider all this messiness. The fourth chapter considers what happens when the relationship between investors and the underlying productive assets they own is mediated by human beings with their own motivations. The resulting emphasis on the relationship between principals (shareholders) and agents (managers) is the problem of corporate governance—and arguably the central problem of modern capitalism. The principal-agent problem, as demonstrated by Mel Brooks's *The Producers* and E. M. Forster's *A Room with a View*, is also a powerful frame for situations in our life when we are, consciously or unconsciously, behaving on behalf of others.

Now that companies have been introduced, we can consider when and how they should combine with each other—an activity known as merging. In the fifth chapter, mergers are paralleled with romantic relationships by exploring how romance and finance have been intertwined from Renaissance Florence to the rise of the Rothschilds to the merger of AOL and Time Warner.

The next two chapters combine the lessons of risk from asset pricing with the messiness of corporate finance by exploring the idea of debt and what can result from excessive levels of debt— bankruptcy. The artist Jeff Koons and William Shakespeare's *The*

*Merchant of Venice* allow us to map the commitments of borrowing to a much more personal setting. And Kazuo Ishiguro's *The Remains of the Day*, the fall of the richest man in colonial America, and a case study of the American Airlines bankruptcy teach us about the risks of excessive borrowing and the rewards of conflicting obligations.

The final chapter attempts to synthesize much of the book by trying to make sense of the disjunction between the nobility of the ideas laid out in the preceding chapters with the reputation of finance today. The stories by authors Leo Tolstoy and Theodore Dreiser manifest the typical reputation of finance, and Willa Cather provides the recipe for living one's life in a manner that is consistent with the nobility of the financial ideas discussed in the preceding chapters. A brief afterword and detailed references (including suggestions for further reading) conclude the book.

With this tour of the molecular biology (asset pricing) and sociobiology (corporate finance) of finance complete, hopefully the field of finance will come alive for you — and will help you navigate the risks and returns of your life.

# 1

# The Wheel of Fortune

In the middle of *The Maltese Falcon*, Dashiell Hammett interrupts his breakneck plot development and spare prose to tell a curious little story. The Flitcraft parable is, according to literary critic Steven Marcus, the "most central moment in the entire novel . . . and one of the most central moments in all of Hammett's writing." Somehow, John Huston chose to omit it in his classic film noir adaptation starring a young Humphrey Bogart as detective Sam Spade.

Spade, the embodiment of the hard-boiled detective, is talking to his femme fatale, Brigid O'Shaughnessy. She has rapidly evolved from being his client into being his lover and, increasingly, his prime suspect. Without any apparent trigger, Spade begins relaying the story of Flitcraft — a successful real estate executive in Tacoma, Washington, who had all "the appurtenances of successful American living." He had a new Packard, two children, a home, a wife, and a promising business. Flitcraft had no secret vices or hidden demons. Indeed, he had a very well-ordered life and was on track for continued success. But, one day, he suddenly disappeared after lunch, "like a fist when you open your hand," without a trace of an explanation and without any romantic or financial motive.

Five years later, someone in nearby Spokane contacted Flitcraft's wife and said that her husband had been sighted there. She then asked Spade to investigate, and he found Flitcraft, who was now a successful automobile dealer with a new family and a new home, living under the pseudonym Charles Pierce. Flitcraft/Pierce expressed no apparent remorse, pointing out to Spade that his previous family was well provided for. Nonetheless, Flitcraft/Pierce was anxious to relay to Spade an explanation, as he'd never told anyone what happened.

Flitcraft explained that on his way to lunch on the day he disappeared, a steel beam fell eight stories at a construction site and crashed on the sidewalk right next to him. He was even left with a small scar from a piece of the concrete sidewalk that flew up and hit his cheek. Flitcraft was shocked — he "felt like somebody had taken the lid off life and let him look at the works."

Flitcraft had created a life that was a "clean orderly sane responsible affair," and now a "falling beam had shown him that life was fundamentally none of those things." We live only because "blind chance" spares us. After the initial shock, he became disturbed by the "discovery that in sensibly ordering his affairs he had got out of step, and not in step, with life." Immediately after lunch, he resolved that he had to "adjust himself to this new glimpse of life." He concluded: "Life could be ended for him at random by a falling beam: he would change his life at random by simply going away." He left immediately by boat for San Francisco and wandered around for several years.

Spade ends the parable by noting that Flitcraft/Pierce ultimately "drifted back to the Northwest, and settled in Spokane and got married," and had a child. Upon learning of these events, his first wife "didn't want him. So they were divorced on the quiet and everything was swell all around." Flitcraft/Pierce didn't feel a sense of guilt or remorse, as he considered his actions to have been perfectly reasonable.

Spade then concludes with his favorite part of the story: "I don't think he even knew he had settled back naturally into the same groove he had jumped out of in Tacoma. But that's the part of it I always liked. He adjusted himself to beams falling, and then no more of them fell, and so he adjusted himself to them not falling."

As I read this story, two images immediately arose in my mind. The first was of David Byrne of the Talking Heads waving his arms, questioning his banal, suburban life, and asking himself, as we all do at different times in our lives, "how did I get here?" Flitcraft's "Once in a Lifetime" experience made him question everything. And the second image was of Gwyneth Paltrow as Helen Quilley in *Sliding Doors* running for a train in London. Soon, we see two alternative realities unfold for her, all because of the chance timing of the Tube doors. Ultimately, the lives of Flitcraft and Quilley are determined by chance.

At least two lessons emerge from the Flitcraft parable. The first is the dominance of chance in our lives. Flitcraft realizes that life is simply not well ordered and that the role of chance is the fundamental reality we must all come to understand. The second lesson is more subtle—Spade's favorite part of the story is how Flitcraft returns to his previous reality despite his best efforts to "change his life at random." In other words, as important as chance is, we just can't seem to escape our own patterns. As Byrne repeatedly chants throughout "Once in a Lifetime," everything is the "same as it ever was."

Like in any good detective story, Dashiell Hammett's key clues to the parable are hiding in plain sight. By choosing the names Flitcraft and Charles Pierce, Hammett added layers of meaning and connected this story to finance. For finance is, at its core, a way to understand the role of risk and randomness in our lives and a way to use the dominance of patterns to our advantage. Flitcraft is a name that has now all but disappeared, but, as a Pinkerton investigator who worked for insurance companies, Hammett would have known that Flitcraft published the bible for actuarial analysis in the life insurance business at the time. Flitcraft was a statistical wizard who published volumes that helped the fledgling insurance industry figure out the odds of living and dying for prospective clients.

And by choosing Charles Pierce as the second name, Hammett invoked a legend who has also been all but forgotten. Charles Sanders Peirce (yes, Hammett reversed the vowels) was 1) the founder of the philosophical tradition known as pragmatism, 2) a mathematician and logician whose work is considered a precursor to many significant developments in twentieth-century mathematics, 3) the founder of semiotics (the study of signs), which undergirds much of modern literary theory, and 4) a founder of modern statistics and the inventor of randomized experiments.

In short, this scientist-mathematician-philosopher was the classic Renaissance man—a man judged by the British philosopher Bertrand Russell to be "certainly the greatest American thinker ever," a man whom philosopher Karl Popper considered "one of the greatest philosophers of all time," and a man whom novelist Walker Percy thought more worthy than Darwin and Freud because he "laid the groundwork for a coherent science of man." Forget Jefferson, Emerson, James, Niebuhr, or Dewey—Peirce was the real deal.

And for Peirce, everything came down to . . . *insurance*. Throughout his life, he returned to insurance, declaring in 1869 that "each of us is an insurance company." How and why did such a broad and deep thinker keep returning to what seems to many of us like the most mundane and uninteresting subject—insurance? Because insurance is anything but mundane and uninteresting. For Peirce, it became a central frame for understanding one's life.

His attachment to insurance is most clearly manifest in a curious turn of events near the end of his life. Peirce had been shunned by academia for romantic adventures that were outside the accepted norm. Vilified by various forces in academia, including the then president of Harvard Charles William Eliot, Peirce had been denied tenure and was living his later years in poverty and searching for income. His friend the philosopher William James tried to funnel some financial opportunities to him and repeatedly suggested that Peirce should deliver a lecture series on pragmatism, given his central role in founding that school of philosophy. After finally convincing the Harvard Corporation to overlook his perceived moral turpitude, Peirce was invited in 1903 to give six lectures.

With much fanfare, his lecture series was announced. James and his colleagues were horrified when Peirce spent much of his first lecture talking solely about probabilities and insurance companies. To the bewilderment of his audience, Peirce used calculus to derive profit conditions for insurance companies in how they set prices for their policies. At the time, calculus would have probably not showed up in the economics department, let alone the philosophy department.

James, never a fan of mathematics, was horrified and suggested that Peirce had lost his mind. He wrote to a friend that Peirce had become a "monster of desultory intellect" and had become a "seedy, almost sordid, old man." Instead of taking advantage of this new opportunity to enter academia and to gain some economic stability, Peirce gave lectures that led to more ostracism. Peirce spent his remaining years in poverty, was shunned by the academy, and died in 1914.

What did Peirce see in insurance? Why and how is an understanding of insurance so vital to the human condition? Why did Hammett invoke insurance so consciously by choosing the names Flitcraft and Pierce? The answer begins with understanding the nature of risk and the idea of probabilities.

In my twenty years of teaching, I have taught courses in microeconomics, finance, tax law, international finance, and entrepreneurship. I've managed to muddle my way through fairly hazardous teaching material but I have always struggled most when I've tried to teach probabilities. Two of my most epic fails were when I tried to advance probabilistic intuitions. In the first case, I tried to develop the idea of probabilities by posing a simple question on the likelihood of me having two daughters. This question rapidly led to a discussion of the empirical regularity that in many countries there are slightly more boys born than girls, and this regularity is not fully attributable to the prevalence of abhorrent means of selecting boys over girls in some cultures. Twenty minutes into this discussion, we were talking about sex ratios, selective abortions, and infanticide — and no one had learned anything about probabilities.

My second failed attempt was an effort to introduce the "Monty Hall" problem. In this problem, you are the contestant on the game show *Let's Make a Deal* who gets to select one of three curtains. One of the curtains conceals a worthy prize while the other two curtains conceal booby prizes. After you select a curtain, the host of the show, Monty Hall, reveals that one of the remaining two curtains concealed a booby prize. He asks you if you'd like to switch your choice to the last curtain. Should you give up the curtain you chose first for the other curtain? This discussion confused more than it enlightened (yes, you should switch — I promise) and veered into a discussion of how one should minimize regret in one's life and just go for it—carpe diem! My finance class had become the *Dead Poets Society.*

If you've struggled as I have with probabilistic intuitions, take solace. For much of human history, simple probabilistic intuitions were elusive. Scholars of statistics have puzzled over why it took millennia for humanity to arrive at the modern intuition that chance is irreducible and omnipresent but can be understood and analyzed rigorously. This revelation, according to the philosopher of science Ian Hacking, is best embodied by none other than Flitcraft's alter ego, Charles Peirce. And the foundation of insurance and much of modern finance is to be found precisely in this revelation. Finance, ultimately, is a set of tools for understanding how to address a risky, uncertain world.

The elusive nature of probabilistic intuition is a particularly deep puzzle as gambling has been practiced for millennia—and there is no activity more suffused with chance and regularity than gambling. So, given how ancient gambling is, why wasn't proba-bilistic thinking discovered earlier? Consider a modern variant of gambling, the *Wheel of Fortune* game show. Fundamentally, you are playing a version of Hangman with the added wrinkle that you have to spin a wheel that changes the rewards for getting the next letter right. Say you know that the hidden phrase is "Carpe diem," you've already gotten $1,000 in the round, and you need to decide if you should spin one more time so you can suggest a "c." Should you do it? You already know the hidden phrase but you have to weigh the probability and rewards of spinning and landing on either "Lose a Turn" or "Bankrupt" rather than landing on a monetary wedge. To answer this question, you have to think about the likelihood of land-ing on those wedges. You have to think probabilistically.

Indeed, the two classic problems of probability are gambling problems that were around for centuries before finally being solved. In the first, the problem of points, two players have contributed equally to a prize and begin flipping a fair coin. They have agreed that the winner will be the player who realizes four of their chosen outcome, heads or tails, first. After three flips resulting in two heads and one tail, the game is interrupted and they have to split the prize. How should they do it? Clearly, the player who chose heads should get more—but how much more?

The other classic gambling problem is the martingale problem. The martingale strategy is one where a gambler enters a casino and bets $10 that the flip of a coin will be heads, while the house takes the opposite side. The strategy is exceedingly simple—after any coin flip that is tails, he will simply double his bet until a coin flip results in a heads outcome. Ultimately, there *will* be a heads outcome and he *will* walk away and *will* net the amount of his original bet, $10, *for sure*. So, clearly, this is a winning strategy and should be employed at all times. So why doesn't everyone do it? Would you do it? For the martingale strategy to win, one has to be able to keep playing for as long as it takes—and if your horizon and wealth are limited, you can lose a fortune.

Gamblers confronted variants of these problems for centuries and simply couldn't come to terms with a clear logic for thinking them through. Why? Part of the problem was that until the arrival of a tractable number system, very sophisticated civilizations, such as the Greeks, didn't have the tools to fully analyze these problems.

But the deeper problem was that, long before Merv Griffin invented the longest-running game show that has spread virally around the world, the original wheel of fortune dominated humanity's imagination. The original wheel of fortune featured the Roman goddess Fortuna, rather than Vanna White, and she was spinning the wheel, not just turning letters. Fortuna's spins of the *rota fortunae* delivered outcomes of either great bounty or extreme deprivation for humans. This wheel is a constant image throughout ancient and medieval times and indicated that chance outcomes were deemed beyond the domain of human reasoning and that divine forces were behind outcomes. Indeed, the wheel looms large in Chaucer and Dante as the explanation for the fall of many characters. How could humans reason through chance outcomes if divine forces dictated them?

The spread of Christianity only solidified the notion that divine forces were at work and that these forces resisted human understanding. The break came with the rise of rationalism and the desire to understand risk-taking as global commerce spread with the Renaissance. Commerce now promised high returns if risk could be well understood, and confidence in the abilities of humans to understand the world provided the fuel for solving these problems. Outcomes previously attributed to divine intervention became amenable to analysis.

The critical breakthrough for probabilistic thinking was the correspondence between two pioneering mathematicians, Blaise Pascal and Pierre de Fermat, about the aforementioned problem of points. In 1654, they created the tools to understand that problem by examining alternative outcomes to derive the expected values of those bets when the game was interrupted. That correspondence then triggered two and a half centuries of rapid-fire developments in probabilistic thinking.

Remarkably, these foundational developments in probability led to an overcorrection in humanity's understanding of chance. The long-standing fatalism reflecting the role of divine forces was replaced with a new kind of fatalism that reflected the discovery of so-called laws of nature. As statistics gained a foothold, more and more phenomena were observed to obey the bell-shaped normal distribution. This simply means that observations of all kinds of phenomena — such as human height and ability — will correspond empirically to the bell-shaped distribution, where observations cluster mostly around an average value and become much less prevalent as you move farther away from that average value.

This set of remarkable discoveries is well embodied by a contraption created by Francis Galton called the quincunx. If you've ever been to Japan, think of a simplified pachinko machine. In

pachinko, balls bounce through a maze of obstacles triggering rewards. Sounds boring, but it's incredibly addictive.

In a quincunx, balls are dropped at the top of a vertical board
that is studded with evenly spaced wooden pegs and bordered with
wooden edges. At the bottom of the board, there are many walled
lanes for the balls to fall into. One might imagine that the balls
would fall willy-nilly across those wooden lanes and ultimately
land in each lane equally—after all, the balls are just bouncing off
wooden pegs randomly on their way down the board.

But the quincunx, like many outcomes that are the product of
multiple random processes, actually results in the wonderfully
soothing bell-shaped distribution where most balls fall in the center.
This regularity was found so often and in so many intriguing places
that it gave rise to a conviction that what seemed like chance was
illusory and that nature followed ironclad laws.

Pierre-Simon Laplace, a pioneer of statistics and probability
during this period, was characteristic of the ironic confusion: the
discoverers of the tools to analyze randomness came to believe in
determinism. Laplace began a famous volume on probability by as-
serting that "all events, even those which on account of their insig-
nificance do not seem to follow the great laws of nature, are a result
of it just as necessarily as the revolutions of the sun." Laws are
everywhere, and they rule, not chance.

Galton, another pioneer of statistics and the creator of the quincunx, waxed eloquent about the bell-shaped curve. To Galton, there
was nothing more impressive than "the wonderful form of cosmic
order" represented by the curve, so much so that it would have been
deified by the Greeks if they had discovered it. As he lovingly describes the curve, he concludes that "it reigns with serenity and
complete self-effacement amidst the wildest confusion . . . It is the
supreme law of Unreason." The will of gods had been replaced with
the laws of nature. Chance was just an artifact because we didn't

know enough — as soon as we figured out the law, all would be clear and order would be created.

Even though he is credited with naming the "normal" distribution, Peirce revolted against this logic. Where others saw laws that made chance irrelevant, for Peirce "chance itself pours in at every avenue of sense . . . it is absolute . . . and the most manifest of all intellectual perceptions."

Peirce was able to keep two seemingly contradictory ideas in his head at the same time — chance and randomness were everywhere (the insight from the former type of fatalism, think Flitcraft), and patterns emerged that suggested regularities in the aggregate (the insight from the latter type of fatalism, think Flitcraft as Pierce). The universe was full of chance and fundamentally stochastic (randomly determined) — but patterns could help us navigate the world.

Galton was clearly brilliant, but his faith in laws led him seriously astray. He became the founder of eugenics, a movement whose followers believe you can improve the genetic quality of the human population by, amongst other things, forcibly sterilizing the part of the population deemed less qualified. This logic became so widespread for a time that even the Supreme Court of the United States upheld the practice in *Buck v. Bell* (1927) when Justice Oliver Wendell Holmes concluded, "Three generations of imbeciles are enough." Galton's ambition was to create "order" and to erase the role of chance and perceived "inferiority" in our populations. And we know the tremendous devastation that logic has wrought through the twentieth century.

Peirce, by contrast, embraced chance and randomness — and that led him to . . . insurance! Indeed, Peirce's understanding of the world — that randomness is everywhere but predictable in aggregate — is the foundation of insurance and modern finance. The tools needed to navigate a world filled with uncertainty is what finance endeavors to provide. Risk is everywhere, it is undeniable, and it shouldn't be ignored or surrendered to—it should be managed. And insurance is the primary way we manage the risks in our lives.

Many of my students flock to finance—but often for the wrong reasons. Their view of finance is that it comprises investors and bankers—they either want to work at investment banks or so-called alternative asset managers such as hedge funds or private equity funds. I am delighted and surprised when a student walks into my office interested in venturing down the path less taken—finance within corporations in the real economy or, even better, insurance.

Going into insurance is the ultimate contrarian bet, given the popular image of insurance executives today—boring, nerdy, and vaguely evil as they profit from the woes of others. It wasn't always so—insurance executives were once heroes, such as the characters played by Fred MacMurray and Edward G. Robinson in the greatest film noir ever, *Double Indemnity*. Now, we have the forgettable, irritating Ned Ryerson of *Groundhog Day* pitching single premium life insurance.

Occasionally, my students are moved when I tell them that the most venerated capitalist today, Warren Buffett, built his business on insurance. Buffett transformed a textile company into an investment vehicle by funding it with an insurance business. Indeed, much of what is attributed to Buffett's investing skill is best understood as his ability to source financing very cheaply through insurance companies. He understood how interesting insurance can be. So did that paradigmatic American, Ben Franklin, who founded the first fire insurance company in the colonies. So, what are you missing when you roll your eyes at the mention of insurance?

As with many innovations in finance, insurance originated with the risks of traveling, often on the seas. Voyages would typically be financed by loans, but the merchant/borrower was personally liable (as in, would be enslaved) if the goods didn't arrive. And travel routes were hazardous. So, a loan was bundled with insurance via a "contract of bottomry." It was a regular loan, but the borrower wouldn't have to pay back in the event the goods were stolen or lost to storms. In turn, the lender would be compensated with a higher interest rate than they would otherwise charge. The risk of losing goods to storms or pirates was now shared and priced. Those better able to bear the risk (would you take out that loan if you knew an unexpected storm could result in your enslavement?)—the financiers —would charge the merchants for assuming that risk.

The other big risk facing commercial shipments was the possibility of running aground and being forced to jettison goods in order to salvage one's voyage. "Rules of jettison" were developed around 1000 BC, known as Lex Rhodia for the island of Rhodes. They persist today and are now called the law of general average. The spirit of this practice is well captured by how it is discussed in the Code of Justinian from more than a thousand years ago: "The Rhodian Law provides that if in order to lighten a ship, merchandise is thrown overboard, that which has been given for all, should be replaced by the contribution of all." If a captain has to throw some goods overboard to save other goods, it's only fair that the owners of the goods that have been saved compensate the owners of the goods that were jettisoned. Even today, ships will declare general average, under the York-Antwerp Rules, and impose these costs on cargo holders.

The practice of general average is a pooling of risk, which is the essence of insurance. Insurance binds people together by mutualizing risk: we're all in this together. The pooling achieved by general average happens forcibly as a matter of maritime law rather than a voluntary insurance contract. So when and how did insurance become more personal and voluntary?

For Romans, the critical risk they faced was an afterlife filled with discontent. And the only way to prevent that outcome was to have an appropriate burial. But how could they be assured that their burial would be taken care of? Enter insurance! Roman burial societies were voluntary associations, particularly common among old soldiers, where the problem of funding funeral expenses was mutualized and shared with people of similar beliefs and social status so you could be assured of having an appropriate burial . . . and, therefore, of salvation.

In fact, the word "assurance" (variants of which I've snuck in twice in this last paragraph) links together insurance and salvation as it means both those things in different domains. It's a synonym for insurance as well as a Christian doctrine that indicates the path to salvation. The idea that salvation is the ultimate insurance payout is the logic of another famous probabilistic puzzle. Pascal, one of those pioneers of probability, famously examined "Pascal's Wager" to suggest that belief in God was worth it, even if the probability of a divine presence was tiny. In effect, Pascal asked, "Is disbelief really worth taking a chance on an eternity in hell?"

Roman burial societies exemplify the organizational form that dominated insurance until the turn of the last century—fraternal, voluntary organizations that provided insurance for their members. Consider the Independent Order of Odd Fellows (IOOF)—yes, odd fellows. The name likely originated with the set of "odd" trades that its members practiced. At the turn of the last century, this fraternal society comprised nearly two million members in North America through sixteen thousand lodges and was the dominant provider of disability insurance, making up for the lost income suffered by workers in the increasingly dangerous workplaces of the industrial era.

The pooling of risks is a natural human impulse, as these risks —for example, how will my family survive if I can't work to provide income?—are too burdensome for most individuals to bear alone. The importance of insurance is also illustrated by the practices it replaced. Several scholars have attributed the decline of the reports of witchcraft with the rise of insurance. Historian Alan Macfarlane notes that "punishment of witches was not merely for past offenses . . . [it] was regarded as a prerequisite for healing from witchcraft and an insurance against future disasters." And historian Owen Davies notes that, with the rise of insurance, "not only was the scope and impact of misfortune mitigated but blame for the experience of misfortune began to be appointed to the failures of these welfare mechanisms." If the alternative is drowning your neighbor after declaring her a witch, complaining about the insurance company denying your claim isn't so bad.

If insurance fills such a basic human need and will be provided by pooling risks across individuals, this still begs the really big question —how much should people pay for it? What should be the dues for the burial society or the IOOF? This, it turns out, is where things get harder—and where that quincunx and the normal distribution come back to help us. Even if we can't predict our own individual outcomes because of the nature of randomness, we can predict aggregate outcomes—because of the omnipresence and promise of that normal distribution. In fact, that's precisely the logic that the insurance industry is predicated on. Using our historical experience for population averages, we can estimate probabilities and price insurance policies—just as Peirce did in that lecture series at Harvard.

But that purely statistical approach misses a key problem: when you offer an insurance contract, you will not know everything about who buys your insurance. The consequences can be severe: sufficiently so, in fact, that they played a pivotal and underappreciated role in bringing about the French Revolution. Louis XVI and his finance ministers overlooked the problem and, as a result, got the pricing of insurance really wrong—and they paid for it, dearly.

The ancien régime's big mistake involved offering insurance for people who were worried about living too long. Living too long? It may seem strange to us to see that as a problem that is worth insuring against. Yet, individuals historically have been more preoccupied with living too long rather than dying early. That's because if we live too long, rather than dying young, we can exhaust our savings and die in poverty—think of what happened to Peirce. That risk, longevity risk, can be solved by "annuitizing" your current wealth. Annuities are contracts where you invest a lump sum and the insurer pays you a fixed annual amount until you die. This can be an effective way to ensure that you will have income until you die.

These annuity contracts were, in fact, a dominant form of public finance for England and France through the pivotal eighteenth century. And they were enabled by the start of record keeping on births and deaths. Indeed, some of the earliest manifestations of those normal curves had to do with mortality. If we knew when people of different ages would die, on average, we could then make sure that the pricing of annuities would work. Every age cohort would get a different annuity rate based on their expected mortality.

As England and France battled through the eighteenth century, they were forced to finance large expenditures on wars, including the very expensive Seven Years' War. In fact, they were engaged in an arms race of sorts, ever escalating the fiscal demands of military adventures. Prior to the eighteenth century, both countries had a track record of reneging on their public obligations in various ways. England reformed their system with the Glorious Revolution and created a public finance system that ensured that expenditures were funded by tax receipts, enacting an early version of a balanced budget system.

France, in contrast, continued to be a fiscal mess and began depending more and more on providing annuities to their populace. The kicker was that they were so desperate for financing that they decided that individuals of all ages could get the same annuity. The same annual payments were offered to a five-year-old as well as an eighty-year-old—for as long as they lived. The annual payment was set based on the idea that the typical group of investors would be interested in these annuities, so, on average, a uniform annuity rate would be okay.

This historical episode provides a particularly brutal example of one of the reasons insurance is so complicated: adverse selection. Guess who provided funds to the French government by buying annuities? Unsurprisingly, old people didn't take up the offer, but young people flocked to it—precisely those who would be the most expensive annuitants for the French government.

It gets better. In probably the earliest example of financial engineers bringing havoc to the world, a group of Swiss bankers bought annuities on behalf of groups of Swiss five-year-old girls who were found to come from particularly healthy stock. They then allowed people to invest in portfolios of these annuities, in what is likely the earliest example of securitization. By the time of the French Revolution, these annuities were the dominant source of financing for the government and the majority of annuitants were below the age of fifteen.

These obligations created a fiscal crisis that led to the reneging of other debt that was held widely by the public. The resulting discontent, in turn, led to the French Revolution. The postmortem on these instruments in the 1790s by future finance ministers decried the imbecility of the ancien régime and the unfairness of these annuities. They looked like giveaways to people like the Swiss bankers who could understand these machinations. Remarkably, one such annuity, one that was extended to the descendants of the buyer in a particularly generous giveaway, remains outstanding today. There is still a budget line item for the French government of €1.20 for the "Linotte rente" issued in 1738, testament to the fact that we still live in the world created by the French Revolution.

Even if the French had annuity rates that differed by age, as they clearly should have, the adverse selection problem would have persisted. Individuals who know they're healthy enough to outlive their expected longevity will buy these annuities, while those knowing that they have histories which would indicate earlier mortality would never invest. In fact, economists Amy Finkelstein and James

Poterba have shown that the United Kingdom's large annuity market still demonstrates this same tendency: people buying annuities live longer than people who don't. That means pricing of the annuities has to try to anticipate how much adverse selection there will be —and that's not easy.

The problem of adverse selection—being unable to make sure that the people who become insured conform to your expectation of who will buy insurance—is only one of the two big problems facing insurance. Problematic French public finance schemes of the eighteenth century provide an example of this second problem as well.

Just to make things more interesting, the French government allowed individuals to buy annuities in groups, and then each individual's payout would go up as other members in the group died. So, the government would pay a fixed amount to the group until the last member died, and, as individuals died, the survivors would get larger and larger shares of that amount. The last survivor would get very large payments until they too passed. These schemes were called tontines.

In effect, this is an annuity with an added kicker that you make out like a bandit when you live longer. It also helps the government because they can predict more easily when the last person will die rather than when an average person will die. Tontine-like arrangements remained common through the turn of the last century in the United States as well as Europe. The original site of the New York Stock Exchange was just outside the Tontine Coffee House, a building funded by the creation of a tontine. Scholars estimate that nine million tontine insurance policies were in effect in the United States in the early twentieth century, corresponding to 8 percent of national wealth.

What could go wrong with these tontines? Well, how would you react if your insurance payouts depended on the mortality of other people? For this wisdom, it's useful, as it often is, to consult *The Simpsons*. If you were Mr. Burns, the evil owner of a nuclear power plant, you'd try to kill all those other parties in your tontine, including Bart's grandfather.

That *Simpsons* plotline provides a great example of how the presence of insurance can create an incentive to alter your behavior, a manifestation of what's known as moral hazard. The example isn't perfect, since usually the insured person takes more risk because of the insurance, as opposed to trying to kill people because of insurance—but you get the idea. Insurance and safety nets of all kinds can lead to more risk-taking, and insurers have to think through that behavioral response in pricing insurance. For more on this, just stream that classic film noir *Double Indemnity* and think about Barbara Stanwyck's character—that's serious moral hazard.

Given the importance of adverse selection and moral hazard, what are the best mechanisms for dealing with them? Ensuring that insurance pools aren't susceptible to people advantageously selecting into policies is what national mandates to buy insurance and employer-provided insurance are all about. Similarly, deductibles make sure that individuals aren't overusing healthcare because they're insured. But what *organization* is best suited to pool risk and counter the effects of moral hazard and adverse selection? It should be one where membership isn't a choice, so that adverse selection isn't operating, and one where you can closely monitor each other's behavior to make sure moral hazard doesn't work against you.

Well, of course, that's the family. You don't get to choose your family, so that takes care of adverse selection. And families provide the intimacy for making sure behavior isn't changing to take advantage of the insurance. Indeed, families have been the most important source of insurance for millennia. Various studies have confirmed that insurance of all kinds is provided within a family and extended families, particularly in developing countries. As one clear example of this, consider what happened to the rate of "household formation" after the financial crisis. We saw a collapse in the creation of new households as children moved back in with their parents in the wake of the financial recession. As Robert Frost said, "Home is the place where, when you have to go there, they have to take you in."

This doesn't mean that families are ideal mechanisms for providing insurance. The benefits of pooling are limited by their size and by the fact that families are complicated. One indicator that families aren't always the best means for providing insurance was the rapid rise of seniors living on their own after the creation of state-provided pensions. Union army veterans from the Civil War were some of the first Americans provided with generous pensions. Economist Dora Costa has shown that they established separate living arrangements from their children at a much higher rate than the general population at the time, suggesting that familial insurance may not be in everyone's interest. Pensions created a choice for how seniors would like to live, and many decided that family-provided annuities weren't as good as government pensions. Sometimes, absence does really make the heart grow fonder.

How does understanding the omnipresence of risk and the nature of insurance help us understand the world? For this, we can return to Peirce. Why did Peirce, the remarkable Renaissance man who was able to embrace both chance and the regularities of the normal distribution, conclude that we should see ourselves as insurance companies?

For Peirce, if "chance itself pours in at every avenue of sense," then it naturally followed that "all human affairs rest upon probabilities, and the same thing is true everywhere." The first lesson from Peirce comes simply from the embrace of randomness. For Peirce, this embrace led to one of his most important discoveries. He employed a deck of cards in the middle of an experiment to ensure that subjects were being assigned randomly, so that the results were not biased and more credible. This is the first instance of randomization in scientific trials, a tool that is now a gold standard of intellectual inquiry. Rather than deny it, Peirce understood that embracing the omnipresence of risk was a powerful approach—it can actually be the foundation of wisdom.

Once you embrace randomness, you are left with the task of making sense of the world and seeking out the patterns that can guide your behavior. That leads us to probabilities as the only way to really understand the world—nothing is entirely certain and we should approach the world probabilistically. If we want to understand how probable things are and how the world works, the only way to figure out these probabilities is through experience, just as with an insurance company. The more experience an insurance company has with a population, the better their understanding of probabilities and the more successful their business. That's why, in effect, we're all insurance companies—experience is the critical method for understanding how to thrive.

Peirce's emphasis on insurance was a natural extension of his philosophy of pragmatism. Pragmatism is the opposite of navel-gazing; in pragmatism, truths are only valuable to the degree they can inform actions, and actions are only valuable if they confirm a truth. Peirce often talks about experience with the statistical term "sampling." Only by sampling what the universe has to offer can we learn anything of value. We should experience as much as possible —just as insurance companies must—in order to make good decisions and understand the world with the right probabilities. Carpe diem, indeed.

Finally, Peirce took the importance of experience to its logical extreme. If our experience is the most important thing for understanding the world, how should we approach others in the world? In a remarkable turn, Peirce builds on a discussion of how the martingale betting strategy requires an infinite horizon and how insurance companies price policies to arrive at an argument for virtuous living —fundamentally because of our own mortality:

> Death makes the number of our risks, of our inferences,
> finite, and so makes their mean result uncertain. The
> very idea of probability and of reasoning rests on the
> assumption that this number is indefinitely great. We
> are thus landed in the same difficulty as before, and
> I can see but one solution of it . . . logicality inexo-
> rably requires that our interests shall not be limited.
> They must not stop at our own fate, but must embrace
> the whole community. This community, again, must
> not be limited, but must extend to all races of beings
> with whom we can come into immediate or mediate
> intellectual relation. It must reach, however vaguely,
> beyond this geological epoch, beyond all bounds . . .
> Logic is rooted in the social principle. To be logical,
> men should not be selfish.

If our own experiences are inherently limited, understanding the
world requires incorporating the experiences and welfare of others. Reacting against the idea of social Darwinism, Peirce instead
thought that the logic of insurance and sampling inexorably led to
"that famous trio of Charity, Faith and Hope, which, in the estima-
tion of St. Paul, are the finest and greatest of spiritual gifts." We
must embrace others to understand the world—the imperative of
experience gathering demands it. For Peirce, insurance teaches us
that experience and empathy are the key methods for dealing with
the chaos of the world.

Wallace Stevens, "the quintessential American poet of the twentieth century" according to critic Peter Schjeldahl, had little use for
much of philosophy. After a 1944 essay on the superiority of poetry over philosophy, a friend rebuked him for not reading the right
philosophers. Stevens responded to his friend that "most modern
philosophers are too academic," but noted one exception: "I have

always been curious about Pierce [sic]." Several critics have noted the deep intellectual links between Peirce and Stevens, but there is also this—Stevens appreciated insurance even more than Peirce. He worked as an insurance company executive his whole life, even when his success as a poet meant that he didn't have to.

Stevens declined the offer to become the Charles Eliot Norton Professor of Poetry at Harvard and, instead, spent most of his days figuring out how the Hartford Accident and Indemnity Company should settle or litigate insurance claims. Fellow poet John Berryman, in his elegy to Stevens, poked at him by calling him a "funny money man" "among the actuaries." So, what did Stevens see in insurance? As we've seen, insurance tries to make sense of the chaos of human experience by capitalizing on patterns and then creating pooling mechanisms for us to be able to manage that chaos. For Stevens, poetry had the same aim of addressing the chaos of the world.

In his preface to the volume *Ideas of Order*, Stevens labeled the volume as "pure poetry" that aimed to address the "dependence of the individual, confronting the elimination of established ideas, on the general sense of order." In addition to the dramatic developments of the first third of the twentieth century (World War I and the Great Depression), Stevens was also sensitive to the chaos of nature and our own minds.

In the poem "The Idea of Order at Key West," Stevens concludes with the fundamental longing of "Oh! Blessed rage for order." Stevens's biographer Paul Mariani characterizes this as a call for the "one weapon against the encroaching chaos not only without but, more frighteningly, within us . . . crying out for a fiction that will sustain us." In the poem, Stevens contrasts "the dark voice of the sea" and the "meaningless plungings of water and the wind" with the voice of a singer who "sang beyond the genius of the sea," suggesting that art—fiction, music, poetry—was the only way to survive the chaos of the world.

Poetry was critical to Stevens because it manifested how imagination could help us make sense of the chaos around us. In his essay "Imagination as Value," Stevens reacts strongly against Pascal's ideas that "imagination is that deceitful part in man, that mistress of error and falsity." Instead, Stevens concludes that "imagination is the only genius" and the "only clue to reality." Why was imagination so important? For Stevens, "imagination is the power of the mind over the possibilities of things" and is the "power that enables us to perceive the normal in the abnormal, the opposite of chaos in the chaos." Stevens almost sounds like one of the early discoverers of the normal distribution.

Perceiving the normal in the abnormal is precisely what insurance is built on and it is what helps us achieve the opposite of chaos amidst the chaos of the world. Peirce too understood that imagination was just as powerful as science and rationalism in dealing with chance and chaos. In contrast to the hyper-rationalism of Pascal, Peirce saw the value of imagination as much as Stevens did, and concluded that "the work of the poet or novelist is not so utterly different from that of the scientific man."

The fundamental problem of life for both Peirce and Stevens — and for Hammett in his Flitcraft parable — was confronting disorder and chaos, making sense of it, not denying it, and living with it. For Peirce, insurance became the central metaphor for explaining that and describing how to handle it — through experience, pragmatism, and empathy. For Stevens, a man who spent his life negotiating insurance claims rather than dedicating himself uniquely to poetry, imagination was the central tool for managing the omnipresence of chaos and for seeking and seeing the hidden order of things amid the chaos. It is no wonder that Stevens concluded that "poetry and surety claims aren't as unlikely a combination as they may seem."

# 2

# Risky Business

I f irresponsible French public finance schemes found their way
into plotlines in *The Simpsons*, what came of the financial instruments that Britain used to fund its government? In fact, these
bonds would figure largely throughout nineteenth-century English literature. Jane Austen's *Pride and Prejudice* famously opens
with the line, "It is a truth universally acknowledged, that a single
man in possession of a good fortune, must be in want of a wife." To

measure his fortune—and thus establish one of the crucial criteria for his eligibility—society usually looked to annual incomes and the security they provided. These incomes were typically generated by investments in British government bonds called the "three percents" or "five percents." These perpetual bonds, called consols, didn't end with death, like annuities or tontines, but went on forever, providing familial stability for generations.

The eligibility created by annual incomes factored critically into the risk management problem that figures so largely in nineteenth-century English literature—the problem faced by young women in the marriage market. Opportunities for financial security had to be weighed against the associated risks of various suitors—navigating that tradeoff is what preoccupies many a heroine and her family in these novels. In what is likely the most cringeworthy marriage proposal ever, Mr. Collins approaches Lizzy Bennet, the heroine of *Pride and Prejudice*, and delivers a hopelessly narcissistic appeal for her hand. Despite Lizzy's protests, Mr. Collins doesn't give up. Rather than praising or wooing Lizzy, Mr. Collins argues that Lizzy must accept his proposal, given the risks she faces.

After again elaborating why he is so worthy, Mr. Collins concludes, "You should take it into farther consideration that in spite of your manifold attractions, it is by no means certain that another offer of marriage may ever be made you. Your portion is unhappily so small that it will in all likelihood undo the effects of your loveliness and amiable qualifications. As I must therefore conclude that you are not serious in your rejection of me, I shall chuse [sic] to attribute it to your wish of increasing my love by suspense, according to the usual practice of elegant females."

In short, settle for me or realize that you might end up with nothing—particularly given your modest means. And surely, Lizzy, you wouldn't be that silly? Lizzy's mother warns her, "If you take it into your head to go on refusing every offer of marriage in this way, you will never get a husband at all—and I am sure I do not know who is to maintain you when your father is dead. —*I* shall not be able to keep you — and so I warn you." As Lizzy's sister Mary warns her, the risks to a woman in the marriage market were huge, as "one false step involves her in endless ruin." Lizzy rejects Mr. Collins handily after gaining her father's permission. She wants to keep rolling the dice.

Mr. Collins ends up winning over Lizzy's best friend, the more risk-averse Charlotte Lucas, with a similar logic just the next day. Charlotte seems well attuned to the pragmatism of Collins. She has already concluded that "happiness in marriage is entirely a matter of chance," so courtship or chemistry is of little use in finding the right mate. And after all, Charlotte concludes, "I am not romantic, you know; I never was. I ask only a comfortable home; and considering Mr. Collins's character, connection, and situation in life, I am convinced that my chance of happiness with him is as fair as most people can boast on entering the marriage state." In short, from her perspective, this is a good trade given her appetite for financial risk and her expected risks and returns of a marital bond. Faced with the risks of the marriage market, Charlotte chooses comfort over further risk exposure, while Lizzy chooses continued exposure in hopes of a romantic outcome.

The risk management problems facing Lizzy and Charlotte in finding a husband are like the tradeoffs we face in many other settings. Is continuing with further education "worth it"? Will the returns on that education compensate for the risks of specialization and indebtedness? Is investing your human capital in that startup company worth the risk that it will go belly-up in the next twelve months? Should you keep looking for the perfect job or accept the offer on the table? These questions implicitly consider risk and return and require you to think about how to allocate your time, energy, and resources given a set of choices in the face of an uncertain future. This allocation problem is precisely the problem at the center of finance.

Insurance, as we saw, is a powerful tool for managing the risks of mortality, longevity, or natural disasters. But what about the risks we face in the labor market or marriage market? There aren't insurance policies available for those risks. Fortunately, finance has adapted the logic of insurance to create the two most important risk management tools available to us — options and diversification. These risk management strategies may seem esoteric and unrelated. Fortunately, Violet Effingham of Anthony Trollope's *Phineas Finn*, as we'll see, is a thoughtful guide to the risk management problem of the marriage market because she managed to intuit both of these strategies well before they were formalized by modern finance. These two instruments also happen to have a common intellectual forefather — an obscure French mathematician who never got the respect he deserved for solving the problem laid out by a British botanist.

If you've ever paused to ponder how dust seems to drift through a shaft of sunlight, you've had the same feeling botanist Robert Brown had in 1827. As he watched pollen emit particles in water, these particles seemed to move about randomly. Why and how were they moving? Soot particles did the same thing, making it clear that the pollen particles weren't autonomously doing something.

The conventional history of subsequent intellectual developments goes like this: in his annus mirabilis of 1905, when he produced four remarkable breakthroughs, Albert Einstein provided the first understanding of the mechanisms of so-called Brownian motion. He demonstrated that many processes that seem continuous (like the motion of dust or pollen) are in fact the product of many discrete particles moving about. In other words, the pollen particles were moving around in a continuous way because they were reacting to tiny water molecules that were bumping them at random. This foundational idea transformed physics by demonstrating the presence of atoms and also provided the machinery to mathematically describe all kinds of seemingly random processes, ultimately giving rise to quantum mechanics.

Finance and economics, forever envious of the rigor and stature of physics, adopted these findings and began aping the physical sciences—thereby marking the beginning of the end. This narrative concludes that finance lost its way by promoting precision and models over human reality by trying to describe inherently social phenomena with physics and quantum mechanics.

This is a convenient narrative that suits those who are dissatisfied with the rise of finance—but it is shoddy intellectual history. In fact, the person who beat Albert Einstein to the punch by five years was Louis Bachelier, a doctoral student in Paris. Rather than studying the movement of particles, he studied the movement of stocks and derived the mathematics to describe all kinds of motion, including the motion of pollen particles observed by Robert Brown. How did he do it? He realized that he could employ and generalize the magical distribution created by the quincunx into settings where outcomes weren't the locations of falling balls, but rather processes of motion that were the result of lots of molecules behaving as if they were going through a quincunx. Even better, his data on stock prices fit that mathematical description extremely well. At the time, the use of stock market data was looked down upon, and Bachelier, despite his breakthrough, never received the recognition he deserved. In fact, leading mathematicians falsely claimed he had made mistakes, leaving Bachelier to operate on the margins of French academia and to die in relative obscurity.

As such, the idea that finance, a study of markets and inherently social phenomena, lost its way by aping physics, a "hard" science of precision, is plain wrong. Instead, as philosopher and historian Jim Holt has described, "Here, then, is the correct chronology. A theory is proposed to explain a mysterious social institution (the Paris Bourse). It is then used to resolve a mid-level mystery in physics (Brownian motion). Finally, it clears up an even deeper mystery in physics (quantum behavior). The implication is plain: Market weirdness explains quantum weirdness, not the other way around. Think of it this way: If Isaac Newton had worked at Goldman Sachs instead of sitting under an apple tree, he would have discovered the Heisenberg uncertainty principle."

Aside from an interesting reversal of conventional wisdom, the story of Bachelier's discovery is also the story of the two most important risk management strategies—options and diversification. Bachelier's ability to describe the movement of stock prices mathematically as "random walks" provided the foundation for him to crudely price the option contracts that were then trading in Paris and had traded since the seventeenth century in Amsterdam. Myron Scholes and Robert Merton would win the Nobel Prize in 1997 for a pricing formula that corresponds to (and considerably improves upon) the mostly forgotten logic laid down by Bachelier. And Bachelier's ability to describe stock prices moving about at random ultimately gave rise to portfolio theory by putting forward the notion that it was hopeless to try to beat the market—the best you could do was hold a diversified portfolio.

Perhaps it's wrong to mock the history of French finance as much as I did in the last chapter. Yes, French public finance schemes were inherently unstable and impractical compared to the English system. But we can thank Parisian financial markets for providing the insights that gave rise to the modern understanding of risk management. Even the British, the inventors of the more stable system, seem to have conceded this. The Royal Coat of Arms of the United Kingdom has the French phrase *Honi soit qui mal y pense*—which translates as "Shame be to him who thinks ill of it."

Violet Effingham of *Phineas Finn* captures the risk management problem of female protagonists such as Lizzy Bennet exceptionally well. As Violet considers the risks she would bear because of a suitor, she concludes, "A child and a man need not mind themselves. Let them do what they may, they can be set right again. Let them fall as they will, you can put them on their feet. But a woman has to mind herself." Violet makes it clear that women had to manage their risks much more carefully because the consequences of failure were considerably greater. Fortunately, Violet also knew how to manage that risk.

Violet dismisses the idea of simply waiting for the "right one." "It does not seem to me to be possible to myself to be what girls call in love. I can like a man, I do like, perhaps, half a dozen . . . But as for caring about any one of them in the way of loving him—wanting to marry him, and have him all to myself, and that sort of thing —I don't know what it means." So, how would Violet ever decide to marry? For Violet, it was all quite simple. At the right time, she would just make a choice amongst competing alternatives. "I shall take the first that comes after I have quite made up my mind . . . After all, a husband is very much like a house or a horse. You don't take your house because it's the best house in the world, but because just then you want a house. You go and see a house, and if it's very nasty you don't take it. But if you think it will suit pretty well, and if you are tired of looking about for houses, you do take it. That's the way one buys one's horses—and one's husbands."

Marriage as a romantic quest to find the "one" was far too risky a strategy for Violet. Instead, the appropriate strategy was to ensure she had a good set of choices when she was finally ready to make that choice. And that is just what she did—having accumulated multiple suitors, she exercised her option for Lord Chiltern when she was ready to marry.

In financial parlance, this is tantamount to creating a portfolio of options and then choosing to invest in one asset at the opportune time. The portfolio of options allows you to wait until you are ready to invest and to see how these assets are evolving—far preferable to committing to one asset prematurely or waiting in the hopes that the "right" asset will come along eventually.

People in finance love options for the freedom and opportunity they represent. And they frame much of their life in analogous terms. By pursuing education, for example, they increase "option value" because more degrees and networks mean that more choices will be available to them. But what exactly are options and how does one use them? The father of Greek philosophy, the Dutch financial markets of the seventeenth century, and the entrepreneur behind Federal Express are excellent guides to understanding that question.

Violet's appreciation of self-knowledge as a prerequisite to the thoughtful use of options has deep historical resonance. Thales of Miletus, acknowledged as the father of Greek philosophy by no one less than Aristotle himself, is often credited both with the phrase "know thyself" and with originating the first options transaction. Thales earned his position as the only philosopher in the Seven Sages of Greece by pioneering the use of natural, instead of supernatural, explanations for phenomena, advocating hypothesis-driven thinking, and even managing to predict solar eclipses with the crudest of instruments.

Despite these remarkable accomplishments, Thales still had something left to prove. According to Aristotle, Thales's poverty led him to be "taunted with the uselessness of philosophy." Seeking to redress this impression, Thales decided to capitalize on his ability to forecast a good olive harvest. "He raised a small sum of money and paid round deposits for the whole of the olive-presses in Miletus and Chios, which he hired at a low rent as nobody was running him up; and when the season arrived, there was a sudden demand for a number of presses at the same time, and by letting them out on what terms he liked he realized a large sum of money." Aristotle's lesson from this story reflects the smug sentiments of philosophers and academics everywhere—Thales demonstrated that "it is easy for philosophers to be rich if they choose, but this is not what they care about."

How does Thales's transaction reflect the nature of options? The "deposit" that Thales first paid secured the right, but not the obligation, to rent the presses. This transaction is the essence of an options transaction—relatively small premia are paid to secure the rights to enter into transactions rather than obligating someone to do something, thereby enabling them to access resources they *might* need but don't know if they will need. A stock option, for example, allows you the right to buy a share at a predetermined price at some point in the future for a relatively small price today.

Options, which today are sometimes regarded as esoteric manifestations of financial engineering, are as old as any traded financial instrument. When trading of financial instruments truly began, in Amsterdam in the late seventeenth century, options were a dominant instrument. Joseph de la Vega, in *Confusion de Confusiones*, highlighted the importance of options. In a dialogue between the philosopher and the shareholder, the philosopher is intrigued by financial markets but is concerned that he won't be able to participate given his poverty and the fact that nobody will "lend me money on my beard." The shareholder tells him not to worry and introduces him to "opsies," which "will be only limited risk to you, while the gain may surpass all your imaginings and hopes." In a detailed explanation of how to purchase the right to buy (calls) and the right to sell (puts) on the Dutch East India Company, de la Vega claimed that these instruments are both "sails for a happy voyage during a beneficent conjuncture and an anchor of security in a storm."

By purchasing a right as opposed to buying the asset itself, options create an asymmetry that enables speculation ("a happy voyage during a beneficent conjuncture") and risk management ("an anchor of security in a storm"). Because an option is a right and not an obligation, you don't have to purchase assets if they decline, but you can still enjoy the possibility of price increases—this characteristic makes it a powerful speculative tool. At the same time, having the right to buy or sell an asset means that during bad times you can be assured of some minimal payoffs—which makes it an effective insurance policy. Think of a warranty when you buy a toaster.

You effectively have the right to sell it back to the manufacturer as a way of insuring yourself against a defective toaster.

In part, people in finance love options because of the nature of this asymmetric payoff. Losses are contained and gains are unlimited. And experiences that create optionality—educational experiences, for example—are valued precisely because of the asymmetric nature of the payoffs. With well-defined losses and no set ceiling on the upside, who knows what could come of such possibilities? Back in 1688, de la Vega highlighted precisely this virtue of options when he traced the etymology of "opsies" to the Latin "*optio,* which means choice," and then further back to "*optare,* which means to wish." Indeed, the "optative mood" is the Greek grammatical form, now lost, for expressing wishes. Purchasing options allows us to wish for outcomes and allows us to imagine what is possible and what might come true. This link between options and the desire to explore what is possible is precisely why Ralph Waldo Emerson called America "optative"—options are for people who want to imagine the outcomes that they desire.

The most distinctive aspect of options is how their asymmetric nature makes them particularly valuable when environments become more risky. Because you have little to lose and much to gain, events that make outcomes more extreme are welcome. In other words, options, because they are a form of insurance, are more valuable when life becomes even more uncertain.

By implication, if you hold an option, you will be encouraged to undertake riskier adventures. So, the real payoff from having options is the risk-taking that it enables. This is particularly evident when you come to realize suddenly that you hold an option. A story from the beginnings of Federal Express, the global logistics company, manifests this relationship between options and risk-taking. In the company's very early days, the CEO, Fred Smith, was struggling mightily to convince suppliers, investors, and customers of the virtue of expedited delivery. On one Friday, things got so bad that fuel suppliers were threatening to shut off supplies, thereby ending the young company, because of an unpaid $24,000 bill. Smith only had $5,000 in the bank. How did he respond?

As the owner of the company, Smith recognized that if he went bankrupt, he would get nothing—but that if he was allowed to live another day he had the possibility of victory. That sounds a lot like an option—an asymmetric payoff with little to lose and much to gain. So, how do you behave if you own an option? Well, you seek out volatility and risk. And where can you find that? FedEx still survives today because Smith went to Las Vegas and converted the $5,000 into $32,000 at the blackjack table. When confronted with the riskiness of the decision, Smith simply said, "What difference does it make? Without the funds for the fuel companies, we couldn't have flown anyway." As the owner of an option, Smith did what came naturally—he took on a great risk; if he won, he would win big, and if he lost, it was no difference to him. Owners of companies only have these incentives when they come close to bankruptcy, as otherwise they bear both losses and gains.

Of course, there are fascinating ethical issues here. By going to Las Vegas, Smith effectively stole from the suppliers, because he was gambling with the money that he owed them. But he was also responding to the incentives in place—incentives that are always in place as any company teeters on the edge. Owners who are underwater become holders of options with little to lose and everything to gain—so why not go to Vegas?

This vignette makes clear that creating options and having them as part of your portfolio allows you, even encourages you, to undertake greater risks. This is why finance people love options and view their lives as enhanced by the presence of these asymmetric bets. Acquiring options can help you assess a set of outcomes beyond your current capabilities, allow you to take more risks than you would otherwise, and simultaneously protect you when you stumble.

• • •

People in finance love options so much that they often overlearn the lessons on the value of options. They become obsessed with "optionality" and the creation and preservation of choices. As one example, my students often describe circuitous paths they will take to their professional destinations, all in the name of creating option value along the way in order to have choices if things go awry. For these students, acquiring options becomes habitual, and the exercise of choice — with the associated death of options that choice entails — becomes difficult.

I am no longer surprised to see students who end up remaining in companies — usually consulting or investment banking firms — that were initially intended as way stations that would create more optionality on the path to their actual entrepreneurial, social, or political goals. They often end up saying to themselves, "Why not stay another year and create more options for down the road?" The tool that was supposed to lead to more risk-taking ends up preventing it.

Any commitment necessarily must overcome the loss of option value that choices close off. So, commitments of various kinds become difficult given the extra burden they bear. It is not uncommon to hear people in finance talk about marriage as the death of optionality. Implicitly, the act of marriage is characterized as the loss of something — future choices — rather than the beginning of something. As a result, a focus on the creation and preservation of choices can ironically lead to an inability to make choices. Alternatively, individuals most unable to make decisions become obsessed with the idea of optionality and frame their inability in terms of preserving optionality.

It is not surprising then that two acclaimed tales of finance feature iconic characters with precisely this problem of an inability to make choices. While Herman Melville's "Bartleby, the Scrivener" is commonly considered one of the great works of American fiction, the subtitle of "A Story of Wall Street" is typically left off. In this short story, a Wall Street lawyer narrates his perplexing interactions with a man he hires as a clerk. For any financial analyst or legal associate familiar with the drudgery of work on Wall Street, the tale cuts all too close to home. Franz Kafka, himself a clerk in an insurance company, couldn't have conjured a more bleak portrait of working in finance. But it's also a story of inaction and the consequences of saying neither yes nor no to life's choices.

While initially quite productive, Bartleby becomes inscrutable and introduces one of the most mysterious lines in American literature as he responds to the narrator's requests for work. Asked to review his work one day, Bartleby simply responds "I would prefer not." When asked if he is saying "no," he repeats his "I would prefer not." He doesn't refuse nor does he accept—he simply says he'd rather not.

After Bartleby is discovered to be living in his office, he is told that he must move out. He simply replies "I would prefer not to." After the lawyer moves offices to relieve himself of the burden of Bartleby, he is told to stop living in the building by the new tenants, and Bartleby simply says, "I would prefer not to make any change at all." Bartleby is eventually sent to jail for vagrancy, and the lawyer secures him meals, but Bartleby "prefers not to dine." The story ends with Bartleby wasting away in the prison and the lawyer finding his dead body.

Much ink has been spilled on the meaning of the cryptic phrase "I prefer not to." Some critics have labeled Bartleby a model of passive resistance, a proto-Occupy protester. Others see him as an embodiment of the depression that Melville may have felt, given the poor popular reception he received. But the interpretation I think is most resonant is that, by not saying either yes or no, Bartleby was preferring the prospect of potential outcomes over real ones. We've all done this at different times—sometimes, the prospect of multiple outcomes is so tantalizing that we resist actually making a decision, preferring to live in a world of possibilities. This is what

Bartleby does—preferring potentiality over reality, preferring optionality over real decisions.

Exactly one hundred years after Herman Melville's publication of "Bartleby, the Scrivener" in *The Piazza Tales*, Saul Bellow published *Seize the Day*, featuring a similarly indecisive protagonist. In this novella, Tommy Wilhelm is a man-child who tumbles through a day in New York that features him regretting his pursuit of an acting career, unsuccessfully asking his father for money, dealing with his wife who is seeking child support, and, finally, losing his last bit of savings to a financial huckster who convinces him that lard and rye are surefire investments. The charlatan, Dr. Tamkin, is a Madoff-like character who combines psychobabble with financial advice that Tommy knows is clearly wrong. Tommy can't resist the con even as he's aware of it.

Tommy realizes that his whole life has been marred by the inability to make choices and the process of stumbling into decisions that are, in fact, non-decisions. "After a long struggle to come to a decision, he [Tommy] had given him [Tamkin] the money. Practical judgment was in abeyance. He had worn himself out, and the decision was no decision. How had this happened? . . . It was because Wilhelm himself was ripe for the mistake. His marriage, too, had been like that. Through such decisions somehow his life had taken form." Tommy concludes that "ten such decisions made up the history of his life." He comes to see his shambolic life as having "taken form" as the result of decisions that were not decisions at all—just stumbles that resulted from his inability to make choices and his overthinking of decisions.

Wilhelm pleads with God to guide him out of his excessive analysis and to lead him toward better choices. "Let me out of my thoughts, and let me do something better with myself. For all the time I have wasted I am very sorry. Let me out of this clutch and into a different life. For I am all balled up." The novella ends with Tommy stumbling into a stranger's funeral, where he breaks down. Completely paralyzed, he is consumed by regret and sadness. "The great knot of ill and grief in his throat swelled upward and he gave in utterly and held his face and wept. He cried with all his heart." He is a broken man unable to make choices and pleads for divine help.

Bartleby and Tommy Wilhelm are shattered individuals—passive actors who are seemingly unable to make choices. But they are also different. Melville provides a fable of inaction and the inability to make choices. Bellow provides a more realistic portrait of what happens when we don't make choices—the world makes decisions for us and we find ourselves caught in currents without any ability to navigate them. This latter version is a result of the temptation that I see many of my students confronting—they choose majors and graduate schools and employers by appealing excessively to a logic of optionality. Soon, these students, like many of us, find themselves undertaking choices unconsciously that they had no idea they were setting themselves up for.

In her discussion of the risks facing young women, Violet Effingham intuited the other risk management tool recommended by finance. As Lady Chiltern notes that Lord Chiltern truly loves Violet, Violet dismisses this criterion and responds that "ten men may love me." Violet then considers the optimal solution before dismissing it: "But I can't marry all the ten." If only she could marry all ten, then her risks would be mitigated. Some husbands would work out well, others wouldn't. If only she could take this indivisible choice and divide it up.

This logic of diversification is the cornerstone of portfolio theory and represents the only true "free lunch" in finance. It's also a logic with a long history as a risk management strategy. The earliest examples, like those of insurance, date back to early shipping where cargo would be divided among ships and routes to mitigate the risks of a loss. In medieval England, the critical risk for farmers was that they were overly exposed to the output of a single plot of land. The remarkable "open field" agricultural system of medieval England was a response to this risk management problem. Serfs tilled narrow strips of land that were spread far and wide across a lord's manor rather than one large piece of land. This method was enormously inefficient because of the added transport costs but provided significant risk mitigation by diversifying a farmer's output across different plots of land.

The use of diversification to mitigate risks runs through to today and appears in unlikely settings. Stringer Bell, the business mastermind of the Barksdale Organization in the television show *The Wire*, employed diversification as a method of risk management. In his cat-and-mouse game with the police, protecting communication was critical, so he used temporary "burner" cell phones. But Bell went further than simply not relying on one phone line to avoid detection —he ensured that the purchases of burner cell phones were spread across multiple stores, so that no clerk would remember a large sale, and he also used multiple SIM cards. His critical risk—detection and monitoring by the police—could be avoided by diversification.

More broadly, his ultimate aim, partially realized, was to diversify beyond the drug trade into real estate and federal contracts, looking for a "game beyond the game." Ultimately, his entire criminal organization is undone because the Barksdale employee who so carefully diversified his burner cell phone purchases failed to diversify where he rented cars from. The use of the same rental car agency again and again is the wedge the police use to break the gang, which leads to Bell's downfall. From medieval agriculture to the techniques of drug dealers, diversification has been a powerful way to manage risk.

Much as options can be understood as a way to get insurance, diversification also relies on the logic of insurance. With insurance, insurers pool risks across individuals and they rely on the regularities of large populations and that magical normal distribution to price risks. With diversification, you atomize your resources and spread them across travel routes, pieces of land, cell phones, or rental car agencies. In order to benefit from pooling across various outcomes, you have to split up what you have.

This logic is especially true for your most precious resource — your time and experience. Stephen Curry is arguably the greatest basketball player active today; did he get there by specializing in one sport and devoting all his energy toward that sport? Contrary to popular sports parenting wisdom, specialization in one sport is not recommended for amateurs or promising high-performance athletes. And it's not the path Curry took.

Rather than spending all his time on the basketball court as a youngster, he also played baseball, soccer, track-and-field, golf, and football. The science appears to back up the virtues of diversified experience, since engaging in multiple sports leads to fewer injuries and may even enhance skills that are primary in some sports and secondary in others. The logic of a liberal arts education is not terribly different — by preventing professional specialization at too early an age, exposure to a broad set of ideas flexes different intellectual muscles and provides alternative perspectives that feed a lifetime of learning.

The insight from finance is not only that diversification can help with risks but that there is actually a built-in bonus from diversifying your assets. This is actually a difficult logic as evidenced by the fact that various thinkers have not understood it — even John Maynard Keynes concluded, prior to the advent of modern portfolio theory, that "the right method in investment is to put fairly large sums into enterprises which one thinks one knows something about and in the management of which one thoroughly believes. It is a mistake to think that one limits one's risk by spreading too much between enterprises about which one knows little and has no reason for special confidence." But the logic of diversification has been intuitive to many for millennia; the advice in Ecclesiastes is to "invest in seven ventures, yes, in eight; you do not know what disaster may come." And in the Talmud, R. Isaac recommends "one should always divide his wealth into three parts: a third in land, a third in merchandise, and a third ready to hand."

The key insight from finance is that diversification of the type recommended in these religious texts not only reduces risks but can actually preserve returns. What could be better than similar returns with less risk? By investing in assets that perform differently, we can benefit from the imperfect relationship between assets. In fact, the best kinds of assets are those that behave very differently from the assets you already own—such assets, when included in your portfolio, reduce risk and can preserve returns. And assets that perform much like what we already own are of limited use for diversification purposes.

That lesson on the virtues of diversification also extends to our personal lives. A dear friend framed his portfolio problem to me in this way: "I know that the most important thing I can do with my time is to spend it with my children—but if I spend all my time with them, I'll screw them up terribly and probably go crazy myself. Why is that?" The finance take on this is that diversifying our experiences and relationships is precisely what we should be doing —relationships don't crowd each other out but they enrich each other. Being a good friend and colleague doesn't diminish your efforts as a parent but may well benefit those efforts.

In fact, the relationships that are most enriching are ones that broaden our perspective beyond our usual experience—those relationships are, in finance terms, "imperfectly correlated assets," precisely the types of assets that most enhance the portfolios of our lives. Similarly, filling our lives with only those people who think like we do and who experience the same world that we inhabit is not nearly as powerful. Just as Keynes found it hard to intuit diversification, the logic of a diversified portfolio of relationships runs counter to many of our instincts. Homophily, or the desire to surround ourselves with like-minded people, is a common social instinct—and one that finance warns against. Yes, it's easier to be around like-minded types, but finance recommends the hard work of exposing yourself to differences, not shielding yourself from them.

The ultimate logic deriving from the emphasis on diversification is known as the capital asset pricing model. Despite its intimidating name, it's a model that I find offers useful insight into our lives outside of finance as well. The gist of that model is that—given the virtues of diversification—individuals will hold many different investments and, consequently, every investment will be measured on the basis of how different or similar they are to the rest of that portfolio. In short, the risk of any investment can't be measured in isolation—the risk of an asset can only be measured by understanding how it behaves relative to a diversified portfolio and how it contributes to that portfolio.

So, here's what that model boils down to: assets that fluctuate very much along with your portfolio are "high-beta" assets that are not highly valued because of their limited diversification value. In fact, they make your exposure to the market even more pronounced —when the market goes down, these stocks go down a lot. The low values of these high-beta assets are the result of the high returns you expect from those assets—since they don't provide much diversification value, they'd better be associated with high returns. And here's the most elusive part of that finance logic—if you need high returns from assets, that can only be accomplished by giving them lower prices today. Lower prices for a given stream of cash flows *create* the higher returns you need to compensate you for the risk presented by these high-beta stocks.

As one example of this, consider companies such as Yahoo!, Clear Channel Outdoor Holdings, or Lamar Advertising. All of them make money by selling advertising online or outdoors—and Google Finance says they all have high betas of more than 1.5. What does a beta of 1.5 mean? These stocks will tend to move up 15 percent when the markets move up 10 percent and move down 15 percent when the markets move down by 10 percent. Why is that? Well, advertising—as the saying goes—is the first thing you cut in a recession and the first thing you bring back in a recovery, so they move in more pronounced ways than the economy itself. Because these companies do particularly poorly when your portfolio does poorly (they are high-beta stocks), they need to compensate you with higher returns, and that means they are less valuable assets.

"Low-beta" assets, in contrast, move with your portfolio but just not as much, so they don't need to generate as high returns and, therefore, have higher prices. As you may already surmise, betas are simply shorthand for the correlation of an asset with your portfolio. At the other extreme, "negative-beta" assets move in the opposite direction of your portfolio—when your whole portfolio does well, these negative-beta assets do poorly, and when your whole portfolio tanks, these stocks do very well. And for that reason these assets are very valuable. Their high value comes from the low expected returns you require of them; that is, since they provide such effective insurance, they don't need to give you explicit returns. In fact, such assets can be associated with negative expected returns precisely because they do such a good job of performing well when the rest of your portfolio is a disaster. It all goes back to the principles of insurance. Assets that provide insurance—by paying off when the rest of your assets do poorly—are very valuable, and you will pay dearly for them. And assets that exacerbate the risks you face in the rest of your portfolio are not highly valued and need to earn a high return to compensate you for all that additional risk exposure.

Gold is a good example of a very low or, even, negative-beta asset. I don't exactly know why people buy gold, but one logic is this: when paper money becomes worthless and we all devolve into a hellish world akin to *Mad Max*, you really want to be holding gold. So, you're willing to live with low or negative returns because gold provides you with that insurance. And even if the usefulness of gold in the *Mad Max* scenario is unrealistic, gold can still behave like a negative-beta asset if enough people believe that it should—by flocking to it at times of uncertainty.

An even more extreme version of this logic is manifest in the expected returns on my life insurance policy. Even if I die on my actuarially appointed date, the policy will have a negative expected return—all those premia over the years and the payout will have a negative return embedded in it. But that's okay, because I tremendously value the fact that when my family is most in need, the insurance policy pays out.

So, who are the high-beta, low-beta, and negative-beta assets in your life? The high-beta assets in your life are likely your LinkedIn network or professional acquaintances. These relationships are largely instrumental; in other words, these individuals are likely to show up when you do well and disappear when things go poorly. Accordingly, they should be given low values—it's not that they can't be a source of great benefits; it's just that they compound the risks you face and don't provide much insurance. When you're down on your knees, these assets provide no relief.

Low-beta assets are considerably more valuable—they are the steady friends who are there for you no matter what happens to you. In fact, this classification of friendships closely mirrors the taxonomy of friendships provided by Aristotle in *Nicomachean Ethics*.

The lowest form of friendship, for Aristotle, is the high-beta, transactional friendship where individuals "love each other for their utility" and "do not love each other for themselves but in virtue of some good which they get from each other." These are friendships that are thin and fragile as "if one party is no longer pleasant or useful the other ceases to love him." When you're succeeding, these high-beta friends surface, but they disappear when you stumble because you become less valuable to them. The much higher notion of friendship is the low-beta friendship where good individuals wish each other well without qualification based on the goodness that these friends feel toward them.

But Aristotle reserves his highest praise for the love that is unconditional—the negative-beta assets in your life. When you stumble the hardest, these people are there for you the most—and when you fly too high, they manage to pull you back down to earth. Noting that "most people seem ... to wish to be loved rather than love," Aristotle contrasts that typical sentiment with mothers who "take delight in loving" and "they themselves love their children even if these owing to their ignorance give them nothing of a mother's due." That sounds just like the negative returns we are willing to live with for negative-beta assets. When we love our negative-beta assets unconditionally—we give and give and give and expect nothing in return—that's negative expected returns.

The reason that the logic of diversification, the capital asset pricing model, and the idea of betas matches the Aristotelian taxonomy of relationships is that the underlying portfolio problem is the same. In finance, we are trying to figure out how to invest our assets and manage toward the best risk-return tradeoff. In life, we are trying to figure out how to allocate our time and energies across many people. It also matches because the underlying logic of insurance is present in both settings. For me, this parallel prompted several questions: Am I providing insurance to my loved ones and friends? Am I there when they need me the most? Am I dedicating too much time to the high-beta assets in my portfolio rather than realizing that they are relatively low-value relationships? And am I valuing the negative-beta assets in my life appropriately?

The story of Lizzy Bennet endures because she navigates her risk management problem as we all hope to. She rejects Mr. Collins as well as her mother as they play on her sense of risk aversion, trying to intimidate her into exercising the first option (Mr. Collins) she is presented with rather than waiting for her true love (Mr. Darcy). She doesn't exercise the option provided by Darcy, her ultimate true love, when he first proposes, as he seems insufficiently dedicated to her and excessively self-obsessed. Instead, she waits until she is ready. She stands by her relationships with her sisters and measures Darcy by his actions toward her family, refusing to choose one over the other and understanding that these relationships should enrich each other. She comes to appreciate Darcy's differences in demeanor rather than being suspicious of them.

Ultimately, she realizes that Darcy is not working against her sisters' interests but is actually a reliable ally. Her visit to Darcy's estate is a critical turning point as she learns of his generous character and steadfast nature from his staff — he is not the arrogant, opportunistic high-beta asset she was wary of. With risks investigated and returns well established, Lizzy gets a second bite at the apple as Darcy presents the option yet again, and now Lizzy doesn't hesitate. Instead of thinking of how much the loss of optionality would cost her, she "hits the bid." She seems to have understood that risk management is not a goal in and of itself — but rather a set of strategies to ensure that one can take the big bets one needs to take to truly create value.

# 3

# On Value

When we think about our talents and how we should use them, we don't consider our financial wealth itself as a talent. Our talents are more personal than a simple calculation of net worth. They are the gifts that make us special and the abilities that we develop over time. If there is a link between money and talents for our modern sensibilities, it is that money and fortune may accrue from the exercise of our talents.

Etymologically, though, talent is deeply linked to money. The original meaning of talent as a unit of weight (approximately 60 pounds) quickly morphed into a monetary unit associated with the value of coins corresponding to that weight. Scholars disagree about precisely how much a talent was worth, but estimates range from $1,000 to $500,000 in today's currency. More familiar monetary denominations — such as shekels and drachmas — were actually small fractions of a talent. So when, how, and why did the word for money become elevated to refer to a gift or an ability that defines us?

As we'll see, the Bible's parable of the talents played a crucial role. That parable, depicted opposite in an engraving by Lucas van Doetechum, corresponds well to the financial logic of value creation. You'll often hear finance practitioners talk about managers who create or destroy value and whether or not they are generating "alpha" or getting paid for "beta." The parable can illuminate that jargon.

The intuition of value creation corresponds closely to another preoccupation of finance — the valuation of assets. How do we know what any asset is worth? Anyone buying a home or a stock or a car must, implicitly or explicitly, be undertaking such a valuation. Is this asset "worth" what I'm paying for it? More broadly, any investment of time or resources requires a valuation. Should I pursue that educational degree? Should you send your child to the Russian School for Mathematics? All those kinds of questions require us to trade off a current sacrifice (tuition today) with some future benefit (your daughter's Fields Medal in 2040) — and that requires a valuation. The process of valuation is the same process that a company like Microsoft undertakes when it purchased LinkedIn for $26.2 billion.

Just as the parable of the talents illuminates finance's idea of where value comes from, the actual practice of valuing assets holds lessons on what is truly valuable in life. But these logics of value creation and valuation, like the parable, are extremely severe. As we'll see, the severity of that parable preoccupied two people — John Milton and Samuel Johnson — whose uses of the parable provide a more humbling take on where and how value is created.

• • •

In the Book of Matthew, Jesus is preparing his disciples for the Day of Judgment with a series of parables, including the parable of the talents. A master is going on a journey and entrusts his property, in the form of eight talents, to three servants—giving them five, two, and one talent, "each according to his ability." When he returns, he finds that two of his servants have taken these talents and doubled them through trading, into ten and four talents, respectively. The master, usually interpreted as God, is pleased and says to each, "Well done, good and faithful servant. You have been faithful . . . Enter into the joy of your master." Those servants are allowed to keep those talents and enter the kingdom of God. But the third servant, who received only one talent, tells God, "I was afraid and I went and hid your talent in the ground. Here you have what is yours" and returns his one talent.

God is not pleased. "You ought to have invested my money with the bankers, and at my coming I should have received what was my own with interest." As punishment, God takes the talent away from the poor servant and gives it instead to the servant who has ten talents, explaining, "For to everyone who has will more be given, and he will have an abundance. But from the one who has not, even what he has will be taken away." Then, God delivers the ultimate punishment: "And cast the worthless servant into the outer darkness. In that place there will be weeping and gnashing of teeth." The poorest servant is deprived of his talent and banished from the kingdom of God. Yikes.

While I wrestle with some dimensions of the parable, the main lessons seem clear—everyone has been endowed with talents and gifts; they are distributed unequally; they are incredibly valuable; and, most importantly, they should be exercised to their fullest extent. We are the stewards of those gifts and must make the most of them. At some point, we'll all be held accountable for what we do with our gifts, and living in fear and depriving yourself and the world of your gifts is sinful. There also seems to be a close connection to our earlier discussion of risk: one can try to insure against and manage risk to some extent, but, ultimately, life entails risks.

What does this Biblical tale have to do with finance? The big questions in finance are: how is value created, and how should we measure value? In particular, when we think of companies whose value goes up over time, it is because they are presumed to be creating value.

Finance's answer to the question of where value comes from is simple—the capital you're entrusted with has a cost because the people who gave it to you have expectations for returns. In fact, the returns they expect are a function of the risk we talked about before, and that risk is measured by how you respond to market fluctuations (remember those betas?). Their expected returns are your cost of capital. You are a steward of their capital, and the sine qua non of value creation is that you have to *exceed* their expectations and your cost of capital if you want to create value.

It's a brutal logic. For example, if you just meet investor expectations, you've done nothing of value. As one example, say your capital providers expect 10 percent for the $100 they entrust you with. If, in one year, you give them $110, you will have provided them with their expected return but not done anything special—you will have just met expectations, and nothing more. You could have stayed in bed.

Only by delivering, say, 15 percent is there value creation, because in that case you've gone above and beyond their expectations. Think of it this way: you start a restaurant and you sell meals at a price that is exactly the same as the cost of your ingredients and labor. That's not terribly exciting and is evidence that you haven't actually created any value beyond the cost of your inputs. That logic holds for capital as well, though the cost of capital is often not explicit.

The logic becomes even more brutal. If you generate a return with your investors' capital that is below their expectations, you've actually destroyed value. In essence, it would have been better if you didn't take their capital at all. You might think that you are doing well if you generate an 8 percent return. In fact, if they expected 10 percent, you destroyed value. You should have stayed in bed.

This logic of value creation has two corollaries. If you just exceed investors' expectations for one or two years, it's not that exciting. True value creation arises if you are a steward of their capital for multiple years and you beat their expectations every year. In a similar vein, if you can grow and continue to reinvest their earnings at a high rate of return, that's even better than simply returning profits to your capital providers—precisely because you're good at beating their expectations.

As one example, contrast the following two cases. In both cases, your investors expect 10 percent but you return 20 percent, so you're handily beating expectations. But in the first case, you do this for five years and only reinvest a quarter of their profits while returning the rest to them. In the second case, you do this for twenty-five years and reinvest all the profits until the very end. What's the difference in value creation? In the first case, you have effectively created value that corresponds to 50 percent of the capital you were entrusted with, while in the latter you would have created value of 900 percent of their investment.

In short, finance has a simple recipe for value creation—1) surpass the expected returns of your capital providers; 2) surpass those expectations for as long as you can; and 3) grow, so you can keep generating returns that are higher than your cost of capital. That's all that really matters for creating value.

There are at least two striking parallels between this logic and the parable. First, we are stewards of resources for others in both cases. That logic of stewardship and obligation is central to finance—we are overseeing the capital that others have entrusted to us, just as the servants must take care of God's talents. As Bob Dylan sang in his gospel classic, everyone's "Gotta Serve Somebody." We are all stewards—links in a chain of individuals charged with tending to our resources.

Second, that role of steward comes with high expectations, is risky, and can be characterized by great outcomes (high returns/salvation) or terrible outcomes (value destruction/damnation). There is a harsh and challenging logic to both: make the most of what you are given, be aware of how much you've been given and how much is expected of you, and make every effort to exceed those expectations.

The finance recipe for value creation can also easily be mapped to the way we think about our lives. The first step, "surpass the expected returns of your capital providers," can be understood as saying that you should give more than you take; that is, return much more to the world than the considerable talents you've been given. The second step, "surpass those expectations for as long as you can," is simply another way of saying never stop giving more than you take. Finally, "grow, so you can keep generating returns that are higher than your cost of capital" is just another way of saying that you should never stop investing in yourself and continue to grow. Postpone harvesting as long as you can — because the returns to investing in your efforts can be enormous.

The founder of Methodism, John Wesley, clearly understood the link between the parable of the talents and value creation back in the 1700s. He explicitly linked the parable to finance in a sermon titled "The Use of Money." The latter two parts of the sermon are summarized as "Do not throw the precious talent into the sea" and "Having, First, gained all you can, and, Secondly saved all you can, Then give all you can." This quote is in fact the origin of the more popular framing of Wesley's logic: "Do all the good you can. By all the means you can. In all the ways you can. In all the places you can. At all the times you can. To all the people you can. As long as ever you can." It is difficult to summarize the financial logic of value creation any better.

There is only a small step from the logic of where value comes from to the logic of how to value anything. Before we establish what finance's approach to valuation *is*, it's useful to be clear about what its approach to valuation is *not*.

Finance and accounting are often seen as basically the same and fundamentally interchangeable. Nothing could be further from the truth. Finance is a direct reaction against accounting and its limitations. Accounting uses balance sheets to tally the value of assets owned and obligations undertaken; income statements calculate annual profits and losses. Accountants take these calculations as fundamental, and indeed many individuals keep tabs on their own financial well-being with these techniques and assumptions.

For people in finance, accounting's approach to value is deeply troubling. Representations on balance sheets deliberately leave out a company's most valuable assets because of the idea of "conservatism": accountants give zero value to assets that they can't value precisely. In fact, the most valuable assets of companies like Coca-Cola, Apple, and Facebook (their brands, intellectual property, and user community) never show up on balance sheets. It gets worse. Because of the principle of historic cost accounting — that assets should be represented at their acquisition price — some assets are listed at values that are completely distinct from current values. You'll see balance sheets with large amounts of "goodwill" (the amount paid to acquire a company in excess of its book value) that may now have little value at all. As such, accounting and balance sheets are static and backward-looking by their nature. They are incomplete snapshots divorced from real value.

Individuals who measure their progress by tallying their own personal balance sheets will make the same mistakes that accountants make. They will undoubtedly emphasize a score-keeping system that prioritizes the many things that they can count precisely — which may well have no true value. Conversely, the score-keeping system ensures that truly valuable assets will never show up on the balance sheets because their value is too hard to put a number on.

Given that accounting is so problematic, finance adopts a different approach to measuring value. Finance's starting point in valuation is that previous accomplishments and what you have today bear little relationship to real value. Finance is completely and ruthlessly forward-looking. The only source of value today is the future. The first step of valuation is to look forward and project what a company or investment will produce in the future.

The second step is to translate those future benefits into today's values. Here's where finance acknowledges that waiting has costs. We are by nature impatient and we also don't like risk, so we charge for that—by means of the cost of capital we discussed before. We punish all future flows by diminishing their value according to that cost of capital to get their associated value today. And the longer you make us wait, the more severe the punishment will be. By translating all those future flows to the present, we will have arrived at what something is worth today—true value. That process is called discounting.

If you look at any valuation model used in finance, it has that basic structure. Ignore the past and present. Look forward to the future and project economic returns. Translate those back to today's value using a "weighted average cost of capital"—a blend of the returns expected by your debt and equity financing. That translation gives you what something is worth today—and if it's more than what you have to pay for the asset, you have a good deal.

Valuing an investment in education has the same structure—project forward the extra wages you will earn because of that education, translate those incremental wages back to today, and compare them to the tuition. If the translated future values are greater than the tuition, you have a good investment. Given how important and controversial educational investments are (and given that I'm in the education business), it's worth pausing to see how those calculations shake out.

A September 2016 memorandum on higher education produced by the Obama administration estimates that, across a career, a worker with a bachelor's degree earns nearly $1 million more than a similar worker with just a high school diploma. For an associate's degree, they earn $330,000 more. Does that tell the whole story? Given that a student has to wait for all those extra wages, it's critical to discount all those wages from the future to the present. When you do, you'll find that the present values of those extra wages are $510,000 for bachelor's degrees and $160,000 for associates degrees. Now, you simply compare that to tuition today to see if you're getting a good deal. Yes, this analysis (contrary to much misleading logic percolating around today) says that a college education is a great deal—but it doesn't mean that *every* college education is a great deal.

Valuing housing has that same structure but is trickier because it's hard to think about the returns to owning a home. To value a home, project forward the rent you won't now have to pay because you'll own a home, along with the property taxes and home improvements you'll have to make, translate them back to the present, and you'll have a home's value today. The comparison to rent not paid is critical—and it's the reason why the housing bubble persisted. People didn't realize that houses were incredibly expensive compared to renting through the early 2000s. If they looked at price-to-rent ratios, they would have seen how expensive buying a home had become.

Finance's approach to valuation is as harsh as the logic of value creation. Whatever you've done in the past doesn't matter and the only thing that matters is the future—and the longer you make me wait for my returns in that future, the greater the punishment via discounting. All value accrues from the future. In fact, any finance practitioner knows that standard valuation models result in the vast majority of value being attributed to so-called terminal values. The value of companies like Facebook, LinkedIn, and Twitter hinges on whatever assumptions we make about what they will do far off in the future—and these assumptions are captured in what people call terminal values. In short, though we project what they'll do in the next several years, the majority of their value is going to come from whatever we think they'll do well down the road. Similarly, in valuing housing, much of today's house value comes from what we think we can sell that house for in several years.

This brief description of valuation allows a taste of the finance approach and how it might refract onto our lives. First, ruthlessly look forward and ignore the past and present in deciding what value is and what actions to undertake. Your previous accomplishments and missed opportunities mean nothing when looking at yourself today. Second, this emphasis on the future means that all estimates of value and decision making are acts of imagination and fundamentally conjectural. Imagining alternative futures is critical for making good decisions, just as it is for valuing investments. Finally, most value arises from terminal values (reflecting returns into perpetuity) and not returns in the short run. We are in a long game, and most enduring value arises from what we leave behind — our legacies — and not what we enjoy while we're here.

I recall my father often telling me something that I now tell my daughters (my terminal values) — "the world belongs to the young." This is an adaptation of a Mao Zedong quote, but the sentiment permeates many traditions and it is an encapsulation of the logic of finance. We are in service of future generations, for it is their world much more than ours.

Parables, by their nature, are open to interpretation — that's what makes them so much fun and also allows them to endure for so long. In the case of the parable of the talents, there are several pieces that still puzzle me.

First, there is the unequal distribution of the talents to the three servants, explicitly suggesting that this distribution reflects the principle of "each according to his ability." Second, there is the redistribution of the talent away from the poorest and toward those who have more — and this is explicitly the goal: "everyone who has will more be given, and he will have an abundance. But from the one who has not, even what he has will be taken away." And finally, there is the harsh punishment of damnation meted out to the poorest servant. This "worthless servant" is cast "into the outer darkness. In that place there will be weeping and gnashing of teeth."

Here is where I find some lessons of the parable more mysterious. Why did the talents get distributed initially the way they did? Why redistribute toward the richest servant? Why deliver the ultimate punishment to the poorest servant who is guilty of, at most, fear?

For some practitioners of finance, these elements of the parable are not puzzling at all and ring true. They would argue: "The answers to your questions are clear. There are fundamental differences in ability across people, and truly talented individuals end up with great rewards because of their ability. As a result, more of society's resources should be under their control, given how talented they are. Individuals who garner fewer economic rewards are not as talented and often squander opportunity." This Randian worldview manifests the machismo that finance practitioners are often known for. Many practitioners of finance pride themselves on the meritocratic nature of their endeavors: the market is a harsh master and the results accord with ability.

But is this necessarily true? And if we don't know for sure, is it a good set of operating beliefs?

In order to explore this, it's useful to consider two remarkably talented and productive people who, as it happens, were obsessed with the parable of the talents. Samuel Johnson—who in eight years single-handedly created a dictionary that was the precursor of the *Oxford English Dictionary*—was haunted by the parable. And John Milton, author of the epic poem in blank verse *Paradise Lost*, repeatedly mentioned the parable in his writings and lost many hours of sleep to its logic.

No matter how much he accomplished, Samuel Johnson feared damnation for not using his talents fully. "He that neglects the culture of ground naturally fertile is more shamefully culpable than he whose field would scarcely recompense his husbandry." Johnson's sentiment is precisely the burden many gifted, privileged people feel. Rather than congratulating himself on being the beneficiary of the unequal distribution of abilities, he framed it as a task to live up to.

Moreover, in his poem "On the Death of Dr. Robert Levet," Johnson flips the lesson of the parable and praises a simple man who was not blessed with the many talents that Johnson knew he himself was blessed with. Levet was a poor man to whom Johnson gave shelter and Levet became a caretaker of sorts for those around him. While in many ways a completely unremarkable man, Levet was worthy of the highest praise from Johnson: "obscurely wise, and coarsely kind," an individual who, through the care and affection he gave those around him, demonstrated "the power of art without the show." Why did Levet deserve such praise? Johnson invokes the parable when he concludes:

> His virtues walk'd their narrow round,
>   Nor made a pause, nor left a void;
> And sure th' Eternal Master found
>   The single talent well employ'd.

Johnson, a man blessed with innumerable talents, took inspiration from a man with little material wealth or natural ability, but with the sole talent of providing care and affection to those around him. For Johnson, the parable is not a recipe for worshipping the "great men and women" of the world who have been given much, but rather a lesson in humility and a reason to appreciate the contributions of those who provide so much despite not being endowed as richly as he was.

Milton went even further in interpreting the parable. The son of a scrivener (a bookkeeper and a money lender), Milton was obsessed with his incalculable debts to his earthly father, who had invested so much in his education, and to his heavenly father, whom he saw as the source of his poetic talent. Milton repeatedly worried that he wouldn't be able to settle these debts and used the parable to voice his concern. He, like many of us, bumbled around for years looking for what at the time was called "credible employment." This concern reached a climax in Milton's forties when he discovered he was going blind. While he had already accomplished much as a pamphleteer for free speech and republicanism during the English Civil War of the 1640s, he had yet to use fully the talents he knew he had for poetry — and the progression of his blindness made him worry that he never would.

In the sonnet "When I Consider How My Light Is Spent," Milton frames his fear of damnation in terms of the parable of the talents. As he is losing his sight, he is tortured by the fear that his "one talent that is death to hide" is "lodged with [him] useless," given his impending blindness.

Milton works his way out of the tortuous bind he faces by switching from the parable of the talents to a totally different parable, the parable of the workers in the vineyard. In that parable, God is a landowner who hires workers for his vineyard. Some begin working in the morning, and others, who have been standing around all day, begin working near the end of the day. He promises to "pay them whatever is right." At the end of the day, God pays all of them the same amount regardless of when they began working, creating rancor amongst those who worked a longer day. God replies, "I will give unto this last, even as unto thee . . . Is thine eye evil, because I am good? So the last shall be first, and the first last."

In Milton's sonnet, the harsh logic of the parable of the talents gives way to the more forgiving message of the parable of the workers in the vineyard. Concerned that God will punish him because he has squandered his talents, Milton pushes back his anxiety and impatience by concluding

> "God doth not need
> Either man's work or His own gifts. Who best
> Bear His mild yoke, they serve Him best. His state
> Is kingly: thousands at His bidding speed,
> And post o'er land and ocean without rest;
> They also serve who only stand and wait."

In other words, there is more to the world than the harsh logic of the parable of the talents, and one cannot live by its lessons alone. There is kindness, generosity, and forgiveness — and the parable of the talents ignores all that, says Milton. The generosity of spirit that Milton gleaned from that second parable may well have allowed him to complete *Paradise Lost, Paradise Regained,* and *Samson Agonistes,* all after he went completely blind.

While the parable of talents corresponds nicely to the intuition of value creation, another important set of ideas in finance directly contradicts the harsher elements of that parable — as well as the harsher elements of the worldview that some in finance tend to exhibit.

That harsh, meritocratic worldview is well encapsulated by the idea of "alpha." Many people in finance, particularly investors, frame their efforts as "alpha generation" and deride those who get "paid for beta." What in the world does this mean? As we saw, beta is a measure of how a stock moves with the market. And that co-movement with the market is the risk that investors can't diversify away and must bear, and therefore demand compensation for. So money managers who get paid for providing returns that are just associated with bearing that risk are doing nothing of value. According to the logic of valuation, they are not creating value. Yet, they are still being compensated handsomely — they are being paid for beta. Returning to our previous example, they are just meeting expectations, yet they think they're creating value.

In contrast to this freeloading logic, "alpha" represents value creation—these are the returns above and beyond expected returns. In short, alpha generators have reached finance nirvana. You are truly generating value, beyond any returns expected for risks borne, when you generate alpha.

The mistake people in finance make all too often is reflected in their appreciation of the more challenging parts of the parable of the talents. They attribute much of their success and returns simply to alpha generation and they pride themselves on it. In reality, finance teaches us that it is very difficult to know the extent to which our efforts are responsible for generating alpha. As a consequence, much of what we label as alpha generation is anything but.

As one example of this, consider the coin-flipping experiment. This experiment is a provocative way to humble any investors who pride themselves on their success as it directly rebuts the idea that alpha is easily labeled or generated. In a room full of a hundred of your friends, ask everyone to take out a coin, flip it ten times in a row, and record their results. You'll find that you're almost guaranteed to have one friend who gets ten heads in a row. Here's the key insight: that friend is indistinguishable from an investor who says they've beaten the market ten years in a row. Why?

Well, it goes back to the nature of randomness and the quincunx. While most balls will fall in the middle and generate the normal pattern, you're guaranteed to have some balls way over on the sides. And when you have tens of thousands of professional investors, you should expect to see many people with remarkably good performance. But it might have nothing to do with their skill; it's entirely possible that it's luck—they are just the balls that landed way off on the side of the quincunx. In fact, if anything, the puzzle is why more professional investors don't do better than the market, based on luck alone.

The lesson from this experiment is that it is very difficult to disentangle skill from luck in finance. First, there is the nature of randomness that will make any measure of success unreliable. Second, there is the inability to identify cleanly which risks have been undertaken, creating ambiguity over what expected returns should have been. Finally, there is now plenty of evidence that indicates that few money managers consistently beat the market, after consideration of their fees.

This last piece is what is known as the efficient markets hypothesis — it is very hard, if not impossible, to consistently beat the market. That hypothesis is much derided today because of the convulsions of the markets and because many professional investors have an interest in making people believe that it is untrue. And naïve formulations of efficient markets — all available information is in prices already — are surely untrue. But the more thoughtful formulations — that it is very hard to beat the market and generate alpha consistently — are well supported.

So, the machismo that heralds market outcomes as clear indicators of effort and ability should be tempered. And the heroism associated with the supposedly meritocratic nature of finance is unjustified. If anything, there is no endeavor where it is easier to recharacterize luck as skill and bad performance as exceptional performance than within the field of finance.

In fact, that is what we see in large chunks of finance. The massive growth of the alternative assets industry over the last three decades is an underappreciated development in our capital markets. That development is predicated on the idea that some investors — such as hedge funds, private equity funds, and venture capital funds — are truly skilled and can generate alpha. That alpha generation serves as the foundation for their fees. Their fee structures — so-called carried interest — are a function of their performance, so, the logic goes, they only get paid when they do well.

Of course, the reality is not quite so benign. These investors have been shown to not outperform reasonable benchmarks on average, and the evidence of skill for most of them is fleeting — except for, perhaps, funds in the top decile of those funds. And their compensation is predicated on benchmarks that don't usually reflect the risks they undertake. Similarly, executive compensation contracts that naively use stock performance to judge how managers are doing are deeply misguided. Separating skill from luck over shorter horizons (less than ten years) is nearly impossible in financial markets. Large chunks of compensation arrangements throughout the economy don't reflect this reality—and have actually contributed handily to growing income inequality.

Finance cautions against attributing outcomes to efforts and skills in a simplistic way. Luck is a dominant and underappreciated part of life and performance. The lesson of finance is one of humility—as it was for Johnson and Milton. The harshest aspects of the parable of the talents—and the worldview of many practitioners of finance—can usefully be tempered with humility, generosity toward others, and a keen appreciation for the force of luck in life.

The logic of valuation is the logic of stewardship and obligation, giving back more than you take, working for future generations, and not confusing outcomes with efforts. The philosophical aspects of finance's approach to valuation should come as no surprise—aren't we all trying to create value in our world? Finance's search for value parallels our own search for meaning.

When we began, we used the etymology of "talent" to find our way to finance. We conclude by using the etymology of "finance" to find our way to meaning. When I ask my students what finance is about, they often reply "money." In fact, finance is rooted in the Latin "finis," which means a "final payment or settlement," as in the settling of a debt with a final payment. The first known use of "finance" is from the medieval story "Tale of Beryn," which is sometimes included in Chaucer's *Canterbury Tales*. In it, one of the characters considers his life and states, "To make from your wrongs to your rights, finance." In short, living up to and settling one's obligations is the road to salvation.

When the Day of Judgment arrives, have you financed?

# 4

# Becoming a Producer

B efore there was Lin-Manuel Miranda's *Hamilton*, there was Mel
Brooks's *The Producers*, the 2001 Broadway hit musical starring Nathan Lane and Matthew Broderick. Yes, *Hamilton* won an incredible eleven Tony awards in 2016, but it didn't break the record
of twelve set by *The Producers*. And before the musical *The Producers*, there was the 1968 film *The Producers*, the hilarious original
production, which was written and directed by Brooks.

In the movie, Zero Mostel played Max Bialystock, a has-been
Broadway producer who is so down on his luck that he's wearing a

cardboard belt. Bialystock charms older women into writing checks for his latest effort but craves a return to lunches at Delmonico's and expensive suits. Leo Bloom, played by a young Gene Wilder, is a meek and innocent accountant who walks into Bialystock's office and stumbles into a big idea.

Bialystock and Bloom decide to sell ownership stakes in a musical to naïve investors that far exceed the 100 percent required for the production. Having raised much more money than they need, Bialystock and Bloom will find the world's worst script, director, and cast and produce a horrible show that will surely be forced to close immediately. Since there won't be any profits to divide up, investors will simply lose their money and will attribute their loss to the bad reception on Broadway. Bialystock and Bloom will then abscond to Rio de Janeiro with all the excess money they raised—and the investors will never know that they collectively own 25,000 percent of this flop, because there won't be any profits to share. As long as there aren't any profits, Bialystock and Bloom will be in the clear, and, surely, it must be much easier to create a flop than a success.

They produce *Springtime for Hitler*, a horrendous and offensive production with sloppy direction, and Bialystock and Bloom fully expect it to close after the first night. The audience, initially offended and unsure of how to react, decide instead to interpret it as a parody and find it hilarious, transforming *Springtime* into a huge hit and destroying Bialystock's and Bloom's hopes. In the final scene, Bialystock and Bloom are in prison replicating the scam by selling too many shares in a production of *Prisoners of Love*.

We've looked so far at matters of risk and return and why investors choose to invest, but there's also the matter of how and why investors get their money back. This might seem like a trivial matter because, obviously, they own their share in a company or a production and are therefore due their share of the profits. But *The Producers* captures an essential truth of finance—investors have few rights and usually have little knowledge of what actually is going on.

So then the puzzle becomes, as economists Andrei Shleifer and Robert Vishny put it, why "suppliers of capital get *anything* back. After all, they part with their money and have little to contribute to the enterprise afterward. The professional managers and entrepreneurs who run the firms might as well abscond with the money." In other words, why doesn't capitalism collapse into an endless series of frauds? Why don't all entrepreneurs do what Bialystock and Bloom tried to do, and why does anyone invest in anything, given the risks that their money might end up in the hands of opportunistic managers or outright frauds?

The answers to these questions illustrate the central problem of modern capitalism—the principal-agent problem—and understanding that problem provides a powerful frame for thinking about our lives.

Once upon a time, capitalism was simple. Think back a few hundred years. Merchants, farmers, and storekeepers owned their businesses and managed their businesses on an everyday basis. Yes, there were departures from that—including slavery and the role of sovereigns in commerce—but I already indicated that this was a fairy tale.

As commerce grew, the scale of enterprise grew as well. That growth of scale required capitalism to adapt to these fundamental changes. It was no longer tenable for one owner to be the only owner, as enterprises required lots of financing to grow. And as the number of owners multiplied, it also became clear that the people who actually ran the businesses would not be the same people as the owners. So now, enterprises previously run by owner-managers have separate owners and managers.

As just one example of this, the largest individual owner of Apple is CEO Tim Cook, but he owns only 0.02 percent of the company. Even the largest mutual fund owner of Apple owns less than 10 percent of the company. There are millions of investors in Apple who have decided to delegate the job of running Apple to managers

—and these investors expect the managers to pursue what is in the best interest of the investors in Apple.

For financial economists, this transition to companies with diffuse owners who delegate authority to professional managers is akin to Adam biting the apple in the Garden of Eden—it represents the end of innocence and the beginning of the modern world.

Why is this change so profound?

Consider the mighty Tootsie Roll, the first individually wrapped penny candy in the United States. Founded in 1896, Tootsie Roll Industries is still publicly traded and now owns other candies as well—including Charms Blow Pops, Dots, and, my personal favorite, Junior Mints. In January 2015, the CEO who had been running Tootsie Roll died, somewhat unexpectedly. How did the shareholders of Tootsie Roll react? Was there a period of mourning? Was there a wave of panic selling over who would take over?

In fact, the stock price went up . . . by 7 percent. What? Joy at the death of a CEO? In fact, this reaction is somewhat common. Unexpected CEO deaths provoke very strong reactions, and very often these are positive. How could that be? Occam's razor would suggest something simple—the shareholders were happy to see the CEO gone. But couldn't they have thrown him out? Wasn't he supposed to be working for the shareholders?

Positive reactions to unexpected CEO deaths, in addition to being vaguely ghoulish, are a manifestation of the basic problem that arises when owners delegate authority to managers—those managers don't always do what they're supposed to, and shareholders struggle to control these managers. This is the problem of corporate governance and a manifestation of the principal-agent problem. It's also the fundamental problem of modern capitalism.

You've undoubtedly come across a version of this problem in your own life. We all grapple with the principal-agent problem when we interact with contractors, lawyers, doctors, and just about anyone who does something for us. In these settings, we (the principals) appoint someone (an agent) to do something on our behalf (build a house, argue a case, take care of our health). The problem has two dimensions—first, they may be motivated to help us but they undoubtedly have their own agenda (providing for their own families, the desire to leave work early); second, we can't always know if they're working on our behalf—we simply can't watch them all the time and they may know much more than we do (Do I really know the quality of concrete they used in my home? Do I really know if I need that MRI? Or, who owns that MRI center?).

Now imagine that same problem on a much larger scale, with the trillions of dollars invested in companies. In all these companies, shareholders can't monitor managers, and managers know much more about what is going on than shareholders ever could—that's called informational asymmetry. How do you know if Tim Cook has the right strategy? How do you know how hard Tim Cook is working? There simply isn't any way to know those things definitively. And managers aren't evil, but they sometimes have their own personal agendas, which may not be coincident with those of the owners. Might Tim Cook build a new headquarters at One Infinite Loop with shareholder funds that is much nicer than required so he can enjoy it and enjoy the adulation of his employees and colleagues? He's not being evil, but you wouldn't be surprised if he thought about himself before he thought about his millions of owners. So, the whole game in modern capitalism is about identifying ways to make sure managers do what they're supposed to do for owners—even when they have their own agendas and owners can't watch them.

In the Tootsie Roll case, shareholders had come to question if the CEO was advancing their interests. The candy industry had been consolidating quickly so that candy companies could counter the massive power of supermarkets and other food companies. Getting shelf space was getting harder and more costly, so candy companies were getting bigger in order to compete for that shelf space. Many companies had expressed interest in buying Tootsie Roll at a very significant premium to current stock price levels. But the CEO of Tootsie Roll wasn't willing to go down that path, even though Tootsie Roll sales had been flat for many years and many investors wanted him to consider selling. Why was the CEO resistant to their pleas?

Well, part of the reason might have been that the CEO knew that selling the company would deprive him of his job—a job that came with $8 million in compensation, including $1.2 million that the company spent annually on a private plane to take him from his home in Massachusetts to Chicago every week. And those numbers are very large when you consider that the company only had $500 million in annual sales. Tim Cook gets paid millions of dollars, but his company's revenues are $150 billion—three hundred times that of Tootsie Roll.

This problem of ensuring that people have the impetus to do what others are counting on them to do—in economese, that's aligning incentives—has become central over the last one hundred years as companies have grown dramatically in scale. That's what the corporate governance scandals of the early 2000s (remember Enron and WorldCom?) were about, as was the credit boom and overleveraging of financial institutions prior to the financial crisis. All too often, managers asked themselves: Why not lend to another unworthy speculative home buyer when it will generate fees today that fuel my salary and the default will come long after I'm gone? The Wells Fargo scandal of 2016 provides yet another example of misaligned incentives with large societal costs.

We've been experimenting with solutions to this problem for the last one hundred years. How might we solve it? In the personal setting, we often rely on reputations—of contractors, lawyers, doctors to help protect ourselves. We also rely on professional codes of conduct. Both mechanisms can help in finance as well, but they are imperfect. For example, will taking the Hippocratic Oath always stop a doctor from ordering that extra MRI from the clinic that he co-owns with the other doctors in his practice? How useful is the reputation of a CEO when it might take more than a decade to know the quality of her decisions—well after she's moved on to her next job?

Agency theory is the part of finance about the ways we can solve that underlying problem of misaligned incentives. Unfortunately, these solutions are only partial—and come with their own set of problems. The most significant way we've tried to solve the agency problem is with stock-based compensation for managers. If managers have skin in the game, they will internalize the interests of shareholders, and the alignment problem will be solved. But that grand experiment over the last forty years has yielded mixed results, to say the least. Yes, perhaps managers are more attuned to their owners' perspective, but now we have a new set of problems. Who decides how much stock managers should get? In theory, a company's board of directors decides, but in practice it can feel like the managers decide how much stock to give themselves, and everyone goes along with it because it's not "real" money, i.e., cash. More dangerously, as managers prepare to sell their stock, they have strange incentives to alter firm performance to their advantage. In short, they can have an incentive to burnish their current performance by sacrificing the future well-being of the company.

Much of what we observe in capital markets are other methods of addressing the agency problem. Why do we see large activist hedge funds causing problems for companies by taking controlling stakes and asking for changes? What about when hedge funds bet against companies by going "short"? These activists actually provide leadership to all the diffuse shareholders—they monitor managers and pressure them to do the right thing. And those evil short sellers may be, in fact, seekers of truth as they try to unmask those managers who are perpetrating frauds. And these short sellers have succeeded, with Enron, for-profit colleges, and others. Many people regard these players as leeches extracting value from productive enterprises — but the other view is that they are solving a deep problem.

Similarly, private equity funds, such as Kohlberg Kravis and Roberts or Blackstone, are predicated on the premise that their abilities as owners will allow them to create value. They provide another solution to the agency problem by replacing the diffuse ownership of public capital markets with concentrated ownership so that they can watch managers carefully. Venture capitalists, who fund early stage companies, are particularly preoccupied with this problem and, as a result, stage their investments in bite-size portions with curious instruments like "convertible preferred stock." The peculiarities of these financial practices are designed to facilitate the monitoring of entrepreneurs and to make sure they are pursuing an agenda that is coincident with their investors' agenda.

Alas, these "solutions," too, have yielded their own problems. Activist investors and short sellers are paid in ways, including contracts that allow them to reap gains over short horizons, that can lead them to place short-term gains over long-term value. Private equity might seem better, but these investors are also paid with similar contracts that provide incentives to harvest investments at particular horizons. And private equity investors often ultimately take their companies public, leading to a set of games they can play because of their informational advantages prior to a public offering.

These activist and private equity investors serve as principals for their managerial agents — but they themselves are agents for another set of principals! These investors are the agents of large pension funds and endowments funds, which have appointed the investors to safeguard their capital and earn good returns. Oh, and those pension funds, which are the principals of those investors, are actually *our* agents, as savers and retirees. In short, capital markets begin to look like a daisy chain of principal-agent contracts, each with significant problems and conflicts.

Let's return to Apple. In 2013, Tim Cook faced a revolt triggered by the actions of David Einhorn of Greenlight Capital, who wanted Cook to start releasing all the cash that was building up inside of Apple. Cook, and Steve Jobs before him, had resisted calls to release that cash. Einhorn was the principal telling his agent, Tim Cook, to return that cash to shareholders. But Einhorn is himself the agent of state pension funds that have delegated to him the job of generating returns. And those state pension funds have our savings invested in them, and we've appointed those pension fund managers to manage our wealth. It is a series of principal-agent relationships—we (the ultimate principal) save through pensions funds (our agents), which appoint David Einhorn (the agents of the pension funds), who monitors Tim Cook (the agent of David Einhorn), who appoints Jony Ive (Cook's agent as Apple's chief design officer), who appoints . . . you get the idea. Once you become attuned to the principal-agent relationship, it's hard not to see it playing out everywhere in life.

In many ways, the biggest debates today on what is wrong with capitalism are actually debates about finance and agency theory. For some, the big problem is that the proponents of agency theory have been too successful: managers now only care about their owners! They should be looking out for workers, customers, and the environment, too. If only managers would be more capacious in their thinking and not just pursue profits, the world would be a better place.

For others, the big problem is that we just haven't internalized the lessons of agency theory well enough: managers are misbehaving all the time and are not focused exclusively, as they should be, on creating value for their owners! We have managers pursuing short-run profits rather than long-term value, investors taking on too much risk because of screwed-up incentives, and pension funds who pay way too much in fees because they are asleep at the wheel.

Who's right? That's the subject of a different book. But, for our purposes, it's worth revisiting the Tootsie Roll story to grasp how all this relates to our lives. It turns out that the story is richer and more complex than I've made out so far. The CEO who died, Melvin Gordon, had married into the Rubin family, that had historically controlled Tootsie Roll. He had been CEO for more than fifty years (he died at age ninety-five) and had repeatedly refused the overtures of Carl Icahn, a notorious corporate raider, who had wanted to sell the company to a larger candy company, like Mars or Hershey's. The Gordon/Rubin family owned a fair chunk of Tootsie Roll, but the key is that they controlled the company with a separate class of shares that had extra voting rights, effectively meaning they would always call the shots.

So the first version of the story — irresponsible CEO ignoring the will of shareholders (an agent not fulfilling the goals of his principal) — is somewhat simplistic. The Gordon family itself was a significant shareholder and had its own agenda, which the CEO was serving. Moreover, the Gordon/Rubin family felt that Icahn and other shareholders would probably not serve the full set of constituents that the family cared for: a sale of the company might lead to the loss of jobs for longtime employees, a relocation of activities that might hurt communities, and a winnowing of brands that would deprive customers of their treasured candy treats. Icahn, in turn, felt that the Gordon/Rubin family, selfishly entrenched with their powerful voting shares, was not taking care of the other shareholders.

As a result, the principals in the Tootsie Roll case (the shareholders) are not speaking with one voice, and the agent (the CEO) may be pursuing his own agenda *or* might be responding to his sense of what *his* principals want (his family shareholders and other constituents). It gets more complex still. Icahn is himself an agent for the pension and endowment funds he manages money for. Is Icahn (now the agent) pursuing a sale of Tootsie Roll for the long-run interests of his principals (his pension fund investors) or is he pursuing his agenda of short-run profits to improve his own track record so he can attract more funds to manage?

What does this complex Tootsie Roll saga tell us? Yes, the principal-agent frame is an incredibly powerful frame to understand modern capitalism. But that frame does not yield simple, clear answers about who is right and who is wrong. In fact, the situation can be quite muddled. Principals can be divided or unclear in their agendas (i.e., which principals should the CEO serve?). It can be difficult to tell if agents are self-serving or honest advocates (i.e., is the CEO doing the right thing?). Sometimes people who look like agents are in fact acting as principals (i.e., CEOs can have other constituents they are serving). And people who look like principals are, in fact, also agents with their own principal-agent problem (i.e., investors are themselves agents with questionable motives).

Welcome to the muddle of modern capitalism! So, returning to the original question: What's wrong with modern capitalism? It turns out the answer is: it's complicated. Screeds about how our financial markets are rigged and opaque may well contain grains of truth—but they miss out on the complexity of the problem we are trying to solve with financial markets.

The principal-agent framework is a powerful lens for understanding the muddle of modern capitalism and the role of finance. The principal-agent framework can help us frame the right questions to ask ourselves about capital markets and, surprisingly, is also extremely helpful in arriving at the right questions when we confront the muddle of our lives.

I've found the lens of principals and agents very helpful in understanding the muddle of life on four dimensions. First, and most obviously, in professional settings, the principal-agent lens is a guide to understanding our roles: When we serve as supervisors, are we empowering our subordinates to fulfill their obligations? When we are delegated a task, are we pursuing it as our supervisors wanted or in a way that serves our own agenda? Second, our roles in families lend themselves to a principal-agent lens, though the actual roles we play at different times shift as we age and take care of children and aging parents.

While these first two settings are about our relationships with particular individuals, the next two applications are about how we navigate our relationships with social expectations and with our own past experiences. Are we serving as principals who articulate our own agendas or as agents of hidden principals? In each case, as with the muddle of modern capitalism, we take up the lens of principals and agents not on a quest for conclusive answers but in order to generate the right questions.

As I've sought different teaching challenges, I ventured at one point into leadership and organizational behavior. One of my favorite cases to teach—so good that even a finance professor can teach it—is about a young hotshot executive with an MBA who has risen quickly and is now struggling with an older subordinate who isn't performing to the executive's expectations. The case is rich in setting the stage, including how the executive has tried to provide feedback to the subordinate. I usually begin the discussion by polling the class on whether they would 1) fire the subordinate, 2) try to coach the subordinate, or 3) work around the subordinate by creating parallel positions. When I press them into role-playing their preferred choices, students who once glibly advocated their answers are usually humbled by the prospect of actually undertaking any of these actions.

But the biggest payoff of the case comes from the ultimate realization that the problem likely isn't the subordinate at all. There are obvious clues littered throughout the case, but students generally just aren't sensitive to them—it usually takes forty minutes or so for someone to realize what has actually been going on. The problem is that the hotshot executive has delegated responsibilities to the subordinate and then proceeded to undercut him at every turn. As a result, the subordinate is frustrated and demotivated—and ultimately leaves the company and industry.

The hotshot executive then gets his comeuppance (in the case update), as this obsession with control is persistent and his senior managers have noted it. The ability to delegate to agents successfully is a critical managerial building block, but the hotshot doesn't appear to know how to do it. He's penalizing his agent for not fulfilling the agenda that he gave him, but at the same time, he is subtly not allowing him to succeed in that role.

When I've taught this case, students seem to immediately see themselves as either the hotshot executive or as the subordinate. For some, it recalls situations where they have been agents caught in a vise of unreasonable expectations and insufficient resources. Others recall their own pathologies in being unable to delegate and then undercutting the very people who could help them. In some sense, the professional world is an aggregation of principal-agent problems—and figuring out whether principals are being reasonable managers is as complicated as figuring out if failing agents are disempowered or incapable. Like the executive in the case study and the individuals in my classroom, we tend to assume that the problem is outside of ourselves—and the principal-agent lens can remind us that the truth is likely much more nuanced.

Several years after my father passed away, my sister and I debated my mother's living arrangements. My mother had a reliable and considerate caretaker, but she was living an increasingly solitary life. We were worried that this solitude might ultimately lead to depression or a shorter lifespan. My sister and I live very close to each other, and we soon stumbled on the idea of moving my mother nearby so she could access her children and her grandchildren easily. It was one of those ideas that, after you have it, you wonder why it took you so long to think of it. She would be able to see all of us at literally a moment's notice, thereby breaking the growing solitude of her life.

I raised the idea with my mother and she reacted cautiously. I pressed my case by explaining all the evident advantages. She continued to resist and I continued to press. Finally, she silenced me with, "But I still see your father in this home. I don't want to leave him." She knew precisely what to say to get me to retreat, and I did.

My sister and I reconnoitered. We were convinced that our mother would like the new arrangement but that she was just resisting the act of change. Once she made the change, we knew she'd be delighted. We contemplated pushing our plan even more aggressively because we knew our mother would, ultimately, do what we wanted.

As we discussed it, it gradually began to occur to me that perhaps she simply didn't value being so close to her children and grandchildren. Perhaps she liked her current life more than the life that we had imagined for her. Even worse, it dawned on me that our plan might reflect our desires rather than hers. Moving her closer would make our lives considerably easier, and my sister and I wanted our children to have maximal exposure to her.

In the name of advancing her interests, were we actually just advancing our interests? Were we truly serving her as her dutiful agents, or were we making her into an agent of our own agenda to improve our own lives? At the same time, it was unclear whether she was even being a good agent for her own interests, since her resistance may have just reflected the costs of change rather than the benefits of the new arrangement in the future. Finally, above it all, it was unclear what my father would have wanted us to do for her. In many ways, he was a hidden principal that I was trying to please. Without us realizing it, the situation had become a muddle — with principals pretending to be agents and a hidden principal with an ultimately unknowable agenda.

These same questions are apparent in child-rearing. Most parents, myself included, like to think of ourselves as dutiful agents on behalf of our children. We want them to be "all that they can be" and the "best versions of themselves." When we speak like that, we are thinking of our children as our principals whom we are merely helping toward their own self-realization.

But in practice I find that version of parenting pretty superficial. Inevitably, children become agents of our agendas as well. Sometimes, that happens innocently—the children become accustomed to choices that reflect parental preferences and then internalize those preferences. They're much more likely to follow our professions and enjoy the things that we like, relative to some random draw from the general population. In fact, for many of us, the chief responsibility of parenting is the act of imprinting a set of values on our children—if that's the case, who's the agent and who's the principal in parenting?

Sometimes the reversal of principal and agent roles happens not so innocently or consciously. Many of us parent with the best of intentions but are guilty of projecting our unrealized ambitions or hopes onto our children. In those situations, we pretend to be agents of our children's dreams and potential, but we are actually the principals trying to force our agents/children into a mold.

The lens of the principal-agent problem can't tell us what the right thing to do is, but it can make us aware of how muddled the situation can be—and how the stories of work and family life that we often tell ourselves are narratives shaped to our own ends. Being aware and honest about our roles as principals and agents might allow us to be slightly better colleagues, spouses, parents, and children than we might otherwise be.

By my count, E. M. Forster uses some version of the word "muddle" nineteen times in *A Room with a View*—and I've used it eight times so far in this chapter. In fact, Forster's whole story is about a muddle —the muddle of whether we choose what society expects of us or what we truly want. It's a muddle because it isn't always clear to us why we're choosing what we choose—because we want it or because society expects us to want it. Are we being agents of social expectations or being true to ourselves as principals?

Lucy Honeychurch is a young woman whose love and passion is triggered by George Emerson, an unconventional and philosophical sort, on a trip to Florence. After returning to England, she sublimates those feelings and follows societal expectations by getting engaged to the charmless and inert, but socially privileged, Cecil Vyse. Lucy finds herself in a muddle—unsure of her feelings toward Cecil and George and unsure what agenda and whose agenda she is pursuing.

Finally, George's father diagnoses what has troubled Lucy all along and articulates the reality that Lucy has been denying. George's father says,

> "My dear, I am worried about you. It seems to me that you are in a muddle . . . Take an old man's word; there's nothing worse than a muddle in all the world. It is easy to face Death and Fate, and the things that sound so dreadful. It is on my muddles that I look back with horror—on the things that I might have avoided . . . Though life is very glorious, it is difficult . . . 'Life' wrote a friend of mine, 'is a public performance on the violin, in which you must learn the instrument as you go along.' I think he puts it well. Man has to pick up the use of his functions as he goes along—especially the function of Love." Then he burst out excitedly; "That's it; that's what I mean. You love George!"

Lucy is convulsed by the realization and resists it but she knows that, in fact, George's father is right. She has been serving society's expectations and ignored her own voice, creating the muddle of her life.

Elle Luna channeled that same sentiment in her imaginative and explosively popular blog post, and subsequent book, *The Crossroads of Should and Must.* She describes our lives as a constant series of such crossroads — and why the path of "should" is alluring but unfulfilling: "Should is how *others* want us to show up in the world — how we're *supposed* to think, what we *ought to* say, what we *should* or *shouldn't* do. It's the vast array of expectations that others layer upon us." That is the safe choice most of us make, and that Luna was making, without even thinking about it. It was also what Lucy Honeychurch was about to do: become an agent of societal expectations.

For Luna, the path of "should" must be rejected in order to pursue the path of "must": "Must is who we are, what we believe, and what we do when we are alone with our truest, most authentic self. It's our instincts, our cravings and longings, the things and places and ideas we burn for, the intuition that swells up from somewhere deep inside of us. Must is what happens when we stop conforming to other people's ideals and start connecting to our own." In other words, "Lucy, go for George" — stop being the agent of social expectations and be your own principal.

The tension between "should" and "must" drives not just *A Room with a View* but has many precedents in literature. In fact, Leo Bloom of *The Producers* was, as you might have guessed, named after Leopold Bloom of James Joyce's *Ulysses.* Mel Brooks gave (at least) two explanations for this. The flip explanation was, "I don't know what it meant to James Joyce, but to me Leo Bloom always meant a vulnerable Jew with curly hair."

Brooks, appearances to the contrary, is a serious intellect who reveres literature and aspired to be a novelist early in his life. The choice of the name Leo Bloom reflected that appreciation of literature as well as this theme of self-realization. For Brooks,

> in the course of any narrative, the major characters
> have to metamorphose. They have to go through an
> experience that forces them to learn something and

change. So Leo was going to change, he was going to bloom. He would start out as a little man who salutes whatever society teaches him to salute . . . but in Leo Bloom's heart there was a much more complicated and protean creature — the guy he'd never dare to be, because he ain't gonna take them chances. He was going to play it straight and trudge right through to his grave, until he ran into Max . . . they catalyze each other . . . so much so that this innocent guy comes up with the idea of making a fortune by producing a surefire flop and selling twenty-five thousand per cent of the profits in advance to old ladies.

Bloom stands at the crossroads of "should" and "must," and Bialystock helps him choose "must" — with all the attendant consequences. Life is, in part, about challenging what is expected of us and given to us in order to find ourselves. As Joyce puts it in the novel featuring Leopold Bloom, *Ulysses*, "What's in a name? That is what we ask ourselves in childhood when we write the name that we are told is ours." Are we being agents of others by following expectations — as Lucy Honeychurch, Leo Bloom, and Elle Luna each come to recognize in the worlds they inhabit — or can we become our own principals? Can we create the meaning of our names?

In the middle of *The Producers*, the playwright of *Springtime for Hitler*, a German with obvious Nazi sympathies, wants to celebrate selling his script to Bialystock and Bloom. He suggests that they toast "the greatest man that ever lived," but, because "the walls have ears," they should whisper the name. The playwright whispers "Adolf Hitler," assuming Bialystock and Bloom will do the same. Bialystock whispers "Max Bialystock," and Leo Bloom whispers "Sigmund Freud." Bialystock's line gets more laughs, but the Bloom line is more telling.

It turns out that Mel Brooks has always been somewhat obsessed with Freud. Many of his earliest routines, including those with Carl Reiner and his 1963 Oscar-winning brilliant short film *The Critic*, feature riffs on psychoanalysis. In describing his source of inspiration for Bialystock and Bloom, Brooks said, "Max and Leo are me, the ego and id of my personality. Bialystock—tough, scheming, full of ideas, bluster, ambition, wounded pride. And Leo, this magical child."

In fact, Brooks spent years in therapy, wrestling with his childhood. His father had died when Brooks was two, and Brooks worshipped his mother, claiming, "If I could go skinny dipping with her, I would." Kenneth Mars, the actor who played the German playwright, remembered Brooks describing his childhood and considered it crucial to understanding him. Brooks told him, " 'You know, my feet never touched the floor until I was two because they were always passing me around and kissing and hugging me.' Mars continues, "I think that's a key: the kind of image he has of himself as the evergreen child, the child who brings you fun."

In this final version of the principal-agent problem, our childhood experiences end up serving as the hidden principals whom we end up serving whether we know it or not.

Nearly everyone involved with *The Producers* seems to have had seriously complex childhoods that shaped their lives. Sidney Glazier, who became *The Producers'* producer, had a harrowing childhood. After his father died, his mother took up with another man and paid an orphanage to take the child off her hands. Movies became "the loveliest and best escape from the troubled life I inherited." But the scars were long lasting. His daughter explained that, while he was "a genius at charming people," he ended up being "impossible to live with"—a man who divorced four times whom she considered bipolar because he "moved between self-destructive tendencies and the will to survive." The other producer, Hollywood mogul Joseph Levine, was a poor and fatherless child who said he couldn't recall "one happy day growing up"—he lived his adulthood doing magic tricks in his office for visitors, experiencing the childhood he never had. Gene Wilder called Mel Brooks "daddy," just as Brooks turned Sid Caesar, the genius behind *Your Show of Shows* who gave him his first break, into a surrogate father.

When I hear descriptions like these, I can't decide if it's all psychobabble or something deep and true. I read Freud in college and found his ideas incredibly alluring. But then I read the ultimate takedown of Freud by the literary critic Frederick Crews, who demonstrated how nonscientific the whole endeavor is. Still, I come across these ideas and they sound right. I even recently found myself channeling them as I complained to a colleague about another colleague (yes, the stereotype turns out to be true—academics can be that petty) and I said, "It's like he's acting out some crap that happened to him as a child." We joked about how, as we get older, we appreciate more and more how influential our childhoods are —and then went back to our catty kvetching about him.

Psychoanalyst Stephen Grosz's book, *The Examined Life*, provoked those same mixed reactions in me. In this short book, Grosz provides mini case studies of his patients and their problems. On the one hand, every case seems to come down to some injustice or memory of childhood that plays itself out in adulthood—it all seems so precious and "just so" that it can't be right. On the other hand, it's an illuminating and resonant set of vignettes about his patients and their struggles—and you can relate to each of them.

At the end of the story of Peter, a young man who unconsciously sabotages his friendships and relationships, Grosz concludes: "Karen Blixen [aka Isak Dinesen, author of *Out of Africa*] said 'all sorrows can be borne if you put them into a story about them.' But what if a person can't tell a story about his sorrows? What if his story tells him? Experience has taught me that our childhoods leave in us stories like this—stories we never found a way to voice, because no one helped us find the words. When we cannot find a way of telling our story, our story tells us—we dream these stories, we develop symptoms, or we find ourselves acting in ways we don't understand."

For me, the lesson of that book is that many of our problems as adults are reflections of unresolved experiences that we had as children. As adults, we turn into unwitting agents of sublimated experiences and much of adulthood is just about figuring out that you *are*, in fact, an unwitting agent of those experiences. Ultimately, it's about learning to not be an unwitting agent—and to be conscious of those past experiences and to become a principal, a conscious architect of your own life.

The best example of this may be the archetype described in *The Drama of the Gifted Child* by Alice Miller. In this short book, Miller describes what happens when intuitive and sensitive children are coupled with a demanding parent. These children become extremely well attuned to the signals and needs of those around them, as it has historically been the key for them to receive love. But they grow up unable to project their own desires and agendas onto the world because they have become so accustomed to fulfilling the needs of others. These children grow up to be exemplary agents, engines of achievement as they seek to be admired. But they can't figure out how to be principals when they are adults. Never having had to formulate their own agenda, they find themselves deeply unsatisfied and frustrated as they only know how to fulfill the needs and dreams of others. They are trapped in the role of agents who don't know how to become principals. And then they repeat that cycle with their children. In short, Tiger Moms beget future Tiger Parents.

Show business marriages must be complicated affairs. Outsized egos and the attention of the press and fans complicate marriages, I imagine. But by most any metric, Mel Brooks and Anne Bancroft seemed to have succeeded for thirty-one years, until Bancroft's death in 2005. Bancroft, best known for her role as Mrs. Robinson in *The Graduate*, was an accomplished actress who won an Oscar and a Tony for the same role, Helen Keller's teacher in *The Miracle Worker*. Later in her life, she took on many producer and writing roles in addition to her acting roles. On top of that, she put up with Brooks for decades, which probably qualifies her for sainthood.

In discussing the differences between writing and acting, Bancroft told the following story to the theater critic Kenneth Tynan. "One evening, I came back late from a difficult rehearsal. Mel had been working at home all day. I was feeling very sorry for myself, and I wailed, 'Acting is so hard.' Mel picked up a blank sheet of paper and held it in front of me. '*That's* what's hard,' he said. I've never complained about acting again."

Without diminishing the art of acting too much, this vignette seems to hit on an essential truth. Yes, it is hard to play a role authored by someone else and be the agent of a screenwriter. But it is harder still to be a principal, where you are called upon to author and produce that story from whole cloth. Sidney Sheldon, the seventh best-selling fiction author *ever* (he knew how to confront a blank piece of paper!), may have been channeling Mel Brooks (or Freud) when he said, "A blank piece of paper is God's way of telling us how hard it is to be God." The act of creating ourselves is a miracle—and, fortunately, we have more than seven days to become principals rather than agents.

# 5

# No Romance Without Finance

F or the truest depiction of Wall Street on film, I think you have to
go way back before *The Big Short* and *The Wolf of Wall Street*.
Mike Nichols's 1988 film *Working Girl* vividly captures most of the
best and worst of Wall Street—the sexism, the snobbery, the self-
indulgence are all there, but so is the emphasis on talent, the competition, and the joy of solving problems. Besides, you get younger
versions of Melanie Griffith, Harrison Ford, Sigourney Weaver, and

Alec Baldwin—all with clothes and hairstyles that only made sense in the 1980s.

Tess (Melanie Griffith) is a secretary from Staten Island anxious to make it in the high-stakes game of mergers and acquisitions. Her boss, Katharine (Sigourney Weaver), is the archetypal investment banker—preppy, brash, selfish, and deceitful. Katharine is in a relationship with Jack (Harrison Ford), the good-guy investment banker who works hard and wants to solve problems for his clients. When Katharine injures herself in Europe, Tess begins acting in Katharine's stead and advises her client, Trask Industries, to merge with a radio station owned by Jack's client. Jack meets Tess without realizing that she's Katharine's secretary, and as they work together on the merger, they fall for each other. Katharine returns and tries to disrupt the mergers, but Trask and the radio station, and Tess and Jack, are already beholden to each other.

In one of the most memorable scenes, Tess is hiding in the closet as Katharine is trying to seduce an unwilling Jack. Katharine gives voice to her romantic sentiments in a way that only an investment banker could. Tired of waiting for Jack to propose, Katharine pulls at Jack and says: "I've been thinking—let's merge, you and I. Think of it, darling: Mr. and Mrs. Fabulously Happy!" While it is one of the least romantic proposals you can imagine (rivaling the proposal of Mr. Collins), the proposal hints at the parallels between the process of merging companies and the process of combining lives in a marriage.

Is it just obsessive investment bankers who see romance and finance as intimately linked? After leaving the Art Tatum Trio, guitarist Tiny Grimes ventured off on his own and partnered with Charlie Parker in 1944 to create one of the classics of bebop jazz, "Romance Without Finance." Grimes's conclusion was unequivocal —romance without finance just didn't make any sense. Without a hint of irony, Grimes sings, "You ain't got no money you can't be mine . . . Romance without finance is a nuisance." Charlie Parker and his bandmates repeatedly affirm the sentiment by shouting in the background, "You ain't kidding brother!" and "It's a drag!"

Fifty years later, the rock band Little Feat released a song with the same title but reversed the Tiny Grimes message, providing a more typically romantic view. Little Feat challenged the Tiny Grimes logic directly with these considerably more anodyne lyrics: "What's money got to do with love? . . . I'll take romance over finance every time."

A similar contrast emerges from the first hits of Ray Charles and Kanye West. For his first hit in 1954, Ray Charles sampled a popular devotional song, "It Must Be Jesus," to create "I Got a Woman," and mixed the sacred and profane in new ways. In that song, he praised a woman for the purity of her love and sang, "She gives me money, when I'm in need. Yeah, she's a kind of friend indeed." Fifty years later, Kanye West, like Little Feat, reversed that original, romantic sentiment by sampling Ray Charles's first hit.

The prelude to the song has Jamie Foxx imitating Ray Charles, but this time he's providing a more cautionary tale by substituting key words. Foxx sings, "She take my money, when I'm in need, Yeah, she's a trifling friend indeed." Fortunately, Kanye turns out to not be quite that cynical. He then goes on to combine the two opposing views of the relationship between love and money in the rest of the song. He repeatedly overlays the sweet sentiment of Ray Charles's "I Got a Woman" with his own more cautionary advice. Just as Jamie Foxx/Ray Charles is lovingly telling us, in the original lyrics, that she gives him money when he's in need, Kanye is adding his own cautionary tale about how she may well be a "gold digger."

At certain times, we might choose to believe the sweet sentiments of Ray Charles and Little Feat. But the pragmatism of Tiny Grimes and Kanye West also resonates. History would seem to be on the side of Grimes and West regarding the deep links between finance and romance. From the financing of Renaissance Florence to the rise of the Rothschilds to the creation of the automobile industry to the early days of the internet, finance and romance have been inextricably linked—and the accumulated financial folklore and wisdom about mergers can provide some hardheaded insight into what makes romantic relationships work.

To understand the linkages between finance, romance, marriage, and mergers, I journeyed to the setting where these linkages were most manifest—the center of the Renaissance, fifteenth-century Florence. While most people associate Italy with passion and romance, they overlook the fact that modern banking has its origins in medieval and Renaissance Italy, where the northern cities of Genoa, Lucca, and, most importantly, Florence witnessed the origins of what we now call a bank. The oldest functioning bank today is based nearby in Siena—the Monte Dei Paschi di Siena—and it recently celebrated its 550th anniversary. Most significantly, the Medici Bank, and the family associated with it, came to dominate Renaissance Florence and, in many respects, are responsible for the cultural awakening and revolution that was the Renaissance.

As I travel to the state archives in modern-day Florence, it becomes clear to me that the romantic aura of Florence is fortified by finance at every corner. I'm crossing from the Pitti Palace (once the home of Cosimo I de' Medici), across the Ponte Vecchio (the bridge covered by the remarkable Vasari Corridor that allowed the Medicis to cross the Arno without mingling with the hoi polloi), to the Uffizi (built by the Medicis), and through the Piazza della Signoria (the Signoria was the political body controlled by the Medicis to great effect—today the Medici Lions overlook the Piazza) to the Basilica of Santa Croce (home of the private Medici Chapel).

I arrive at my destination, the Archivio di Stato di Firenze. Originally housed in the Uffizi, the archives have been moved to a hulking, brutal, brown monstrosity of a building built in the 1980s with rust-colored external staircases. Even the Italians made bad stylistic choices in the 1980s. Francesca Klein, the generous archivist who has agreed to meet me, has kindly arranged a tour of fifteenth-century Florence, where one of the most ingenious manifestations of the deep links between finance and romance was born—the Dowry Fund, or the *Monte delle doti.*

We begin by reviewing several letters of the Strozzi family, once one of the richest families in Florence. After all the men of the family were exiled because they were perceived as too great a threat to the Medicis, Alessandra, the matriarch, wrote numerous letters to her son Filippo about his sister Caterina and her uncertain marital future. Francesca explains that marriages were a dominant concern for families during that time as they were critical to extending and strengthening the businesses and power of the merchant families. In effect, marriages created business alliances.

Sixteen-year-old Caterina's marital prospects, Francesca explains, were particularly problematic, as her family was in exile and, consequently, held in some disrepute. Finally Alessandra writes, overjoyed, as an engagement with Marco Parente has been arranged —along with a dowry of one thousand florins. Dowries (payments from a bride's family to a groom's) were a dominant social institution in Florence, and Francesca shows me numerous archival records of all the dowries paid in Florence in the fifteenth and sixteenth centuries.

The importance of marriages and dowries gave rise, along with other circumstances, to the Dowry Fund. The Dowry Fund—an early feat of financial engineering—solved three seemingly unrelated problems. First, parents of daughters were faced with a marriage market where young women significantly outnumbered eligible older men, in part due to the plague. As one reflection of this, dowries were escalating in price rapidly, creating more risk for fathers and their daughters. Without a sufficient dowry, either the nunnery or a life of prostitution awaited a daughter. As one example, Francesca shows me dowry records featuring the payment of 833 florins to one Paolo upon marriage to Magdalena, and the payment of 50 florins to a nunnery upon the entry of Margherita to that nunnery. Failure to match in the marriage market was costly in many ways.

Increasing and uncertain dowry prices gave rise to a second major concern. As dowries became more important, men became even more concerned with ensuring that they extracted substantial dowries upon marriage from the bride's families. Indeed, several examples emerged of grooms waiting years for dowries to be paid. Finally, the Florentine state was teetering on a fiscal disaster. Mounting debts from wars with Milan and Lucca were now threatening the state.

The confluence of uncertain dowry prices, groom anxiety over dowry transfers upon consummation of marriages, and unstable government finance gave rise to the Dowry Fund.

In 1425, the government of Florence inaugurated the *Monte delle doti*. Citizens could loan money to the state for fixed interest rates at the time of their daughter's fifth birthday, and these accounts would mature ten years later, along with their daughters (giving new meaning to the idea of "yield to maturity"). The account could only be redeemed upon consummation of a marriage and would be paid directly to the groom by the state. In this way, the state had a powerful new fundraising tool, fathers were insured against rapid dowry inflation by generous interest rates as well as a precommitment to save, and grooms were guaranteed the payment of the dowry by the state rather than by a father who might renege.

Talk about financial innovation. As Francesca shows me yet more letters concerned with marriages and dowries, I am comforted by the fact that we only have to think about 529 plans for our daughters instead of dowry funds.

Initially, though, the *Monte delle doti* was a bust — only two fathers participated. Rates weren't sufficiently attractive at 11 percent, and, more importantly, the contract stipulated that the death of the daughter prior to maturity resulted in the fathers forfeiting their principal. With high mortality rates, this just wasn't a good deal for an anxious father. Facing even more fiscal pressure, the government revised the *Monte delle doti* in 1433 to allow for repayment of the principal upon the death of daughters and raised interest rates to as high as 21 percent.

The Dowry Fund then exploded in popularity and became a dominant form of the financing of Florence in the fifteenth century. In a city with a population of fifty thousand, nearly twenty thousand accounts were established over one hundred years. Art historians have speculated that *The Arnolfini Portrait* by Jan van Eyck that opens this chapter, one of the most famous paintings of a wedding, actually reflects the payment of a *Monte*-linked dowry.

Ultimately, the *Monte delle doti* proved unstable—like many government-funded deals that appear too good to be true—and had to be restructured . . . several times. But the central role of the *Monte* was clear. Observers regarded the fund as "the heart of this body which we call city" and believed that without it, Florence would have been "deflowered" (i.e., overtaken by a rival). Aside from being central to the survival of fifteenth-century Florence, the *Monte* did much more. In the words of Julius Kirshner and Anthony Molho, the leading scholars of the *Monte,* "the dowry fund was the principal institutional vehicle preventing the morcellization of the collective patrimony of the ruling class while concurrently encouraging class endogamy."

Translation from academese: the *Monte* allowed elites to keep inmarrying (endogamy), rather than marrying up-and-comers with large cash dowries, and thereby perpetuated the economic strength of the elites rather than diluting that power. Indeed, these scholars point to the *Monte* as the reason for the durability of the elites of Florence relative to other elites in other city-states.

The dowry fund encouraged what is known as "assortative mating," where individuals mate with people like themselves rather than at random. As a result, elites could stay in power by creating strategic alliances between elite families. Marriages were, in effect, mergers between powerful families, and the *Monte* was the financing mechanism that allowed them to keep pursuing those mergers.

Indeed, marriages as mergers between economic interests are common through much of history. Most obviously, royalty preoccupied with sovereign strength have always viewed marriages through this lens. The French phrase *choix du roi* reflects the notion that having a son first and a daughter next was the preferred choice for French sovereigns. The firstborn son ensured continuation of the royal lineage, and the second-born daughter was an asset to be deployed strategically via marriage with would-be allies.

That same prism on marriage characterized the view of the most important financial family since the Medicis—the Rothschilds. During an era when marriages became more romantically oriented, the Rothschilds chose a different path. While many families viewed marrying within their community as important, the Rothschilds took that process much further. As the individual responsible for transforming a family firm that traded antiquities into the largest banking empire of the nineteenth century, Mayer Amschel benefited enormously from his marriage. He married the daughter of a court agent, a critical person responsible for the financial dealings of local peerage. As historian Niall Ferguson puts it: "In addition to the benefits of association with her father, the match brought Mayer Amschel vital new capital, in the form of a dowry of 2,400 gulden. It was to prove the first of a succession of carefully calculated Rothschild marriages, laying a foundation of prosperous kinship every bit as important as the foundation of royal patronage represented by the title of court agent."

During a critical phase in the family's dominance on the financial scene, the Rothschilds were inspired by royal examples to inbreed, to a degree that was unprecedented at the time. Beginning in the 1820s, there were nearly twenty marriages within the family, largely between uncles and nieces, designed to ensure that the five branches of the family stayed together and that power and wealth remained consolidated. In short, their standards made it appear, as Ferguson puts it, that "only a Rothschild would really do for a Rothschild."

When Hannah Mayer chose to marry outside of the family in 1839 (almost straight out of the plotline of a nineteenth-century romantic novel), the family reacted violently, to ensure that the message was clear. James, one of the Rothschild leaders at the time, wrote to his brother: "I and the rest of the family have . . . always brought our offspring up from their early childhood with the sense that their love is to be confined to members of the family, that their attachment for one another would prevent them from getting any ideas of marrying anyone other than one of the family so that the fortune would stay inside the family. Who will give me any assurance that my own children will do what I tell them if they see that there is no punishment forthcoming?" Indeed, inmarriage did stave off the Buddenbrooks-like decline that most family firms experience, as the Rothschilds ended up flourishing for several generations to come.

If you think marriages as mergers of economic interests are something relegated to the distant past or to sovereigns and quasi-sovereigns (like the Rothschilds), think again. In a fascinating study of the role of marriages in the business elite of Thailand, several Thai scholars found that for family businesses that rely on connections (such as construction), almost all the children of those families marry other elite families in those connected industries, as opposed to children in non-connected industries. And it pays off. When children of elite family businesses marry the children of other elite family businesses, the share price of those family businesses appreciates significantly on the announcement of the marriage. No such stock price appreciation happens when these children marry "commoners."

It's not just in the cultures of Asia. Modern America is increasingly characterized by marriages of individuals with similar financial power. In fact, one of the major drivers of increasing income inequality recently has been the revival of assortative mating. With more marriages happening between individuals of similar earning power and educational pedigree, economic power has become more concentrated. Some estimates suggest that if mating were to happen as randomly as it did in 1960, household income inequality would have changed little over the last fifty years. In other words, it's not just Nicky Hilton marrying James Rothschild—it's all of us marrying people in the same social and educational strata. Just take a look at the weddings section of the Sunday *New York Times*—a section known as the M&A pages to people in finance, and one that is the subject of matrimonial Moneyball analyses where pedigree is quantified and analyzed.

This lens of marriages as mergers opens the door to applying the wisdom of finance to our romantic lives. In fact, the determinants of successful mergers are a bread-and-butter topic in finance and the closest we come to seeing the emotion and tumult of romantic love and marriage in the commercial world. And we know a lot about what goes right and wrong in mergers—and maybe that can help us understand marriage.

The parallel between mergers and marriages was never more clear than (*cue wavy dissolve accompanied by romantic music*) . . .

*ONCE UPON A TIME*, in Paris, the City of Love, our two lovers met for the first time. It was the beginning of a classic "May-December" romance. The age difference between the lovers was twenty years, but, to many, it seemed more like they were children of completely different eras. Our "December" had already been through two very complicated marriages and was desperately seeking rejuvenation as he pondered his longevity and the meaning of life. Our "May" was at his peak power of attraction, in full bloom. He had burst on the society scene over the last decade and become the center of that world's attention. But May knew his power was fleeting and he sought the steadiness and status of an older man.

Initially, May was in hot pursuit, chasing December to Beijing, so that May could "accidentally" bump into him again. May quickly realized that he would have to be more straightforward. May arranged a dinner in New York in a private dining room so they could share stories about their histories and visions of the future. Discovering a foundation of common values, May dropped all pretense and just popped the question. And December readily agreed, only two months and three meetings after the initial meeting in Paris.

Their extended families were shocked at the sudden decision, but close family members came together quickly and celebrated the engagement privately at May's home over a 1990 bottle of Château Léoville–Las Cases. In a few days, news of the engagement was spilled all over the wedding section of the *New York Times* and other society outlets. It was the marriage of the decade, and perhaps of the century.

The cracks began to appear early, but the momentum of the public's expectations was too much to stop them. December hadn't tried to find out much about May and discovered along the way that May was a tough negotiator who reneged on key promises. But the promise of their union overshadowed any warning signs. It was only months after the actual wedding when the wheels fell off the marriage. May had obscured the less flattering aspects of his background and found December's ways to be old-fashioned. December had less tolerance, and less use, for May's youthful exuberance than he had first imagined. The thrill of their whirlwind romance quickly disappeared. After just one year, it was clear that the union was in serious trouble, but they muddled along, as unhappy couples sometimes do, for eight years until the divorce became final. Both May and December came to rue the day they had met in the City of Love.

That whirlwind romance, impulsive marriage, and massive flameout constitute a thinly disguised story of the merger between AOL and Time Warner in 2000. I've dressed it up as a fairy tale, but, otherwise, the actual story was that dramatic. Our "December" was Jerry Levin of Time Warner, and "May" was Steve Case of AOL. Aside from their age difference, the companies were truly from different eras. AOL had grown up in the previous decade as the most prominent example of what the internet could be, with its twenty million subscribers. Time Warner was a stodgy media company with prized assets that just couldn't figure out the internet.

The AOL–Time Warner merger was enormous, a combined value of nearly $350 billion, and magical. Veteran venture capitalist Roger McNamee said at the time, somewhat breathlessly, "Let's be clear: This is the single most transformational event I've seen in my career." Ted Turner, the swashbuckling entrepreneur whose company Levin had acquired earlier in the decade, was on the board of Time Warner and owned $9 billion of Time Warner stock. When asked if he found it difficult to vote for the merger, Turner said, "I did it as enthusiastically as when I first made love some forty-two years ago."

By the time it all was done, views had changed. Turner, having lost a good chunk of his wealth but not his hyperbolic manner, declared "the Time Warner–AOL merger should pass into history like the Vietnam War and the Iraq and Afghanistan wars. It's one of the biggest disasters that have occurred to our country." Somewhat more moderately, the most capable manager of both companies, Jeff Bewkes, said, "It was the biggest mistake in corporate history." Depending on how you count it, over $200 billion in market value was destroyed. It's little solace to the shareholders and employees that got crushed in the AOL–Time Warner merger, but the truth is that many, and some say most, mergers fail. And the failures of AOL–Time Warner are representative of the most common mistakes.

So, what went wrong in the marriage of AOL and Time Warner? Just about everything—and, in fact, the mistakes read like a playbook for disaster drawn from the finance folklore of what makes mergers succeed or fail. With only minimal revision, the mistakes of AOL–

Time Warner might just as easily be a playbook for disaster drawn from matrimonial folklore of what makes marriages succeed or fail —just substitute people for the companies and see if works for you.

1. *Due diligence is critical:* Time Warner never did appropriate due diligence—the thorough investigation and vetting of a target company's financials and operations—and subsequently found fairly significant accounting fraud. That fraud was the result of an aggressive sales culture at AOL that was fostered as the blistering growth rates of the mid-1990s began to cool. When companies put themselves up for sale, they routinely flatter their financial statements. Only due diligence can serve to avoid extremely costly mistakes —Hewlett Packard spent $11 billion on Autonomy only to find it had bought something closer to $1 billion in value.

2. *Filling a hole in your organization is not a merger strategy:* Levin had struggled with adapting to a digital media age and thought that, in one fell swoop, he could compensate for being behind fast-paced technological change. Efforts to build that capability internally were always short-circuited and not given the resources to succeed. But Levin was willing to bet the company on the AOL merger so that he could fill the gaping hole in his organization.

3. *Racing against the clock leads to bad decision making:* Levin felt pressure to do something, as his tenure at Time Warner was coming to an end. Case knew that it was only a matter of time until the sky-high valuations of internet companies would come crashing down. They proceeded with little outside advice (within their companies or from advisors) and on impulse decided to merge their companies.

4. *Synergies are always overstated . . . :* The pervasive buzzword in mergers is "synergies"—the increases in value that will

result from an acquirer's ability to grow revenue or cut costs when the entities are combined. The 1 + 1 = 3 logic is tempting—we will quickly change the other organization to help realize the great value that can emerge from the union. For AOL and Time Warner, it was the promise of cross-selling opportunities and content sharing. Those opportunities were never realized for cultural and marketing reasons. In many ways, AOL and Time Warner effectively remained separate entities, never growing together in any meaningful sense.

The illusory promise of quickly changing a target to realize synergies is usually accompanied by flowery language and sentiments that obscure the underlying challenges. Dick Parsons, who became CEO of the combined entity, provides a vivid example. When asked about the merger, he said:

> We need to marry up with all of that kind of content that exists in the Time Warner space and then we need to create a unified platform and we need to sort of drive convergence. It's not like convergence is anything more than the ultimate expression of vertical integration. It's just that instead now we have this big stack, we smoosh it all into one thing. The merger is about these larger notions of creating a truly vertically integrated company that is built offensively and defensively powerful in terms of protecting itself not only today in terms of the way the business is prosecuted and the way content is delivered, but going forward in the converging world.

Right.

5.  . . . *and the costs of integration are always understated:* The hard work of mergers never shows up in the forecasts done by bankers at the time of deals. Integrating the headquar-

ters, merging sales forces, and combining back offices always sounds easy but is costly and takes longer than anyone expects. In the AOL–Time Warner example, it became clear early on that integration would be painful when they couldn't even adopt a common email platform. This is also known as "unreasonable expectations are your enemy."

6. *Asymmetric mergers are easy but of limited value, and mergers of equals are horribly difficult but potentially very rewarding:* Mergers where one organization dominates another —also known affectionately as "bolt-on acquisitions"—are easy because the dominant organization can simply force changes and savings. But they also don't occasion that much value creation. Mergers of equals are incredibly hard, given the joint decision making they imply—but they are the only occasions when the logic of 1 + 1 = 3 is even feasible. AOL and Time Warner had the worst of all worlds—AOL went in thinking that they were dominant, and Time Warner became dominant as soon as the deal was consummated and the tech bubble burst.

7. *Serial acquirers are problematic:* Levin was on his third big deal, having risen through his adept handling of the huge Warner Brothers and Turner Broadcasting mergers. Serial asymmetric acquirers who bolt on targets easily might actually learn something along the way that will make them more efficient at these transactions. But serial acquirers who take on large mergers, as Levin did, are likely addicted to the thrill of the deal and have little appetite for the hard work of a real merger and the management of a combined entity.

8. *Ultimately, it's all about culture, "doing the work," and execution:* For all the finance in mergers, any practitioner will tell you that culture and execution are everything. Dick Parsons said that AOL and Time Warner were "like different spe-

cies, and in fact, they were species that were inherently at war." The supposed opportunities for cross-selling and synergies that motivated the merger were also reflective of deep cultural differences. But it wasn't just cultural differences —no one seemed up to the gigantic task and hard work of executing on the merger. When AOL and Time Warner split in 2009, Steve Case concluded, in a tweet, no less, "Thomas Edison: 'Vision without execution is hallucination'—pretty much sums up AOL/TW—failure of leadership (myself included)."

While the AOL–Time Warner debacle provides a cautionary tale about mergers and serves to embody the folklore around mergers and marriages gone wrong, it leaves open many deeper questions. Why merge at all? When should firms combine operations and when can they simply do business with each other? In finance, these questions reflect the problem of the "boundaries of the firm." When should we draw the boundaries of an organization so that a given customer, competitor, or supplier is outside the boundary or inside the boundary? This framing makes clear that there is always an alternative to a merger, such as contracting with an outside party. If you can contract with someone for given services, why should companies merge at all?

To frame this in a more personal setting, consider your daily transportation needs. Putting aside mass transit, how can you fulfill those needs? Today, one can wake up in the morning and decide to use Uber and contract with them on the spot. There is no membership fee to Uber, and I can transact at will and immediately, or not —that's a spot market transaction. Alternatively, I could enter into a twelve-month lease with an automobile dealer. I don't own the car but I have the ability to use it at will within certain parameters, such as mileage limits. Finally, I could buy a car and have complete control of that asset. That continuum—from a spot market transaction to a contractual arrangement all the way to ownership of the asset —is the continuum that we all live on for everything we need from another party.

Very roughly speaking, this continuum of spot markets (Uber) vs. contracts (car leases) vs. mergers (car ownership) corresponds in the personal relationship setting to Tinder vs. living together vs. marriage. Obviously, marriage does not involve "owning another person" but it does correspond to a decision to merge with another person —which is what the logic of the boundaries of the firm is all about.

So when should you do which and why? The story of General Motors and Fisher Body in the 1910s and 1920s is, for economists, *Anna Karenina, Middlemarch,* and *Jane Eyre* all rolled in one—the classic story that explains the nature of flirtation, commitment, marriage, and love.

After its founding in 1908, General Motors continued to acquire distinct car companies through the 1910s—including the companies that would become the Cadillac and Chevrolet divisions. During this period, they were purchasing auto bodies (think of a car's skeleton) from various suppliers, including Fisher Body, a firm run by the Fisher brothers. Fisher Body grew quickly during the 1910s, becoming the exclusive supplier to Cadillac and producing 370,000 auto bodies by 1916.

Auto bodies were changing in the 1910s and 1920s, as all-wooden bodies were giving way to wooden bodies with metal skins and, ultimately, to all-metal bodies. While wooden auto bodies were relatively simple to make, metal bodies weren't, and every car model had different metal body needs that couldn't be adapted from other models, like the more flexible wood bodies could. So, body manufacturers soon had to invest in metal dies and factories that were specific to a given model. By 1919, GM needed Fisher to invest a fair amount to manufacture these new bodies, particularly as open metal bodies (think convertibles or imagine a Model T) were giving way to closed metal bodies.

These technological changes in body manufacturing required a change in the relationships between Fisher and GM. Previously, GM was effectively transacting in a spot market for bodies, putting in orders for bodies as they needed them. But, in 1919, GM and Fisher entered into a ten-year contract for buying bodies, and GM bought 60 percent of Fisher, though the Fisher brothers would continue to run their company. The contract had two major provisions—GM committed to buying all of their closed metal bodies from Fisher (an "exclusive dealing" provision), and Fisher guaranteed a price that was their cost of manufacturing and transporting a body, plus a 17.5 percent markup of those costs, or what they were charging for comparable bodies to other auto makers (a "price protection" provision).

By the mid-1920s, closed metal bodies were exploding in popularity, far beyond GM's expectations, as they came to constitute two-thirds of the overall market. And Fisher had a 50 percent market share in the closed bodies market. GM wanted Fisher to build a new dedicated plant closer to GM's operations in Flint, which would reduce transportation costs and also result in lower average costs, given the much larger scale they could now operate at.

But Fisher had no incentive to do that—and in fact liked things as they were. Because of the nature of the price protection provision, they had every reason to keep transportation costs and manufacturing costs high, given the predetermined markup—and GM had to buy from them under the exclusive dealing provision. By 1926, GM decided that the situation was intolerable and merged with Fisher Body, making it into a division.

Much like George Eliot's novels generate annual conferences to debate the meaning of her books, the merger of GM and Fisher Body continues to mesmerize and divide economists. Much ink has been dedicated to alternative interpretations of this story, with all the stereotypical academic cattiness. Indeed, the *Journal of Law and Economics* dedicated a special issue to alternative accounts and interpretations of this merger—a remarkable fact given economists' skepticism about anecdotes. While there are innumerable variants, there are two primary interpretations of this romance that progresses from spot market transaction to long-term contractual arrangements and then all the way to merger. Each of these interpretations—the transaction cost approach and the property rights approach—is associated with a Nobel Prize (Ronald Coase in 1991 and Oliver Hart and Bengt Holmström in 2016), so, by academic standards, this is a prize fight.

The considerably less romantic interpretation is that GM merged with Fisher in 1926 because the ongoing costs of contracting with each other just became too high. Yes, they could have stayed separate and just kept contracting and renegotiating contracts, but it's so costly to write these contracts, and if they merged, they wouldn't have to keep writing new contracts all the time. At some point, mergers are motivated just by the savings from avoiding repeatedly writing those detailed contracts.

In short, why pay two rents when we can live together? I can be on your health plan and that's much cheaper. And, if anything happens to you, the government will recognize my rights. Avoiding all the frictions of staying apart and contracting justifies the decision to go beyond contracts to merge. In short, it's a marriage of convenience.

The more convincing, and more romantic, interpretation is that the growing richness of the relationship between Fisher Body and GM demanded escalating levels of commitment. Why did GM and Fisher first enter into a long-term contract in 1919? The growth of metal bodies meant that Fisher had to invest in a factory that was only good for GM models, as opposed to wooden body factories that could be adapted across customers. Economists call that, and I'm not kidding, "relationship-specific investment." If they built that factory, Fisher would be concerned that, once it was completed, GM would have too much bargaining power over Fisher. The exclusive dealing provision of the initial contract guaranteed that GM couldn't exercise that power, because they committed to buying all their metal bodies from Fisher.

GM, in turn, was worried that the exclusive dealing provision meant that Fisher could exercise its power over GM by charging GM exorbitant prices once GM was locked in. The price protection clause ensured that Fisher wouldn't be opportunistic in that way. In short, as they came to need each other more and more (the rise of metal bodies created further entanglement between them than wooden bodies), increasing levels of commitment to each other ensured that they could realize the full benefits of that relationship. In economese, that would be: the presence of relationship-specific investments generates a need for a long-term contractual arrangement, rather than a spot market transaction, to ensure the largest joint surplus.

But then things got more complicated. The contract didn't anticipate the massive rise in demand for metal bodies. And the contract had this weird incentive for Fisher—they were getting paid more if their labor and transportation costs were higher. As a result, they didn't want to build a new, more efficient plant nearer to GM. In short, the contract didn't fully anticipate everything and was necessarily incomplete. In fact, the very nature of contracts is that they are incomplete. We can't envision every eventuality, and that essential incompleteness means that many scenarios exist where we rely on each other so much that we need to merge—incomplete contracts just won't do.

This merger happened when their dependence on each other grew so much that it was important to curtail distinct one-sided incentives and to create one entity. For Fisher to take the next leap to a completely relationship-specific investment (a new, dedicated factory for auto bodies right next to GM's Flint operation) required a level of certainty and commitment that was beyond the scope of a necessarily incomplete contract between two separate parties. That leap, and all the attendant investments it would generate, would create a much larger joint surplus for both parties. But that leap of faith required a merger.

The merger was highly successful, with the Fisher brothers continuing to work with GM for two decades. GM CEO Alfred P. Sloan considered the merger "decisive" in their ongoing competition with Ford. GM flourished for the next several decades, becoming the largest automobile company in the world. Indeed, until the early 1980s, GM cars continued to feature a stamp of "Body by Fisher." This version of the merger, and the one I prefer, is not a marriage of convenience but a marriage of love.

*AND THEY LIVED HAPPILY EVER AFTER.*

In truth, not all automobile romances turn out so well. When Henry Ford was just tinkering around with prototypes in 1896, Harvey Firestone provided him with his first pneumatic tires. Firestone went on to establish Firestone Tire in 1900, and Ford created Ford Motor in 1903, and they remained close — so close that Firestone was awarded the original tire contract on the historic Model T, a model that sold a remarkable 14.7 million units from 1909 to 1927.

Their business and personal partnership blossomed. They jointly scouted locations in California in the mid-1920s, a move that led to them both creating large facilities near each other's operations in Los Angeles. Thomas Edison, Firestone, and Ford (the three acknowledged leaders of American industry at the time) joined with the naturalist John Burroughs and became the Four Vagabonds —

taking extravagant annual camping trips in the 1910s and 1920s to explore nature, with, on occasion, U.S. presidents joining in the fun. The partnership between Ford and Firestone remained very strong through the 1970s and even through the sale of Firestone to the Japanese company Bridgestone in 1988. But the partnership was tested severely in the late 1990s. Up to two hundred deaths were associated with the Ford Explorer SUV and their Firestone 500 tires. Explorers were rolling over at an uncommonly high rate, and the cause was unclear—were the Explorers unusually prone to rolling over? Or were the tires unusually prone to tread separation and that, in turn, led to the rollovers?

Instead of Ford and Firestone jointly figuring out the problem, the partnership shattered. Ford accused Firestone of manufacturing poor tires, and Firestone accused Ford of recommending incorrect inflating levels (the original Deflategate) to allow for comfort over safety. The press labeled it a historically ugly divorce that ended a hundred-year partnership—and it had all the recriminations that only the dissolution of a long partnership can engender.

Firestone ended all supply relationships with Ford with a letter that accused Ford of engineering a cover-up by improperly shifting attention to the tires. The letter concluded, "Business relationships, like personal ones, are built upon trust and mutual respect. We have come to the conclusion that we can no longer supply tires to Ford since the basic foundation of our relationship has been seriously eroded. This is not a decision we make lightly after almost 100 years of history." With that bitter note, one of the great partnerships in American commerce came to an ignominious end.

There is but one remnant of that corporate partnership, but it appears to be a very durable remnant. The grandson of Henry Ford, William Clay Ford Sr., and the granddaughter of Harvey Firestone, Martha Parke Firestone, met each other through their mothers. After covertly writing letters to each other, they married in 1947, while still students. That marriage was, by all accounts, very happy and produced four children—and the ownership of the NFL Detroit Lions along the way. One of those four children was William Clay Ford Jr., who—wait for it—happened to be chairman of Ford Motor Company as the rollover scandal was erupting. So, a man who was the product of the romance between the grandchildren of both Harvey Firestone and Henry Ford presided over the messy dissolution of the corporate partnership begun by his great-grandfathers.

Perhaps there really is romance without finance.

*THE END*

# 6

# Living the Dream

Meetings can be mind-numbing, but the July 12, 2013, faculty meeting at the University College of London may have represented a new low. One faculty member was literally carried to the meeting from his usual location down the hall, seated next to the outgoing provost, said not a word, and was counted as "present but not voting." While that may sound quite typical (or ideal, depending on your perspective on meetings), this particular faculty member had also been dead for close to two hundred years, and it was his preserved skeleton, usually ensconced a few doors down the hallway, that attended the meeting.

What kind of individual would be accorded such respect and also be eccentric enough to have ensured that this odd legacy could be implemented upon his death? Who could have been so bizarre as to have carried around a pair of glass eyes in his pocket so that his preservation could proceed apace? This unusual gentleman was Jeremy Bentham, an Enlightenment philosopher who had the foresight to advocate for universal suffrage and the decriminalization of homosexuality in the early nineteenth century.

As the founder of utilitarianism, he established the idea that social policy should be evaluated by the improvement in human welfare aggregated across all individuals. The simple maxim that "the greatest happiness of the greatest number is the foundation of morals and legislation," a phrase Bentham attributed to Joseph Priestley, was remarkably radical for its time and still serves as the foundation of much economic and philosophical analysis.

Bentham was also the first great defender of the use of credit and the idea of leverage. In his showdown with Adam Smith on lending, they take quite uncharacteristic positions. The typically eloquent exponent of markets (Smith) advocates for limits on markets, while the radical reformer (Bentham) embraces the unfettered market for debt.

In *The Wealth of Nations*, Smith had argued that interest rates on loans should be capped at 5 percent. His logic manifested the deep historical bias against borrowers. Smith ventured that if interest rates were allowed to be higher, only "prodigals and projectors" would take the loans, and people with reasonable projects wouldn't take loans. Allowing borrowing at all different rates would turn things upside down, according to Smith—worthy risks wouldn't be able to borrow, and bad risks would dominate the economy. In this regard, Smith was channeling millennia of distaste for the act of borrowing.

In a series of letters to Smith that were published, provocatively, as a "Defence of Usury," Bentham decimated Smith's arguments for limits on interest rates. Bentham pointed out that Smith had overlooked how lenders would have an incentive to select and monitor borrowers to protect their capital. Bentham noted that "there are, in this case, two wits set to sift the merits of the project . . . and of these two there is one, whose prejudices are certainly not most likely to be on the favourable side" of wasteful projects. More broadly, Smith's arguments were inconsistent with the liberty that Smith himself had championed. Bentham reminded Smith, using Smith's own words, that "it is the highest impertinence and presumption . . . in kings and ministers, *to pretend to watch over the economy of private people* [Bentham's emphasis]."

But Bentham's most blistering and convincing argument cut to the core of why credit markets are important. By limiting access to only the best credits, Smith was privileging the position of "old-fashioned" borrowers with traditional needs and impeding the innovators and upstarts with well-grounded but risky projects. Smith had applied a "stamp of indiscriminate reprobation" upon "all such persons as, in the pursuit of wealth, strike out into any new channel, and particularly, into any new channel of invention" in favor of those "whose trade runs in the old channels, and to the best security which such channels can afford." Outlawing high interest rates and demeaning borrowing prevented innovation and growth, was inconsistent with liberty, and was unnecessary since lenders could take care of themselves.

The conflict between Smith and Bentham on leverage finds no better dramatic treatment than William Shakespeare's *The Merchant of Venice*. The play is driven by developments surrounding the loan by Shylock to Bassanio, which is guaranteed by Antonio. When Antonio is unable to repay the loan, Shylock tries to exercise his right to take a "pound of flesh," an outcome that is only avoided because of the quick wit of Bassanio's new wife, Portia. Shylock's antipathy for Antonio is driven by a disagreement, as with Bentham and Smith, over the propriety of interest. As Shylock relays it, he hates Antonio because "he lends out money gratis and brings down / The rate of usance here with us in Venice." The trial that follows

Antonio's default is a mockery of justice that results in the chummy, Christian world of Venice cruelly punishing the outsider Jew for his vengeance. Venetians vilify the Jews for providing a function that they know they need, reflecting the same anti-debt bias that Bentham reacted so strongly against.

But the role of debt in *The Merchant of Venice* runs far deeper than a plot device. The plot proceeds through the accretion of not only financial obligations but also personal obligations. Bassanio borrows from Antonio, who borrows from Shylock, who borrows from his friend Tubal. Antonio's bond with Bassanio, as the poet W. H. Auden notes, is an "infinite obligation that links utility to duty" and is founded on love. Bassanio is personally indebted to Antonio for funding his romance with Portia, and then Portia, by virtue of her marriage to Bassanio, is obliged to save Antonio. And Antonio ultimately is bound to Portia because she saves him. Portia and Antonio are effectively competing for Bassanio's affection, a battle that she wins because, as critic Harry Berger Jr. puts it, she knows how to "sink hooks of gratitude and obligation deep into the beneficiary's bowels." And the marriages of the play provide for much wordplay about "bonds" but they also, because they represent claims on another person, mirror Shylock's claim on Antonio's body.

Auden saw a play superficially about debt but more deeply about bonds between people. He notes that "there are few plays in which the word love is used more frequently." Contrasting it with a feudal order, Auden concludes that "in *The Merchant of Venice*, you are free to form the relationships you choose, but your obligations are then enormous." Debt, it turns out, is about much more than money —it is about the ties that bind.

People in finance love leverage even more than Bentham. Aside from the many substantive benefits of leverage, which we'll discuss shortly, using the term "leverage" allows finance people to sound much more impressive than if they simply said "borrowing other people's money." But the truth is, that's all that leverage is in finance — borrowing money. Nonetheless, financiers sometimes get emotional at the mention of leverage — and with good reason. Many fortunes have been made and lost through leverage, and the appropriate management of leverage can be the difference between spectacular economic failures and successes. But what constitutes the appropriate management of leverage?

Let's begin with the most fundamental question. Why do finance practitioners call borrowing "leverage"? As with many things in finance, the answer is easier than you think. A lever is an instrument — think of a crowbar — that allows you to move an object that you have no business moving. In some sense, levers are magical — you can do things you had no idea you could do, because they multiply the force you are capable of exerting on your own. As Archimedes suggested, and as depicted on the cover of this book, "Give me a lever long enough and a fulcrum on which to place it and I shall move the world."

This is precisely the aspiration of many people — students, homeowners, and businesspeople — who borrow. Let's start with homeowners. Imagine you have $100 and you want to buy a home (add as many zeros as you'd like to these numbers if that makes it more interesting to you). If you can't avail yourself of leverage, how large a home can you buy and what does your balance sheet look like after you purchase that home?

Well, if you can't borrow, then you can only buy a $100 home, and your balance sheet consists of assets of a $100 house, and you have financed it with $100 of equity. Now, let's introduce some leverage — or the ability to borrow when you purchase your home. Just to keep things simple, let's say you can finance a home purchase with debt of up to 80 percent of the value of the home. Well, now you can buy a $500 home, and your balance sheet looks considerably different. You have assets of a $500 home, an obligation to pay back $400, and $100 of equity.

| Assets | Liabilities and Net Worth |
|---|---|
| House $100 | $100 Equity |

| Assets | Liabilities and Net Worth |
|---|---|
| House $500 | $400 Mortgage $100 Equity |

While in both cases you still have $100 of value (your equity), in one case you get to live in a much larger and, presumably, nicer house. In many ways, leverage allows us to live in homes we have no right to live in.

Borrowing for education is the same thing: we can't afford the tuition based on our current income and wealth, but completing an education may well be the path toward a much higher income and a better life. So, we borrow to access that opportunity. This same logic of wanting to access opportunities beyond our current resources is what finance is for companies and entrepreneurs—controlling more resources than they'd usually be able to can be much more rewarding than staying within their current means.

But it gets better. Not only do you get to live in a house you have no right to live in, leverage also increases your returns substantially. Say house prices rise in value by 10 percent. Without leverage, your wealth would rise by 10 percent—the house is worth $110 and your equity is worth $110 (i.e., balance sheets have to balance). But if you employed leverage, your wealth would have increased by 50 percent—the house is worth $550 and your outstanding loan is for $400—so your equity has gone from $100 to $150. Now you get a sense of why finance people love leverage. You get to live in a larger house *and* you get higher returns. Of course, house prices don't always rise. Imagine instead that house prices fall by 20 percent. In the case without leverage you would have lost 20 percent, or $20. With leverage, you would lose all your wealth of $100. Leverage amplifies returns in both directions.

And of course, there's that other thing about borrowing—it's a very meaningful commitment. To protect themselves, lenders have rights that allow them to limit what you do with their money—so-called covenants—and if you violate them, they can extract a penalty or even seize your assets. For example, you usually can't take on additional indebtedness without getting their approval. These mechanisms allow lenders to make sure you don't do something crazy with their money. Most seriously, lenders have rights and claims on you and your assets if you fail to make ongoing payments. For homeowners, this can mean losing your home. For companies, this can mean declaring bankruptcy if they don't provide periodic interest payments.

So how much leverage should a company take on? The simplest finance answer for firms is that they trade off two contrary impulses—the tax advantages of using debt versus the risk that debt imposes on organizations. Because interest payments are tax deductible for firms and individuals, it can be advantageous to use debt. In short, by taking on debt to finance equipment purchases or a home for an individual, you are allowed by the government to pay less in taxes and to shift value from the government to yourself.

On the other hand, excessive debt can create difficulties. Highly indebted companies can suffer even before they reach bankruptcy. As the companies become less stable, highly valued employees might leave, customers stop buying as they anticipate the disappearance of the company, and vendors stop selling as they fear not getting paid for their sales. Trading off these costs of financial distress and tax benefits gives one a sense of what the right amount of leverage is for a company.

Getting that tradeoff right is particularly important for the private equity industry. In private equity transactions, underlevered firms are often "taken private" by borrowing against those companies' assets and buying out the old shareholders, through a "leveraged buyout" (i.e., borrowing to buy out the owners). What kinds of firms are candidates for such transactions? The best candidates are firms that have lots of profits, so that the tax motivations are operative, and have very stable business models, so that the likelihood of financial distress is mitigated. Think tobacco or, better yet, casinos —lots of profits, little technological innovation (so disruption risks are low), and addicted customers. Casinos are promising candidates for leverage—as long as you don't get greedy with too much debt and you know how to run those businesses. Otherwise, you might go bankrupt—several times over.

The central question facing borrowers—how do I access opportunities beyond my current resources?—is analogous to a question that inspires many of us: How do I live the fullest life? Much of what life has to offer requires the help of others. Being married, starting a family, engaging in meaningful friendships, working in organizations, starting a business are all value-generating activities that one simply can't do alone. Getting that help creates a set of commitments—and those commitments come with constraints. In short, how you are able to embed yourself in broader networks and relationships through commitments will determine your ultimate trajectory—much as debt shapes the trajectories of firms by providing resources in return for commitments.

The parallel between firm leverage decisions and the commitments we take on in life is evident in the stories of two very different artists—George Orwell and Jeff Koons. Orwell's journey to completing *1984* demonstrates the costs of interdependency and the virtue of a low-leverage life. It's the story of just how important solitude and independence are to achieving great things—and how important it can be to insulate yourself from the world. As World War II ended, Orwell was struggling to make a living as a journalist and wrote over 110,000 words in 1945 alone to support himself. But he knew all these efforts were enervating him. Orwell told Dorothy Plowman that he was "smothered under journalism," and told his friend Andrew Gow, "I have become more and more like a sucked orange."

To write *1984*, he knew he had to retreat from the world. He wrote to his friend Arthur Koestler, "Everyone keeps coming at me wanting me to lecture, to write commissioned booklets, to join this and that, etc — you don't know how I pine to be free of it all and have time to think again." In 1946, Orwell retreated for several years to the island of Jura in the Scottish Hebrides — a location he described as "extremely ungetatable." And there he found the recipe for creativity and for the writing of *1984*. That is a low-leverage life of few commitments and obligations — and it worked incredibly well for Orwell.

Artists who choose the low-leverage life find the alternative extremely difficult. Saul Bellow wrote amazing novels, but he also tried writing plays, an activity involving much more interaction with directors, producers, and actors. His efforts led him to appreciate being a novelist even more: "Alone with his page, between four walls, [the novelist] is compensated for his solitude by a high degree of autonomy. In the theatre, he discovers the happiness of collaboration . . . The price of all this delight is a reduction in one's exclusive powers." Similarly, in celebrating the virtues of independent filmmakers over larger, more collaborative efforts, Bellow notes that "a large team must inevitably have a leveling effect on the imagination of any single member of it . . . [and the large budgets are] enough to change the giddy artist into a sober bureaucrat." By increasing the number of interactions he was subject to, Bellow found that his imagination was mediated into mediocrity.

While Bellow didn't come to appreciate the benefits of commitments, collaboration, and leverage, other artists have ridden leverage to great heights—perhaps no one more so than Jeff Koons. Described by critic Peter Schjeldahl in 2014 as the "signal artist of today's world," Koons produces enormous installations such as *Play-Doh*, a ten-foot-high aluminum construction that took twenty years to complete. How does he undertake such ambitious projects? With lots of leverage.

In the early 1980s, Koons was facing escalating costs for the Hoover vacuum cleaners and other found objects that he was transforming into art. To finance the art he was working on at night, he began working as a cotton futures trader in the day. Unsurprisingly, the lessons of leverage from Wall Street were not lost on Koons. Building on a sales experience that began as a nine-year-old when he sold wrapping paper and chocolates door to door, Koons became an expert salesman. In this case, he was selling futures contracts. Futures contracts commit you to selling goods in the future at a set price, regardless of whether you own those goods now. With the exception of the set price, this is what Koons went on to do with his art.

Koons describes himself as "the idea person. I'm not physically involved in the production. I don't have the necessary abilities, so I go to the top people, whether I'm working with my foundry—Tallix —or in physics." His large installations require him, as Schjeldahl describes, "to constantly escalate deluxe materials and expert fabrication in his work, with a pattern of selling works in advance in order to secure the cash to execute them, usually in small editions. (Collectors have waited years for their purchases.) The more money he makes, the more he spends, maintaining a Chelsea workshop that employs a staff of a hundred and twenty-five." Koons characterized the leverage of his production process as "a system to control every gesture as if I did it."

Talk about loving leverage—in comparing him to Andy Warhol, Schjeldahl concludes that Koons "surfs the market, with bets that have occasioned more than one near wipe-out." Indeed, his dealers are notorious for going bankrupt under the pressures he puts them under, and customers often have to continue investing to finance his escalating costs. As writer Felix Salmon describes, Koons sold work to collectors before he even knew how to build it—thereby turning the traditional business model of artists upside down.

Salmon notes that "the Koons model is a little bit like the patronage model, where a wealthy patron will pay an artist's expenses in return for his artistic output. But Koons flipped that model: he had the collectors working for him, more than the other way around. They weren't calling the shots: he was." While some ridicule Koons, I think Salmon gets it right: "Koons does something very interesting, which very few other artists do. He turns money into art, rather than just turning art into money."

Koons's factory and financing methods are the antithesis of Orwell's efforts. And their distinct choices represent the kinds of choices we face in creating our lives. Orwell's path of solitude can be deeply enriching—one has complete autonomy and the pleasure of knowing that the resulting efforts are singularly one's own. Koons, in contrast, operates on a completely different scale by embedding himself in rich networks, accepting the tradeoffs that this implies, and operating an organization in the service of his art. Seen in financial terms, Orwell is the all-equity financed firm exempting himself from any constraints and commitments in order to flourish, whereas Koons is the leveraged buyout, piling up commitments and constraints in order to attempt larger and larger things, with associated risks and rewards.

So, who are you, Koons or Orwell? Either life can be very rewarding for the right person. Most of us will choose to end up somewhere in between, much as firms do with their leverage choices, and the choice will be manifest in your professional and personal lives. The nature of successful marriages and friendships are that they require interdependencies that are associated with compromises —but also provide experiences that are unattainable without those interdependencies. Choosing to have children is the most obvious example of levering up your life. You make an unimaginable set of emotional and financial commitments to them, and they open up a world that is beyond imagination.

Professionally, your own talents may lead you to great places, but embedding yourself in an organization can amplify your potential impact on the world. At the same time, these organizations will require you to surrender autonomy and accept compromises. Successful entrepreneurs are Orwells who must become more like a Koons. Ideas may germinate in your head, but creating a business out of them will certainly require innumerable interdependencies with other people.

I sometimes see my life in this way and am aware of the risks I am running. My wife and I have three young children and full-time demanding careers. We try to be good friends to those around us and to our extended families. Ultimately, we are trying to live a highly levered life, by our standards. We have made significant commitments to many individuals and our employers and, most of all, to our children so that we can live a life where we aspire to have the maximum impact on the world, given our means. But it is complicated and it might not work. I often ask myself if we are making the most of our lives by living a highly levered life or simply taking on too much at the cost of the people closest to us.

What kinds of mistakes do people make in levering their lives? Most obviously, they can take on too many commitments and obligations and may not be able to live up to those obligations. We'll return to that in the following chapter when we talk about financial distress and bankruptcy. But what mistake do people make *on average*? One of the central facts about corporations and their financing decisions maps particularly well to our lives. By most measures, firms are dramatically underlevered. They don't appear to take the full advantages that the tradeoff theory implies and, as a result, remain underlevered. Many individuals may well do the same thing—they retreat from commitments and obligations, and in the process, they limit what they can do. Studies of regret show that regret mostly arises from commitments avoided—untaken educational opportunities, missed love connections, and inattention to children.

Is leverage just a benevolent tool to help you achieve your dreams? Is it all just that simple? Anyone who's labored under the weight of loans can attest to the difficulties leverage can create. The pressure of student loans and mortgages can change the shape of our lives. The commitments of leverage can even preclude you from pursuing the dreams you might have otherwise pursued—mired in student debt, you may ask yourself if you can take on additional commitments to pursue those dreams. That problem is known by the ominous name of "debt overhang." The idea of debt overhang is that you can prevent yourself from doing things you should do because of the shadow of a preexisting commitment.

Think of a homeowner who buys a $100 home with a mortgage of $80. If that home falls in value to $70, he will be underwater—he owes more than his asset is worth. Now, let's say he could add an extension to the house that would cost him $25 but would add $30 to the value of the house. Should he do it?

Normally, you'd say, "Of course he should. This is a great investment. He puts in $25 and gets $30." But in this case, he puts in $25, but the lender effectively gets the first $10 of returns. And the owner only gets $20. So, it turns into a bad investment for the homeowner. The real curiosity is that the lender would be better off if the owner did the extension, but lenders often hesitate to make the compromises required to make the owner have the right incentives. The shadow of that preexisting commitment prevents the owner from doing the things he needs to do. This idea of debt overhang, in part, is why the housing crisis was so scary—with nearly one in five owners underwater in 2009, we might have seen many more neighborhoods with highly levered homes just continue to deteriorate because of these crazy incentives.

What's the answer? Well, the lender should accept a loss on its loan so that the homeowner will return to a setting where it's possible to pursue projects that are in the homeowner's own best interests. And the lender is better off for taking that loss. Unfortunately, lenders often are unwilling to take those losses.

There exists no more gut-wrenching a portrait of debt overhang —and the shadow of preexisting commitments—in our personal lives than Kazuo Ishiguro's portrait of Mr. Stevens in *The Remains of the Day*. Mr. Stevens is a model butler in Oxfordshire in the interwar years who has dedicated himself to Lord Darlington. The book is told by an older Mr. Stevens, who recounts his past and slowly realizes the missed opportunity of his love for the housekeeper, Miss Kenton—and the missed opportunity of his life.

Before describing his first memories of Miss Kenton, Mr. Stevens digresses and notes that "marrying amongst more senior employees can have an extremely disruptive effect on work," and that people who are searching for love are "a blight on good professionalism." For a man preoccupied with the idea of dignity and obligated to serve, such relationships were simply beyond the imagination. Miss Kenton, after more than a decade of working with Mr. Stevens, falls for him and wants more than a life of service. Miss Kenton provides numerous opportunities to a clueless Mr. Stevens, who remains in denial of his own growing feelings.

Finally, Miss Kenton begins seeing someone else but wants to provide one last chance to Mr. Stevens. She tells him of this budding romance and baits him with this: "It occurs to me you must be a well-contented man, Mr. Stevens. Here you are, after all, at the top of your profession, every aspect of your domain well under control. I really cannot imagine what more you might wish for in life."

Having been served up this easy pitch, Mr. Stevens whiffs. His commitment to Darlington and his profession prevents him from pursuing the opportunity in front of him. "As far as I'm concerned, Miss Kenton, my vocation will not be fulfilled until I have done all

I can to see his lordship through the great tasks he has set himself. The day his lordship's work is complete, the day *he* is able to rest on his laurels, content in the knowledge that he has done all anyone could ever reasonably ask of him, only on that day, Miss Kenton, will I be able to call myself, as you put it, a well-contented man." The commitment to professionalism and Darlington were paramount.

On two of the most important nights of his life, Mr. Stevens's professional obligations crowd out his personal needs as he fails to attend to his father on his deathbed and fails to follow through on the final opportunity presented by Miss Kenton. Curiously, those two nights end up filling him with a "sense of triumph" for the professionalism he is exhibiting. This absolute dedication borders on martyrdom—or maybe masochism.

Decades later, we see that Miss Kenton left Darlington Hall for a marriage that turned out to be an unhappy one. Darlington turns out to be a misguided amateur diplomat who dies mired in shame because he is known as the architect of Neville Chamberlain's appeasement policy toward Adolf Hitler. And what of Mr. Stevens?

After seeing Miss Kenton again and realizing what he did not pursue, Mr. Stevens concludes: "I gave [Darlington] the very best I had to give, and now—well—I find I do not have a great deal more left to give . . . I've given what I had to give. I gave it all to Lord Darlington . . . I trusted in his lordship's wisdom. All those years I served him, I trusted I was doing something worthwhile . . . Really —one has to ask oneself—what dignity is there in that?"

Leverage is dangerous for two reasons—as we'll see in the next chapter, it can lead to bankruptcy where the commitments you've made become untenable. But the danger of debt overhang is much more general. Negotiating our existing commitments to allow us to take on new ones is the critical life skill that finance highlights. Debt overhang is the manifestation of not being able to renegotiate those commitments to take on new opportunities—and the resulting loss for everyone involved. And Mr. Stevens is the manifestation of the fear that taking on new commitments is inconsistent with pre-existing commitments—a belief that leads him to a life of emotional poverty. Fortunately, even if lenders are sometimes too silly to change their expectations, we can renegotiate our commitments —to loved ones, to jobs, to society—when we need to so that we can invest anew. Sometimes, as with Mr. Stevens, fear is the only thing that is stopping us from trying to do so.

The advantages and disadvantages of leverage are manifest in finance's predictions on the best use of leverage over the life cycle of firms. Because leverage can compromise firms by limiting investment (as we just saw), firms facing lots of uncertainty with lots of potential investment needs, particularly young firms, should limit their leverage. Similarly, unstable firms nearing their economic end will find that leverage will hasten their demise. We expect a hump-shaped trajectory for firm leverage—young, dynamic firms avoid debt, mature firms lever up with debt, and older firms where economic decline has set in are best advised to reduce their debt levels.

A related pattern is apparent in our financial lives because of what is known as the life-cycle hypothesis of consumption smoothing. One of the puzzles in economics is how consumption (not just the food we eat but everything we consume—housing, experiences, etc.) remains stable over the course of our lives. Despite large fluctuations in income in our lifetimes, we basically don't change how much we consume. How do we do that? Well, we borrow when we are young and need to consume and don't have resources—and then, as we age, we repay debt and save for retirement so we can continue consuming at roughly the same level.

Our sequencing of commitments and leverage in our own lives has a slightly distinct pattern but manifests a similar logic. We expect nothing of our babies and try to ensure they enjoy years of pure nurturing. As they grow, we begin to introduce commitments and obligations, within a safe setting, so they get used to the idea. In our middle years, we lever up with commitments to spouses, children, our careers, and our communities. And as we age, we delever as the stress of those commitments, even the simplest ones, becomes too much. I've seen these same dynamics at play in my family. As our parents aged, we (in truth, it was really my sister) tried to relieve them of some of the concerns that they faced, including simple financial management that they would have excelled at years ago. Fortunately, they planned so well—moving to smaller homes ahead of the need to, saving aggressively, and simplifying their lives—that our efforts were only on the margin.

And I see this with our girls. When and how should we introduce the idea of commitments and obligations to them? How do you structure chores and responsibilities so that they become accustomed to them but they don't crowd out the joy of childhood? We constantly walk the line between introducing them to leverage and shielding them from it.

Most of all, I think of this problem with my girls and their investment in themselves—what is known as their human capital. My wife and I married at later ages and started a family relatively late. As a consequence, we were free of commitments through our twenties and were both able to invest heavily in our human capital and our careers, the benefits of which we now are reaping. The tradeoff seems clear, at least in retrospect—we now have young children at an age that may not be optimal for bringing up children and we will have them at home until I'm close to retirement. But we were able to invest in ourselves and careers in very advantageous ways. Had we levered up earlier with family commitments, I don't think either one of us would be where we are professionally.

When one of my daughters comes to me at age twenty-four and says she wants to get married and start a family, I'm not sure what I will say. I know in my heart I'll be thinking that the commitments she is about to undertake will crowd out investment in herself . . .

and there will be time later to lever up her life. But then I'll just think about the possibility of another terminal value and will jump for joy.

Until now, leverage has appeared to be a set of tradeoffs. You can take on debt to buy a house, but that doesn't increase your wealth. Yes, you get to live in a nicer house, but it comes with associated risks. Similarly, for companies taking on leverage involves a tradeoff between tax benefits and creating risk. And, as Bellow emphasized and Koons demonstrates, leverage in life can mean operating on a whole different scale—but these commitments come with obligations and a loss of autonomy that can be limiting. It all depends on who you are and what kind of life you want to lead.

But modern finance suggests there's something more to leverage —a leverage bonus of sorts. In observing how little leverage firms were using, the economist Michael Jensen concluded that leverage could help solve the major problems of modern capitalism. In his view, managers were not always serving shareholders well—the principal-agent problem we saw previously. The reluctance of managers to use leverage reflected their desire to be free of obligations in order to pursue other activities that might not serve their shareholders. A natural corollary to that was that leverage could be used to limit managers' ability to do things that served themselves and not shareholders. In effect, leverage ties the hands of managers and enforces a discipline on them to serve their masters best. In Jensen's words, "the threat caused by failure to make debt service payments serves as an effective motivating force to make such organizations more efficient."

Jensen provides a nice example from the oil industry. After oil prices came down in the 1980s, managers resisted the economic logic of stopping their drilling efforts. Companies continued to invest in exploration, and in unrelated companies, well beyond the point they should have instead of returning cash to shareholders —in part, because there were so many profits sloshing around and no commitments to anyone. Tying their hands with mandatory debt payments would have prevented them from destroying lots of value. That's the leverage bonus.

Leverage in life involves a similar benefit. Jensen's insight is predicated on the conflict produced when managers pursue agendas that are contrary to shareholder interests. That kind of conflict can often play out within ourselves. We frequently know what the right thing to do is and even agree that we should do it—but for myriad reasons, we don't actually undertake the action, be it exercising, stopping smoking, or spending more time with our children. Indeed, the problem of self-control is fundamental for many of us, and the best solution to it, as much research has documented, is to make meaningful commitments to others to ensure that we do the right thing. These commitments might be expensive bets with friends, costly memberships in health clubs, or forced savings plans. Such commitments effectively do the same thing that debt does in the modern corporation—they restrict choice to increase the odds that you'll do the right thing.

The logic of the leverage bonus extends further. By embedding yourself in demanding relationships and making commitments, you may well just become a better person. In offering advice to young people, Thomas Watson, the founder of IBM, said, "Don't make friends who are comfortable to be with. Make friends who will force you to lever yourself up." Commitments to smart and demanding people keep us from doing stupid things—we gain from those commitments. Leverage is not a zero-sum game.

In addition to allowing you to be more productive and raising your own standards, embedding yourself in meaningful relationships is simply good for you. George Vaillant, a research psychiatrist, helped conduct the longest longitudinal study of emotional and physical development by continuing the so-called Grant Study of

Harvard undergraduates in the late 1930s. By tracking physiological and emotional data over more than seventy years, Vaillant and his colleagues provide some of the best evidence on what matters for longevity and happiness. And the answer he arrived at, as described by Joshua Wolf Shenk, is deceptively simple.

> Vaillant's other main interest is the power of relationships. "It is social aptitude," he writes, "not intellectual brilliance or parental social class, that leads to successful aging." Warm connections are necessary — and if not found in a mother or father, they can come from siblings, uncles, friends, mentors. The men's relationships at age 47, he found, predicted late-life adjustment better than any other variable, except defenses [mechanisms for reacting to adversity]. Good sibling relationships seem especially powerful: 93 percent of the men who were thriving at age 65 had been close to a brother or sister when younger. In an interview in the March 2008 newsletter to the Grant Study subjects, Vaillant was asked, "What have you learned from the Grant Study men?" Vaillant's response: "That the only thing that really matters in life are your relationships to other people."

Commitments to others yield not just the power to accomplish more but also the emotional sustenance that we need to survive and thrive.

The logic of leverage's power extends most strongly to one's relationship with the world. Perhaps the most valuable lever imaginable is the esteem your colleagues, friends, and community regard you with. It enables you to mobilize resources, and you are provided remarkable latitude because of how individuals understand you and regard you. Indeed, Thomas Jefferson's observations on the value of reputation bring us back to Archimedes and the power of leverage. In a letter to José Corrêa da Serra in December 1814, Jefferson wrote: "I have ever deemed it more honorable, & more profitable too, to set a good example than to follow a bad one. The good opinion of mankind, like the lever of Archimedes, with the given fulcrum, moves the world."

Living the fullest life is what many of us aspire to. As Bentham suggested, living beyond our current resources via leverage is not immoral—it can be a recipe for a productive and rich life. How you choose to employ leverage by committing to meaningful relationships reflects your own preferences and tastes that may range from Orwell's to Koons's. But don't be afraid to use leverage—it's a powerful force to accomplish much more that you're otherwise able to. Most of all, leverage may actually make us better people by holding us accountable as we commit ourselves to others with high standards. It also just might enable us to live longer and richer lives than we can imagine—and to move the world in the process.

In the early 1990s, Jeff Koons stumbled badly. In 1994, he was struggling through a divorce, and his father passed away just as he was at a professional breaking point. Koons had begun an ambitious effort to create the *Celebration* series—a series of massive, colorful sculptures of eggs, balloon dogs, and Valentine hearts. But his perfectionism was starting to cost him. He scrapped one egg after thirty-five thousand man-hours of painting because it wasn't perfect. In the process, several of his dealers and the foundries he used for the sculptures went bankrupt. Koons's own workshop, once more than one hundred people, was whittled down to two.

But Koons didn't give up on the high-leverage life. He found yet another dealer to finance his work and then spent the next ten years completing the series that would become his most well-known work. In 2014, the Whitney Museum of Modern Art dedicated the entire building, an unprecedented act, to showcase Koons's work. His high-leverage bet had paid off fantastically.

Koons seems to have understood the power of leverage well and linked it to art itself. In commenting on his iconic Popeye sculpture, which has the cartoon character dipping into an open can of spinach that is transforming him into a superman, Koons linked the power of art and leverage. Koons commented as he viewed the piece, "You have a sense of transcendence taking place here . . . he eats that spinach and he transcends into the strength. I think that's the art. The spinach is the art. Art can change your life. It can expand your parameters. It can give this vastness to life." A better description of leverage is hard to find. Who knew spinach, art, and leverage were all connected?

As a coda, casino magnate Steve Wynn purchased *Popeye* for $28 million in 2014. Wynn's father had built a small empire of bingo parlors in Connecticut on leverage. When Wynn was nineteen, his father died more than $300,000 in debt, which led to Wynn dropping out of college. Wynn, undeterred by this trauma, went west to Las Vegas and built an empire of his own, starting with the Golden Nugget, through the savvy use of leverage. *Popeye* stands today at the entrance of the shopping esplanade of the Wynn Hotel in Las Vegas, the home of dreams fueled by leverage.

# 7

# Failing Forward

In 1789, George Washington set out to form a cabinet that would help the new and unsteady nation gain a more solid footing. He knew the country faced critical financial difficulties, so he created a Treasury Department. Given the country's dire fiscal straits, the choice of who would be the first secretary of the Treasury would be momentous. Fortunately, Washington had an obvious candidate in mind—a dear, trusted friend with a remarkable life story and impeccable financial bona fides: Robert Morris.

Robert Morris? Who? Wasn't Alexander Hamilton the obvious candidate?

If not for a few fateful choices, Morris would now be on the ten-dollar bill, not to mention the marquee at the Richard Rodgers Theatre. Like Hamilton, Morris had a troubled childhood and was abandoned by his parents. Through a stroke of good fortune, he secured an internship at a leading shipping and finance company in Philadelphia, where his quick wits helped elevate him to running the company alongside the owner's son. Morris was an ardent patriot and became one of only two individuals who signed not only the Declaration of Independence but also the Articles of Confederation and the Constitution. Washington appointed Morris the first superintendent of finance (a precursor to the position of Treasury secretary) in 1781 under the Articles of Confederation, and in that capacity Morris set up the first U.S. central bank, the Bank of North America, an institution designed to address the fiscal woes of the young republic.

But those roles were not the roles that led Washington to call him the "financier of the revolution." Morris literally underwrote the Revolutionary War by using his own credit to secure munitions at crucial moments, including using personal IOUs to enable Washington to turn the tide at the critical Battle of Yorktown in 1781. Why were his IOUs as powerful as other currencies? At the time, Morris's commercial success was such that, according to legal scholar Bruce Mann, "the American economy did not see his likes again until J. P. Morgan and John D. Rockefeller, Sr., a century later . . . he was the most modern economic figure of the early republic."

Washington clearly had good reason to turn to Robert Morris when he needed a Treasury secretary. But Morris declined the offer. Anxious to focus his attention on rebuilding the fortune that had been depleted during the Revolutionary War, Morris recommended Hamilton in his stead. Already you might be slapping your forehead and asking yourself, "What was he thinking?" But this dramatic tale of choosing money over service gets even better.

Initially, Morris was wildly successful in recouping his fortune. His North America Land Company was the largest land trust ever in American history (and arguably the first Real Estate Investment Trust) with more than six million acres of land (as a point of comparison, New Jersey is smaller than five million acres). Separately, he owned large chunks of western New York and 40 percent of what would become the country's permanent capital, the District of Columbia.

How could such a patriot, financier, and public servant have escaped your notice? Don't feel too bad: this giant of the Revolutionary War period has been relegated to footnotes in many accounts of that era. As is often the case, history is written by, and about, the winners, and Morris did not end up a winner. His real estate company was predicated on a mountain of leverage, and several of his partners duped him in various ways. By the mid-1790s, only five years after being offered the Treasury secretary position, Morris could not service his debt and he had to retreat to his country home to avoid his creditors.

Ultimately, Morris's creditors got to him, and he found himself where debtors unable to service their debts usually found themselves during those times: in prison, where he paid fees to his captors for the privilege of staying there. His fall from grace was complete. Beset by commitments that he could not meet, Morris spent three years in debtors' prison. Released in 1801, he lived another five years in obscurity and modest circumstances, and is now buried in a relatively nondescript plot in Philadelphia's Christ Church, a few blocks away from the site of the jail that housed him.

A man who was once the wealthiest man in the young republic and could have been the first secretary of the Treasury died penniless and became less than a footnote in most history books. Talk about the road not taken . . .

But Morris does have an underappreciated legacy that remains to today. The bankruptcy of Robert Morris was, according to the prominent nineteenth-century Philadelphian Joshua Francis Fisher, "like a little earthquake, everybody trembled and feared their roofs would fall about their heads." George Washington even went to the prison to dine with Morris, risking yellow fever in the process. The magnitude of the fall from grace shook the nation to the core. Morris's main legacy is that he triggered, because of the height from which he fell, a thorough reexamination of how the young country should think about failure and financial distress. That reexamination resulted in the modern notion of bankruptcy, which proves to be a remarkably good guide to understanding failure generally. And the complexities of bankruptcies, as manifest in a case study of American Airlines, illuminate the conflicting commitments that are essential to our lives.

The first national bankruptcy law, which the young nation had struggled to formulate for ten years, came to pass quickly in 1800, as explained by Bruce Mann, in direct response to Morris's imprisonment. "That Morris could fall so far was, for many, inconceivable . . . When Congress finally met to take up the bill in December, it did so in the shadow of 'the great man' himself, pacing the prison courtyard two blocks away. For the first time the debate was substantive."

Until 1800, borrowers who could not service their debts were moral failures. As a consequence, imprisonment was common for debtors. In fact, punishments through history have ranged from forfeiture of property to being pilloried to imprisonment to dismemberment, and even to death. Puritan sermons were filled with the logic that no fate could be worse than debt, and that debts must be fulfilled no matter the circumstance. That Morris could fall to such depths led to a change in the way bankruptcies were treated, and it created, Mann indicates, "a milestone in the law of failure."

Failure would be redefined away from a moral failing or a sin and toward a more natural consequence of risk-taking with the 1800 act. If failure was a consequence of risk-taking, then the law needed to be reformed to not be so creditor-centric. Punishing debtors for their sins was neither constructive nor terribly humane. Indeed, the new republic desperately needed risk takers, and punishing them so severely froze commerce in the late 1790s. If the young country was to flourish, failure had to be redefined, and the moral stigma associated with it had to be lessened.

As one example of this shift, creditors were historically the only ones who could put a debtor into bankruptcy. The 1800 act opened the door to allowing debtors to put themselves in bankruptcy. Today, we take that as a given—companies and individuals can opt for bankruptcy, rather than being chased into declaring it. But until the 1800 act, debtors couldn't seek protection through bankruptcy—the law had been all about protecting creditors from ruthless and irresponsible debtors.

Along with the shift on how debtors could initiate bankruptcy, the "discharge" of debt could be accomplished with the approval of creditors, so that commercial agents could begin with a clean slate. Indeed, Morris left jail in 1801 after more than $3 million of debt was discharged, as the court, and his creditors, realized that he had no assets to service that debt. Morris was then free to live out his life with his wife on a small stipend provided by a friend.

This reorientation of the legal attitude toward failure has a deeper resonance. Failure, when we encounter it in ourselves or in others, should not be understood or seen as a moral defect. Inevitably, risk-taking will lead to failure, and failure should be viewed as a bad outcome with an abundance of lessons. Conflating the bad outcomes of risk-taking with a sense of moral failing limits our willingness to take on risks and we lose out on the opportunity to learn from failure. If we punish ourselves for our failures, this is no different than pillorying debtors or placing them in jail.

Organizations that stigmatize failure actually tend to repeat failures rather than learn from them. My colleague Amy Edmondson has studied attitudes toward failure in settings ranging from the *Challenger* shuttle disaster at NASA to medical errors in hospitals. Her conclusion is that one has to acknowledge "the inevitability of failure in today's complex work organizations. Those that catch, correct, and learn from failure before others do will succeed. Those that wallow in the blame game will not."

Bessemer Venture Partners, a leading venture capital firm, takes this to the extreme by celebrating all the companies they had the opportunity to invest in but didn't. Their "anti-portfolio" consists of Google, Apple, eBay, Facebook, and FedEx, all of which they passed on. Failures can't be stigmatized if they are to be the source of learning.

The natural corollary of defining failure away from morality is to understand that bankruptcy should provide for an opportunity for rebirth rather than signaling a death. Allowing for the discharge of debts is just one example of how bankruptcy law became centered on allowing for rebirth and away from declaring death. For bankruptcy to be oriented toward rebirth, the most important change had to be around the process immediately following the declaration of failure. Insolvencies ranging from Robert Morris's to Lehman Brothers' demonstrate how important it is to create an orderly process for that rebirth. The language of death and rebirth might seem extreme, but in fact it permeates the legal literature and practice of bankruptcy. As Bruce Mann notes, "The fundamental dilemma of bankruptcy law has always been about whether it is about death or rebirth." That's also the reason why investors who buy up distressed companies don't flinch when they're called "vultures."

Prior to the 1800 act, debtors were often hounded by their creditors. When Morris left his Philadelphia home and his family to barricade himself at his country house, he avoided capture by accepting written communication only through a bucket lifted from his second-story window. At one point, creditors commissioned a constable and six men armed with pickaxes and sledgehammers to retrieve Morris from his rural residence. In relaying this incident, Morris recounted how fortunate it was that he had guests staying with him at that time because "they [the constable's men] would have had me in five minutes if every pistol and gun in the house had not been manned and fixed at them."

The standoff with his creditors was costly to everyone, including his creditors. Morris's land was occupied by squatters, and tax collectors seized land in a disorganized way, leading to a loss in the overall value of the estate. Morris's experience demonstrates that the problem in bankruptcy proceedings is often not about protecting the creditors from those unscrupulous, immoral debtors—but more about protecting debtors from unreasonable creditors whose impatience lessens the value of the overall assets.

The colossal Lehman Brothers insolvency of 2008 provides a more recent example of how costly a disorderly, chaotic bankruptcy can be, even under a better bankruptcy regime. Coming in the aftermath of government-assisted sales and bailouts through 2008, the Lehman Brothers bankruptcy was unprecedented in scale and extremely disorganized because everyone was surprised by the sudden failure. The papers for the bankruptcy that governed $600 billion in assets were drafted and filed in one day without any advance preparation. Unsurprisingly, an estimated $75 billion of value was lost to the claimants because of the chaotic weeks that followed the unplanned bankruptcy.

So, what constitutes an orderly bankruptcy? Four of the defining features of the modern corporate bankruptcy are designed to ensure the possibility of rebirth amidst the chaos of insolvency—and they have parallels to what we need when we stumble and fail in our own lives. First, the declaration of a bankruptcy is accompanied by an "automatic stay"—a period during which creditors are prevented from filing claims against debtors, to ensure that chaos doesn't ensue and that the debtor can outline an orderly process. Second, the process of bankruptcy is overseen by impartial observers who serve as referees—indeed, the judges and trustees who oversaw bankruptcies were called referees until the twentieth century. These referees are meant to ensure that competing concerns are all balanced.

Third, professional advisors are called in—lawyers, bankers, accountants—to provide assistance, so that the best outcome can be arrived at. That external help and advice are viewed as so important that advisors' fees become the senior-most claim on the company's assets. Finally, debtors are provided with a stay so that they can put forward a plan—and this plan is the lynchpin for any company seeking to emerge from a bankruptcy. The plan should address how, in a forward-looking manner, the company can generate the greatest overall value, rather than concentrating on how to carve up the carcass amongst claimants.

The chaos that bankruptcies trigger—with debtors flailing about under an unsustainable set of commitments and creditors making immediate and conflicting demands—also characterizes our lives when we stumble. Living a levered life can lead to situations in which we have commitments beyond our capabilities. The same logics that guide constructive outcomes amid failures in commercial settings will sound familiar when it comes to our own lives. Acting rashly after failure is unwise. Seeking help in creating a forward-looking plan is critical. And this plan must acknowledge failures and commitments broken, but should be aimed at ensuring that you are making the most of who you are for the future. Rather than taking failures as occasions for self-flagellation, see them as opportunities for rebirth. Create some breathing room (an automatic stay), get help (from family, friends, and professionals), and start looking toward the future instead of backward (author a plan for your recovery).

My most significant academic failure came as I attempted to transition from an MBA program into a PhD program. I had made the unorthodox choice of going to India for a year after graduating with an MBA, and then I returned to do a PhD in political economy. I knew that I didn't have the recommended mathematical and statistical background, but I had no idea how out of my depth I was. I found out in my first semester of my PhD program, when I utterly bombed my microeconomic theory midterm. I stared at the blue booklet and simply froze. I scribbled something down that was barely relevant. I received a B–, but it was clear that the grade was extremely charitable and that it was the lowest grade in the class.

I had already questioned myself so many times about the unorthodox path I was on, knowing full well that other paths were available to me. I was ready to call up the recruiters who had offered me a job not so long ago, but first I went to talk to the professor. That conversation has always stayed with me. He didn't question me about my background; he didn't try to assess my suitability for the program; he wasn't impatient with me. He simply shrugged and said, "These things happen." He didn't try to induce guilt or breed doubt—nor did he reassure me. His great kindness was in implicitly telling me to put it behind me. Because of his kindness and wisdom, that exam debacle marked a fresh start for me and not a lasting disappointment.

So far, we've seen that the processes governing bankruptcy and financial distress have as their premise the principle that our failures shouldn't be stigmatized, that they are occasions for a fresh start, and that outside help, patience, and thoughtful planning are the recipe for a cooling off in the aftermath of a crisis. But is it really all so simple? Should we so readily forgive those who fail and allow them a fresh start? Is that all there is to bankruptcy?

While some may come about through pure misfortune, most bankruptcies and failures are morally complex. Consider the decision of homeowners who can continue to service their mortgage but whose house is worth less than the value of the mortgage—a fate facing many in the wake of the 2008 financial crisis. Should they walk away from the house and let the bank suffer the loss or should they continue to pay their mortgage? Such situations are complex, because walking away from our commitments raises several moral questions: What does it mean to make a commitment? Who suffers if I renege on that commitment? Who suffers if I don't renege? In the housing example, it's some version of "Will my neighbors suffer if I walk away from my home? Will my children suffer if I don't?"

Gerard Arpey joined American Airlines in 1982 at age twenty-four. By 2001, he had become the head of operations and made the courageous decision to ground all American Airlines flights on September 11, 2001, well before the Federal Aviation Administration had demanded it. As CEO during the 2000s he was tested again. All his major competitors had declared bankruptcy so that they could renegotiate (some would say renege on) expensive pensions and labor contracts with unionized labor. American was alone in not using bankruptcy to gain bargaining power with the unions. For Arpey, it was a moral question: "Call me old-fashioned. But I think companies ought to pay people back. And I think companies ought to make good on commitments to employees and communities."

By 2010, American continued to struggle as many of its competitors declared bankruptcy and then merged with each other. Arpey was still being pressured to use bankruptcy as a restructuring tool, but he continued to resist: "I still believe in principles in a business that will often push you to compromise your principles. I believe in the long run it will serve our institution and our stakeholders that we honored our commitment to our creditors, funded our pension plans and have done our very best to do everything consensually." This led many to praise Arpey as a paragon of CEO virtues. David Boren, former U.S. senator and American Airlines board member, said that "he's a very rare person in corporate America in his real loyalty to his company and the people who work there . . . This country would be so much better off if we had more people who had Gerard Arpey's sense of responsibility and character as well as ability."

By 2011, Arpey's hand had been forced by Tom Horton, the very president whom he had appointed, and his board of directors. On November 29, 2011, Horton and the board voted to put American Airlines into bankruptcy, and on that same day Arpey resigned. Arpey left without severance, and Horton, who had advocated for the bankruptcy, took over. American's bankruptcy lawyer said, "We are talking about an emergency and the survival of this company." In fact, American declared bankruptcy with close to $5 billion in cash on hand. As Horton made clear, the untenable nature of their position was actually "their cost position relative to their competitors," a gap reflecting labor contracts and pension obligations. Bankruptcy would allow them to renegotiate those contracts and put unions under increased pressure to agree to concessions. One of the first steps they took was to nullify several parts of their collective bargaining agreements with labor, something that was inconceivable without the protection of the bankruptcy code.

Arpey reflected, "I believe it's important to the character of the company and its ultimate long-term success to do your very best to honor those commitments. It is not good thinking—either at the corporate level or at the personal level—to believe you can simply walk away from your circumstances." His commitment earned him many admirers. The *New York Times* published an op-ed about Arpey the day after the bankruptcy titled "A CEO's Moral Stand."

The story of American Airlines' bankruptcy, and Arpey's resistance to it, captures why many of us feel queasy about bankruptcies. Yes, finance teaches us to be forgiving of those who fail and to prioritize a fresh start for them. But isn't it wrong to just give up on your commitments? Shouldn't people be held responsible for those commitments? If we allow people to go bankrupt or fail in other ways without any stigma or punishment, won't they take advantage of that option even when they shouldn't? Then bankruptcy isn't about failure anymore—it becomes a strategic renegotiation tool. In fact, bankruptcies like American's are called strategic bankruptcies. It all sounds positively Trumpian.

The moral queasiness provoked by the American Airlines story can be a familiar feeling in other contexts as well. I experience it in the only part of my job that I don't like—dealing with students on grading and attendance. Harvard Business School has a very strict attendance policy, so signing up for a class entails a considerable commitment to attend it. That commitment is amplified because productive discussion of a case study requires effort and participation from everyone. HBS also has a forced grading curve, where the bottom 10 percent must receive a failing grade, and missing class can be a critical factor in moving you into that bottom 10 percent. As a consequence, I am inevitably in the position of administering academic justice at the micro level.

Sometimes, it's simple: Should a student be excused for an absence because of a death in the family? Of course. But usually, it's not so simple: "A potential employer has asked me to fly to see them for an interview—can I have an excused absence?" "There is a once-in-a-lifetime opportunity to see my venerated venture capitalist speak on campus—can I have an excused absence?" "I woke up with a pounding headache—can I have an excused absence?" "I have a project due tomorrow and need the extra time to finish it —can I have an excused absence?" These are minor examples of what we all face in our professional lives—people who ask for forgiveness when they renege on a commitment they've already made to a joint endeavor.

My general response to this is, "Sure, go ahead." But in my mind, I'm asking myself, "Really?" Why does that commitment take precedence over the one you made to our class? You knew what you were getting into, so live with the consequences. Indeed, by letting them not pay a price, am I enabling an irresponsible spirit of reneging? And aren't I implicitly penalizing those who do make the effort to come and stand by their commitment, despite their pounding headaches? Am I just saying "sure" because I know those kinds of students who seek excused absences are the ones who will inevitably come by to complain about grades after the end of the semester? And what kind of incentives am I propagating by saying "Sure, go ahead"?

In short, I'm asking: "Why can't they all be more like Gerard Arpey?! Why can't they live up to the commitments they make?" And then I realize that holding them responsible for not being Gerard Arpey is the only part of my job that I don't like, and I return to glibly saying, "Sure, go ahead."

These are trivial examples compared to the kinds of situations we can find ourselves in. A close friend seeks your advice as he contemplates a divorce from his spouse of ten years — a divorce that will inevitably have significant consequences for their two young children. How do you advise him on how to think through his commitments to his children and spouse? Can one simply say, "You need to do what's right for yourself." Or, "You can't do that as you've made a serious commitment to them."

Ultimately, that's why bankruptcy decisions are so fraught — and so interesting. Bankruptcies are evocative because they are about our attitudes toward our commitments and how conflicting obligations should be navigated. Categorical moral codes like "you should always stand by your commitments" or facile answers like "go ahead, don't worry about those commitments — do what's right for you" are insufficient. The hardest moments in life are about competing duties and obligations and how to navigate them — just as the essence of the bankruptcy decision is how to navigate the competing, and seemingly unsustainable, set of commitments that a company or an individual has made.

In her book *The Fragility of Goodness*, philosopher Martha Nussbaum considers precisely this difficulty of conflicting duties, taking to task Immanuel Kant, among others, for his absolutist ideas on duty. Nussbaum is very tough on Kant, but her basic point is right: a literal reading of Kant suggests that there are no such things as conflicts of duty. If you're experiencing a conflict, it's just because you haven't thought through the correct prioritization of your duties — think it through, and there will be no conflict. For Kant, being moral is about fulfilling your duty, and those imperatives are clear and categorical. Kant would have liked Arpey.

Nussbaum argues that the world is much more complex, and she uses examples from Greek tragedy to demonstrate that a good life is not about simply correctly prioritizing one's obligations and then fulfilling them accordingly. Life is not well ordered; it is messy and complicated, so competing obligations will be the natural condition. Nussbaum argues that, perhaps counterintuitively, navigating those competing obligations is precisely what makes for a good life.

In Aeschylus's *Agamemnon*, for instance, the gods demand that Agamemnon sacrifice his daughter Iphigenia as he leads his soldiers into war in order to assure safe passage. Agamemnon is torn between competing duties to the gods, to his army, and to his daughter. If he refuses to sacrifice his daughter, many will die, including his daughter. Agamemnon agonizes: "A heavy doom is disobedience, but heavy, too, if I shall rend my own child, the adornment of my house, polluting a father's hands with streams of slaughtered maiden's blood close by the altar. Which of these is without evils?"

The centrality of struggles between conflicting duties is also evident in the Bhagavad Gita, a central text of Hinduism. This story centers on the warrior Arjuna, who struggles on the battlefield as he realizes that he is about to kill many family members fighting on the other side. Just as the Chorus counsels Agamemnon to speedy action, Krishna advises Arjuna to follow his duty to fight his family despite the conflicting obligations — or, as T. S. Eliot famously paraphrased it: "Not fare well, fare forward, voyagers." Agamemnon ultimately chooses to kill his daughter, and Arjuna goes into battle against his family. Nussbaum outlines how the tragic circumstances of these conflicting duties are the nature of our lives and resists the idea that Agamemnon or Arjuna could have consulted a hierarchy of duties to better handle the situation.

How can these seemingly outsized dramatic stories relate to our lives today? In her 1988 interview with Bill Moyers, Nussbaum analogizes between Greek tragedies and her own struggles as a working mother. Rather than fall back on facile recipes of "leaning in" or "trying to have it all," Nussbaum acknowledges the fundamental tension between these competing obligations and embraces the constant struggle surrounding them. She views that struggle as a reflection of how full and rich a life she is leading. To feel the confusion of competing obligations deeply is, to Nussbaum, the essence of the good life. In *Fragility*, she writes, "the richer my scheme of value, the more I open myself to such a possibility [of conflicting obligations]; and yet a life designed to ward off this possibility may prove to be impoverished."

You can also see some fraction of this wisdom in the story of the American Airlines bankruptcy. On November 29, 2011 (the day of the filing), the share price of American Airlines fell by 80 percent, to $0.26, and many bondholders suffered significant losses. But in fact all of 2011 had been problematic. The stock price began 2011 at $7.76 and had already dropped to $1.25 *before* the filing. As Arpey resisted filing, there were rising threats to American — efforts to renew American's old fleet were hampered as aircraft manufacturers expressed doubts over whether the airline would survive long enough to pay for the planes; partner airlines began questioning code-sharing agreements with American; rumors percolated that pilots would undertake a mass retirement to create senior pension obligations while American was still solvent; and there were questions about whether credit card companies would continue to facilitate payments for American tickets. These potential developments would signal an immediate end to American, given how disruptive their impact would be.

In fact, many claimed that Arpey's resistance to bankruptcy was putting the enterprise at much greater risk — and that he should have declared bankruptcy much earlier to allow American the best long-term chances at survival. Internally, Arpey's subordinates referred to their strategies prior to bankruptcy as "kick-the-can-down-the-road" strategies that were governed by "the art of what we thought the possible was, not what we thought was necessary."

The actual unfolding of the bankruptcy was remarkable. Smelling blood in the water, the CEO of US Airways, a considerably smaller airline, proposed a merger of equals to capitalize on American's weakness. Horton, the CEO who succeeded Arpey, rejected US Airways, given the much larger size of American. Horton immediately moved to change work rules and renegotiate with labor to reduce American's labor cost per seat mile (how much American spends for labor for every mile flown by a passenger) from $4.25 closer to where other major carriers were, at $3.50. Pensions were gutted.

Angered by these moves that were enabled by the filing, and seeking more negotiating leverage, American's unions secretly negotiated directly with the CEO of US Airways to design a merger. When the CEO of US Airways revealed this, Horton came back to the negotiating table, realizing a merger was inevitable. Operational improvements at American during 2012—which were created by lower labor costs, newer planes, renewed alliances, and a windfall from dropping oil prices—gave American more negotiating leverage with US Airways. In the merger ultimately announced, American ended up with 72 percent of the combined entity rather than the 50 percent that was originally proposed. After gaining antitrust approval, American emerged from bankruptcy on December 9, 2013. With so much bad blood between Horton and the unions, the CEO of US Airways became the new CEO of the combined entity. Horton had been in the job for slightly over two years.

Ultimately, individuals who bought American shares and bonds at the filing made five to ten times their investment in two years. Equity holders who hadn't sold quickly recouped all their losses. Labor, though, fared worse: estimates suggest that American saved more than $1 billion annually by renegotiating labor contracts.

Today, American Airlines is the world's largest airline. At the time of the bankruptcy filing, American Airlines and US Airways (including their regional airlines) together employed 115,530 people, 100,896 of whom were full-time workers. By the end of 2015, American Airlines (including regional airlines) had grown to 118,831 employees, 102,744 of whom were full-time workers. In 2015, American Airlines reported profits of more than $7 billion, a figure that the CEO claimed was the largest profit ever reported by an airline.

What to make of this tragic tale? And who's the hero? My former student Jim Dubela is a twenty-five-year veteran pilot of American Airlines. Today, Dubela reflects on Horton and Arpey in this way: "A lot has been spoken about who really was the 'good guy.' As someone who lost a huge portion of their pension, it's logical to side with Arpey. However, as a student of business, I feel Arpey should have been more pragmatic . . . . Horton saw what needed to be done and did it. You have to be decisive as a CEO and clearly communicate the battle plan. Or you lose. We did not have the unity of effort under Mr. Arpey. Actually it hurts to say this, because I respect Mr. Arpey. A lot. As for Mr. Horton, his decisiveness worked, but he never was able to regain the trust of his employees."

Did Horton do the right thing? Did Arpey? Did Agamemnon?

So, what do these tragic tales of a bankrupt patriot, a failing airline, and a father who sacrifices his daughter tell us about how to live a good life? Nussbaum suggests that the lesson is not to shirk the struggle of competing obligations but to embrace it. In her discussion of Euripides's *Hecuba* with Bill Moyers, she distills what it means to live a good life. The story of Hecuba is hardly a story to which one might think to look for inspiration. Hecuba suffers a tremendous fall in grace—losing her husband and transitioning from queen to slave—and reacts with equanimity to her fate. But when she sees that her youngest child has been killed by her friend King Polymestor, to whom Hecuba had entrusted him, all equanimity is gone. She revenges herself on her friend by stabbing him in the eyes and killing his two children. What lesson does this appallingly violent tale teach us? Here is what Nussbaum suggests:

> I think it's pretty clear that this comes about not because she's a bad person, but in a sense because she's a good person, because she has had deep friendships on which she staked her moral life. And so what this play says that is so disturbing, is that the condition of being good is such that it should always be possible for you to be morally destroyed by something that you couldn't prevent. To be a good human being is to have a kind of openness to the world, an ability to trust uncertain things beyond your own control that can lead you to be shattered in very extreme circumstances, in circumstances for which you are not yourself to blame. And I think that says something very important about the condition of the ethical life. That it is based on a trust in the uncertain, a willingness to be exposed. It's based on being more like a plant than like a jewel, something rather fragile, but whose very particular beauty is inseparable from that fragility.

We are all fragile creatures, all teetering on the edges of bankruptcy, struggling to navigate between competing obligations that arise when we care deeply about things in our lives. The mistake is to reject uncertainty—just as the philosopher Charles Sanders Peirce suggested—by not caring deeply enough to feel those competing obligations.

Returning to American Airlines, Arpey seems to have considered himself a jewel, perfectly resolute with unshakable confidence in how to navigate the future, and a Kantian, with categorical rules of duty. But Nussbaum suggests that, while such absolutism is appealing, in fact it is a cop-out to not acknowledge all the competing obligations and struggle with the hard choices they present. In that sense, Horton may well be the plant struggling with all these competing obligations, wrestling in the muck of a bankruptcy proceeding, to figure out a way through the morass for a struggling airline. Perhaps Horton is the CEO who more fittingly deserved the *New York Times* op-ed on his "moral stand."

I don't mean to recommend bankruptcy, or Horton as a role model, to you. Nor do I think Nussbaum would recommend Hecuba's path. But Nussbaum does suggest that tragedy can be a manifestation of having tried to live the good life: "I must constantly choose among competing and apparently incommensurable goods and those circumstances may force me into a position in which I cannot help being false to something or doing something wrong . . . all these I take to be not just the material of tragedy but everyday facts of lived practical reason." In that same way, bankruptcy is a process that can't be approached with a simple moral frame or set of decision rules. Instead, it is a process of navigating deeply felt competing obligations — much as a good life is.

# 8

# Why Everyone Hates Finance

In this final chapter, I'd like to take a step back from thinking through the intersections of finance with our everyday lives and ask a different kind of question. If the ideas of finance are as noble as I've made them out to be, why does the impression of finance in the world tend to be so one-dimensional and negative? To take it further, if the ideas of finance are so life-affirming, why does everyone hate it? And what do we do about it?

In a letter to his daughter in 1935, the Irish author James Joyce recommended a particular story as "the greatest story that the literature of the world knows." Joyce, no literary slouch himself, was recommending a story that is steeped in finance and many of the ideas that we've been discussing. And it's a story that illustrates why everyone hates finance.

The tale begins with a peasant, Pakhom, expressing discontent that he always has to pay fines to a nearby estate owner because some of his farm animals wander improperly onto her property. When it becomes clear that the estate owner may sell her large property, Pakhom begins to think of purchasing a fraction of her land in order to be free of this continued imposition of fees. But he knows that he can't afford a lot of any size.

Finance to the rescue! Anxious to seize the opportunity and buy a large lot of land, Pakhom borrows large amounts to finance his purchase, providing a vivid example of the power of leverage. The transaction proceeds with Pakhom paying a deposit to secure the right to purchase the land while he secures financing, just as Thales did more than two millennia ago when he pioneered the use of options to create choices and enable risk-taking. Pakhom borrows more to buy seeds and, after a successful harvest, succeeds in paying back all his creditors, making him into a "landowner, in the full sense of the word." Pakhom is "filled with joy . . . Before, when he had ridden over that land, it had seemed the same as any other. But now it was something special."

The remainder of the story is filled with even more finance. There are fire sales after the bankruptcies of other peasants, discussions of risk exposures created by crop choices, an example of risk pooling via a commune, and more purchases of land that require valuations. Indeed, the story could serve as an introductory finance textbook.

The peasant, however, does not remain happy. As a landowner, he now finds himself imposing fines on other peasants, creating conflict, and becoming antsy. Pakhom moves away to another area where there is more land available. After another artful use of leverage to purchase more land, "everything seemed wonderful. But no sooner had he settled down to his new life than he began to feel cramped even here."

Pakhom meets a merchant who tells him of a faraway land run by a tribe of Bakshirs who have abundant, fertile land and are quite gullible. Pakhom leaves his wife and sets off to their land with many items to bribe the Bakshirs into giving him plenty of land. He ingratiates himself with the Bakshirs and then settles down to negotiate a purchase with a Bakshir elder. When Pakhom asks the elder about prices for land, the elder responds, "We have a set price—a thousand rubles a day." Pakhom is confused as he expects a per-acre price. The elder explains that Pakhom can have as much land as he can circumnavigate in a day for a thousand rubles.

Pakhom is overjoyed at the prospect of that much land and readily agrees, though there is one important caveat. If he does not return to his starting point by sundown, his money is forfeited and he gets no land at all. After a restless night filled with bad dreams, he sets off with the Bakshirs to a starting point and begins walking at sunrise.

While all begins well, he quickly becomes enamored of all the fertile land he sees. He exhausts himself under the hot sun and, as the sunlight fades, runs back to the starting point. Dehydrated, breathless, and frightened, he pushes himself past his limit, reaching the starting point just as the sun is setting.

And then, he drops dead.

The last line of the tale, written by Leo Tolstoy, answers the question that is posed by its title, "How Much Land Does a Man Need?"

"Pakhom's workman picked up the spade, dug a grave for his master—six feet from head to heel, which was exactly the right length—and buried him."

Tolstoy reveals more detail earlier in the story than I did. The Devil, who visited Pakhom in his dreams, was behind it all. Early in the story, Pakhom had told his wife, "If I had plenty of land, I shouldn't fear the Devil himself!" Hearing this, the Devil responds, "I'll give you land enough; and by means of that land, I will get you into my power." The Devil plants the seeds of envy and greed in Pakhom during these early successful transactions and watches them bring Pakhom under his sway.

Many of us have, in fact, said the same thing Pakhom said in a slightly different way. It takes some form of "if only we had $X more, we could do Y." It also comes in the form of discussions of "the number"—a common discussion amongst people in finance about how much they need to accumulate so that they can pursue their true dreams.

The story of insatiable desire in Tolstoy's tale is a widely held cultural frame on finance. This is particularly true for stories that are explicitly about finance.

My favorite novel centered on finance is Theodore Dreiser's *The Financier*, published in 1912. A former journalist, Dreiser modeled his main character, Frank Algernon Cowperwood (Cowperwood's middle name is a reference to sunny, naïve Horatio Alger stories), on robber barons and got all the finance details right. The son of a prudent banker, Cowperwood searches for meaning and is dissatisfied when his mother tells him that the story of the Garden of Eden is the best source of wisdom. Instead, he becomes obsessed with a scene unfolding in a nearby pet store. A lobster is slowly eating a squid as the squid struggles to live. The squid finally dies, and, to Cowperwood, this scene captures everything—"The incident made a great impression on him. It answered in a rough way that riddle which had been annoying him so much in the past: 'How is life organized?' Things lived on each other—that was it."

As a thirteen-year-old, Cowperwood walks by an auction, buys seven cases of soap for $32 with money he doesn't have (but secures ultimately with a loan from his father), and walks to the family grocer and sells them to him for a note worth $62. He then uses that note to pay back his father. Having risked zero and made $30 in one day with leverage, he's hooked. Cowperwood's bets become larger and larger, and he wins and loses fortunes several times over, some of them illegally. He gets caught in a "short squeeze," misuses public funds, goes to jail, and then makes it all back again. Stories of his insatiable appetite for money are interwoven with stories of his sexual appetites, tales of adultery, and his acquisitiveness for art. Dreiser completed the Cowperwood story in three novels, christened, in case there was any confusion, as *The Trilogy of Desire.*

What was Dreiser trying to capture in *The Financier?* For Dreiser, post–Civil War finance reminded him of the fall of Rome. Dreiser considered Cowperwood's story, and finance more broadly, as evocative of "the strange, forceful ruthlessness of the human mind when it has freed itself from old faiths and illusions, and has not accepted any new ones. There you get mental action spurred by desire, ambition, vanity, without any of the moderating influences which we are prone to admire—sympathy, tenderness and fair play." This characterization sounds very much like the way many view finance today.

There is a fairly straight line from Cowperwood to the Gordon Gekko of *Wall Street,* the Patrick Bateman of Bret Easton Ellis's *American Psycho,* and to the Eric Packer of Don DeLillo's *Cosmopolis.* Cowperwood is actually a fully rounded character, whom it is easy to sympathize with. Gradually, the finance protagonists have become less sympathetic and realistic, and more ghoulish and robotic. But the constant across all these characters is the untrammeled desire for more. With each new portrayal, finance reaches a new low. That fall in grace reflects the ever-increasing dissatisfaction with finance in society. More than half of Americans are now convinced that Wall Street does more harm than good for the economy.

And we shouldn't be surprised by the miserable reputation of finance. As both Mark Twain and Philip Roth have noted, reality is providing even more fantastic characters than can be dreamt up by a fiction writer. The latest and most perfected version of the finance archetype is the real-life Martin Shkreli. A son of Albanian immigrants, he launched a hedge fund, was indicted for securities fraud, ran a pharmaceutical company, raised prices on a lifesaving drug by 5,000 percent, pled the Fifth Amendment when called to testify before Congress, purchased a onetime edition of a Wu-Tang Clan album for millions (and won't share it), and livestreamed his life, which included flirting with underage girls, all by the age of thirty-three. With real finance characters like this, who needs fiction?

Given how pervasive the theme of insatiable desire is in modern-day depictions of finance, it begs the question: Does this theme of insatiable desire reflect an idea grounded in finance? It is tempting to conclude that in fact finance is all about the individual pursuit of more. After all, when Gordon Gekko of *Wall Street* says "greed is good," isn't he actually framing a key insight of economics — that the pursuit of self-interest in some settings can lead to good outcomes?

In fact, the most fundamental idea of finance questions the pursuit of more. It is an idea so foundational that it is often not taught and just left unsaid — as I have done so far.

As we've seen, finance is primarily the story of risk and its omnipresence. Insurance and risk management (options and diversification) are activities we undertake to deal with risk. Costs of capital and expected returns reflect how we charge for the risks we are asked to bear. Underneath it all, however, is the notion that risk is not something that we like to bear. That's why we undertake risk management and charge people when we bear risk. If we were indifferent to risk, much of finance would collapse. Insurance and risk management would be unnecessary and we would not charge for risk at all.

Where does our distaste for risk arise from? One way to understand this is to return to the links between finance and gambling. Would you accept the following bet: "I am going to flip a fair coin. If

it's heads, I give you $1,000, and if it's tails, you give me $1,000."
Given that heads and tails are equally likely, your expected payoff
is zero.

So would you do it? Would your answer differ if it were $100,000?
$10? If you were indifferent to risk, you would happily enter into
this bet. If you loved risk, you would actually pay to be able to
take on this bet, because it would provide you with some benefit by
inducing uncertainty. And if you were risk averse, you would have
to be paid to take the bet. How would you get paid? By making the
payoff to winning larger than the cost of losing, your expected value
would be more than zero. You are getting paid to take on the bet.

There are many controversies about these kinds of thought experiments, including the question of whether the gaming industry
is an indicator that some people must love risk. But risk aversion
and the pricing of risk reflect the intuition that most of us would
need to be paid to take on that bet. And finance is largely predicated on that idea of risk aversion. Again, without it, insurance
wouldn't need to exist.

But what does that risk aversion suggest about our underlying
preferences? What does it say about us that it is more costly to lose
$1,000 than it is valuable to gain $1,000? We are trading off losing
dollars when we're poorer against winning dollars when we're richer
— and risk aversion reflects the fact that those dollars are not worth
the same amount to us. Losing a dollar when we're poorer is more
painful than gaining a dollar when we're richer. Said another way,
every incremental dollar of wealth we get is worth less and less to
us. More formally, that's called the "diminishing marginal utility of
wealth."

Again, there are caveats — in fact, much of behavioral finance
is about amending this idea to incorporate, for example, distinctive
responses to losses.

But underneath all of finance is this underlying idea: the pursuit
of more will yield less and less. And any expectation other than

that is not consistent with the ideas of finance. The game of accumulation is one that will leave one less and less satisfied as one gains more and more. To search for ever-greater satisfaction through accumulation is folly. That is the bedrock idea in finance. And it runs completely counter to how individuals in finance often act and how they are perceived.

Why, then, does this bedrock idea of finance get lost amongst practitioners, as perceived by much of the world? To me, this is the big question—and it's one that I don't have an answer to, at least not a complete one.

One overly simple answer is that everyone gets finance wrong. It is actually a noble profession where people are behaving by worthy ideals but being slandered nonetheless. The slander reflects an age-old bias—dating back to Socrates's characterization of money as barren—against activities that don't produce tangible goods. The demonization of finance has been with us forever and reflects this ignorant bias.

Another overly simple answer is that finance attracts people who are one-dimensional and who have deep, insatiable desires. The practice of finance is not bad. It just attracts a disproportionate share of bad eggs.

I think there are grains of truth to these possibilities—and I wish they were the whole story.

But I'm afraid they're not. I think that finance can breed insatiable desire in people who venture into it. I think the experiences of Pakhom and Cowperwood are ones that we are all susceptible to. Outsized successes fueled by leverage create enormous wealth at all-too-early ages—just as with Pakhom and Cowperwood. The problem then becomes how to make sense of that success. The human tendency, as well documented by psychologists, is to attribute it to oneself as opposed to the situation. People will most naturally view their successes as related to their abilities as opposed to luck. So-called attribution errors occur everywhere in life.

But the scope and magnitude of those errors is nowhere greater than in the world of finance. People in finance are continuously fed feedback by the markets on their decisions. And those decisions result in both significantly good and significantly bad outcomes. Bad outcomes are rationalized quickly as being the result of situational factors, while good outcomes are understood to be the result of one's own actions. And it's entirely feasible to continue in this pattern of self-deception for years. Indeed, one *needs* to continue in this mode to stay confident and succeed in finance. Otherwise, it is simply too humbling. My most successful friends in finance never seem to talk much about their losing investments.

The frequency and magnitude of attribution errors differentiate finance from virtually all other endeavors. In business, law, teaching, and medicine (with the exception of surgery), we are confronted only after months and years with measures of our success or failure. In finance, particularly for investors, these attributions can happen every day, in perfectly quantifiable ways, and with amounts that are far larger than any individual would usually command. Moreover, the "discipline of the market" shrouds all of finance in a meritocratic haze. Investors come to see their outcomes as reflecting their ability, given the chaotic, competitive market they work in, rather than acknowledging the dominant role of chance. Ultimately, all those attribution errors result in successful people who are susceptible to developing massively outsized egos and appetites.

Of course, not everyone in finance evolves in this way. There are plenty of humble, wonderful people in finance — and there are some people who are truly skillful in finance. But there are enough real Cowperwoods and Pakhoms to create the stereotype. Financial markets can even allow this pattern to spill over into other parts of the economy. Consider the Silicon Valley entrepreneur who comes to believe the hype of ever-escalating valuations. Financial markets, with their patina of quantitative accuracy, let loose our desire to link our outcomes with our character.

Consider this the asshole theory of finance. It's not finance that's bad. It's not the people who finance attracts who are bad. It's just that finance fuels ego and ambition in an unusually powerful way.

If that's the case, then the real question becomes: How do we protect ourselves from the particular kind of personal risk a life in finance creates? I think the best way to insure ourselves against that risk is through works—and the work—of imagination, just as Wallace Stevens suggested. Finding narratives that allow us to stay attached to what is meaningful in finance can insulate us from the feedback loops of attribution error—and perhaps help save us from becoming caricatures like those in the more common and dispiriting depictions of finance.

So, are we left with just a bunch of antiheroes in finance? Are the only stories to tell in finance cautionary tales about insatiable desires? Is it all Pakhoms, Cowperwoods, Packers, and Shkrelis? Can't even one author find his way to depicting a character who uses finance skillfully and not just for his benefit—a character who manifests, through his behavior, the wisdom of finance?

Fortunately, there is one shining example of a character who does exactly that. It's just that the author who provided it is not a he but a she, and the character is not a hero but a heroine.

*O Pioneers!*, Willa Cather's portrait of Alexandra Bergson, is the story that truly belongs in every finance textbook. Alexandra is a first-generation immigrant from Sweden living on the plains of Nebraska, responsible for a family farm and three younger brothers at the turn of the last century. She is a model financier who employs many of the lessons of finance without slipping into the traps that those antiheroes do.

Consider Alexandra: just as her brothers exhort her to sell their land at rock-bottom prices during a crisis, she proposes a plan to catapult her family from struggling farmers to independent landowners by using leverage to go in the exact opposite direction by buying more nearby land. Her brothers think she's crazy as Alexandra recommends selling all their cattle and borrowing as much as they can in order to "raise every dollar we can, and buy every acre we can." Her complex financing plan, which involves mortgaging the homestead, features debt service payments well into the future that will only work if she's right about the future of land prices.

How does Alexandra know it will work? How does she assess the risks? She samples. She and her youngest brother, Emil, take a trip to explore all the neighboring counties and "talked to the men about their crops and to the women about their poultry. She spent a whole day with one young farmer who had been away at school, and who was experimenting with a new kind of clover hay. She learned a great deal."

She discovers option value in the nearby land. Other properties hold limited risk and limited return. "Down there they have a little certainty, but up with us there is a big chance." Alexandra sees an option-like payoff with little downside and lots of upside.

Her brother Lou seeks certainty about her prediction: "But how do you *know* that land is going to go up enough to pay the mortgages?" Alexandra knows that the risk is insoluble and replies, "I *know*, that's all. When you drive over the country you can feel it coming." Experience and imagination allow her to confront the uncertainty. After her plan succeeds, her love interest, Carl, whose family left instead of taking that same risk, says, "I would never have believed it could be done. I'm disappointed in my own eye, in my imagination."

She values diversification tremendously and consults Ivar, an older man with unorthodox ideas and behavior whom everyone ridicules, because she values his unusual perspective on farming.

When confronted with the opposing views of her brother Lou, Alexandra replies, "Lou and I have different notions about feedstock, and that's a good thing. It's bad if all the members of a family think alike. They never get anywhere. Lou can learn by my mistakes and I can learn by his." The family and her life are strengthened, not diminished, by differences and by a diversity of views.

After Alexandra's success, she divides the land among the siblings, but her brothers assert that the wealth she created after that division also belongs to them. They try to bully her by looking backward and tell her, "Everything you've made has come out of the original land that us boys worked for . . . The property of the family really belongs to the men of the family, no matter about the title. If anything goes wrong, it's the men that are held responsible." Alexandra refutes this backward-looking logic that emphasizes downside risk and stands by her account of all the value she has created since that division of land. She has conviction about all she has done to create value in the land and stands up to her brothers' threats.

The elder brothers, clearly not favored by Cather, adopt bourgeois acquisitive habits but at the same time rail against finance. Lou tells Carl, Alexandra's love interest, "If you had any nerve you'd get together and march down to Wall Street and blow it up. Dynamite it, I mean." Occupy! Carl responds, "That would be a waste of powder. The same business would go on in another street." Writing in the midst of a great progressive moment, Cather doesn't paint finance as the enemy.

When Carl asks her to explain her remarkable success, Alexandra doesn't attribute it to herself. She responds, "We hadn't any of us much to do with it, Carl. The land did it. It had its little joke. It pretended to be poor because nobody knew how to work it right, and then, all at once, it worked itself. It woke up out of its sleep and stretched itself, and it was so big, so rich, that we suddenly found we were rich, just from sitting still." She understands that luck might well explain her success just as much as any notion of skill.

How does Alexandra respond to her success? While her brothers make ostentatious purchases including newfangled bathtubs, she keeps her home, the richest farm in the area, "curiously unfinished and uneven in comfort."

And what are all of Alexandra's efforts in service for? When she finally connects with Carl, she says, "I don't need money. But I have needed you for a great many years." Her most significant accomplishment is not her wealth or status, but she expresses her greatest happiness when she enables her youngest brother to go to college and law school, because "that was what she had worked for."

After her neighbor mistakenly kills Alexandra's best friend *and* her beloved brother Emil, Alexandra is crushed but is not filled with vengeance. Instead, she feels compassion for the killer. "He was in a strange country, he had no kinsmen or friends, and in a moment he had ruined his life." Alexandra vows to him, "I am never going to stop trying until I get you pardoned." Despite her tremendous emotional loss, she forgives her neighbor and attempts to get him a fresh start after his catastrophic mistake.

Finally, as Alexandra contemplates what to do with her land and the legacy of her success after she is gone, she considers gifting it to her nieces and nephews. "Suppose I do will my land to their children, what difference will that make? The land belongs to the future, Carl; that's the way it seems to me. How many of the names on the county clerk's plat will be there in fifty years? I might as well try to will the sunset over there to my brother's children. We come and go, but the land is always here. And the people who love it and understand it are the people who own it—for a little while." She understands herself to be a steward, a link in an ongoing chain, charged with taking care of resources.

Alexandra Bergson is our ultimate finance hero. She is a master risk taker who knows how to assess risks through experience and imagination and how to use leverage to change the lives of the people she loves. She values diversification and sees option value, but doesn't hesitate to make the big decision. She knows how value is created and she knows that she is ultimately only a steward for the capital she is entrusted with. She is filled with forgiveness for those around her who fail, and she knows her success is difficult to attribute to her skill. She is not addicted to risk-taking and does not develop insatiable desires. She remains invested in her deepest relationships with close friends and family. She is everything that Cowperwood, Bateman, Packer, and Shkreli are not.

If you approach the New York Public Library from East Forty-First Street (also known as Library Way), you are provided with an excellent view of that majestic structure. If you take a moment to look down at the sidewalk, you'll see ninety-six plaques sculpted by Gregg LeFevre with literary quotes from authors around the world. Willa Cather and *O Pioneers!* is represented there.

The quote comes from Alexandra's Carl, who, in a nostalgic moment, says, "There are only two or three human stories, and they go on repeating themselves as fiercely as if they had never happened before, like the larks in this country, that have been singing the same five notes over for thousands of years." In his representation of the quote, LeFevre repeats the quote again and again and again, reinforcing Cather's sentiment.

For Cather, there are ultimately only a few stories that all of our lives end up resembling. Some of them, as we've seen, are tales of hollow accumulation and insatiable desire. Some are tales of heart and hard work. It is up to us to choose amongst them wisely. I recommend Alexandra Bergson's story.

# AFTERWORD

By most measures, C. P. Snow was a true Renaissance man. Trained as a physical chemist, he was a fellow in chemistry at Christ College, Cambridge University. He served as a parliamentary secretary in the House of Lords and held various positions in the civil service. He wrote a biography of Anthony Trollope, a mystery novel, and a series of novels on academic life. He was short-listed for the Booker Prize. Not a bad life's work.

But Snow is best remembered for a short essay that came out of a lecture he delivered in 1959. In "Two Cultures," Snow railed against the division of intellectuals into two warring camps—literary intellectuals and scientists, a division that his own life disavowed. Scientists had come to feel that "the whole literature of the traditional culture doesn't seem relevant to their interests. They are, of course, dead wrong. As a result, their imaginative understanding is less than it could be. They are self-impoverished." And literary intellectuals were willfully ignorant of the natural sciences, viewing them as pedestrian disciplines lacking any real unifying vision. For Snow, a scientist's ignorance of Shakespeare was no less a crime than a literary intellectual's ignorance of the second law of thermodynamics.

For Snow, "this polarization is sheer loss to us all. To us as people, and to our society." Why did Snow consider the stakes so high? Snow believed that "at the heart of thought and creation we are letting some of our best chances go by default. The clashing point of two subjects, two disciplines, two cultures—of two galaxies, so far as that goes—ought to produce creative chances. In the history of mental activity that has been where some of the breakthroughs came." Snow goes even further than this, driven by the apocalyptic worries of the Cold War. Given the war with the Russians, the union of the two cultures must be consummated "for the sake of the intellectual life, for the sake of this country's special danger, for the sake of western society living precariously rich among poor, [and] for the sake of the poor who needn't be poor if there is intelligence in the world."

In short, "when these two senses have grown apart, then no society is going to be able to think with wisdom."

The chasm that exists between finance and the humanities today will surely not lead to the decline and fall of civilization. I can't quite muster Snow's outrage and apocalyptic vision. But the lost opportunities for wisdom seem clear to me.

In my life, I revisit that chasm most days as I cross the Charles River in the American Cambridge. On one side of the river, I teach at Harvard Business School, where wonderful students and faculty members seek to understand the world of commerce, but are sometimes impatient with lessons that aren't easily translated into actionable advice. Consequently, they doubt the value of what the other side of the river offers.

When I cross the Charles to teach at Harvard Law School, I walk through a university that can be deeply skeptical of business, business academia, and the encroachment of practical knowledge. When I launched a course at HBS for undergraduates and tried to get it into Harvard College's core curriculum, the presence of case studies that depicted business situations was initially considered inconsistent with a liberal arts education, precisely because of its practical dimensions. Wiser minds prevailed, but it gave me a sense of the nature of that chasm.

The consequences of that chasm exist beyond our universities. Finance has convulsed the economy repeatedly, and there is tremendous skepticism about its value. Indeed, it has become fashionable to deride the value of finance in intellectual circles, political campaigns, and even amongst businesspeople. All this would be fine if that skepticism weren't built largely on an edifice of ignorant conceptions of what finance actually is.

Similarly, finance, in the academy and in practice, has become more specialized, less easily understood, and more divorced from people's lives. Threatened by the skepticism in society today, financial professionals have their back against the wall and are responding with silly notions of how finance is "God's work." To be clear, there is much wrong with finance, but the current chasm only promises ill-conceived responses to fixing finance.

Forty years after Snow's lecture, E. O. Wilson framed a response. In *Consilience*, Wilson began to outline his effort at nothing less than the unity of all knowledge, taking particular aim at the problem Snow had identified. Wilson traces his project to the "Ionian Enchantment," an idea that all of the world's workings can be explained by a few laws. And to whom did Wilson attribute that idea? The original source is none other than Thales of Miletus, our innovator of option securities and derivatives. Perhaps everything is connected.

Wilson went on to explain his efforts to rectify the problem identified by Snow: "There is only one way to unite the great branches of learning and end the culture wars. It is to view the boundary between the scientific and literary cultures not as a territorial line but as a broad and mostly unexplored terrain awaiting cooperative entry from both sides. The misunderstandings arise from ignorance of the terrain, not from a fundamental difference in mentality."

What was the goal of this effort? For Wilson, this terrain held the promise "of the elegance and beauty and power of our shared ideas and, in the best spirit of philosophical pragmatism, the wisdom of our conduct."

I can hardly claim any unified theory of anything. Nor can I claim all that much wisdom. But I can issue you the invitation to cross into the terrain between finance and the humanities to develop your own wisdom. If you've made it here, you're on your way. The references and resources are designed as fuel for your further expeditions. Safe travels.

# ACKNOWLEDGMENTS

I am deeply grateful to the many individuals who underwrote this effort. Tim Sullivan and my agent, Jay Mandel, initiated me into the ways of the book publishing industry and provided steady and wise counsel throughout this process. Most importantly, Jay introduced me to my editor, Rick Wolff, who has been an incredibly thoughtful, encouraging, and understanding guide during this process. Rick provided a perfect combination of avuncular wisdom, detailed feedback, and hardheaded, deadline-oriented thinking. My deep thanks to the entire Houghton Mifflin Harcourt team, particularly Rosemary McGuinness and Adriana Cloud, whose patience I must have exhausted many times. Alexandra Kesick, Zach Markovich, and Rohan Reddy all provided excellent research assistance as I prepared the manuscript. Zoe Dabbs went above and beyond the call of duty in helping me complete the manuscript.

Long phone calls with Amanda Irwin Wilkins transformed this book and my views on reading and writing. Joshua Margolis gave me the initial impetus to explore these ideas and provided support and comments all along the way. Several long lunches with Joshua Rothman provided inspiration and opened the world of storytelling to me. My interactions with Amanda, Joshua, and Joshua were pivotal in transitioning this effort from a lecture to a book.

Many colleagues provided generous support to these efforts, but Lynn Paine, Cynthia Montgomery, Nien-He Hsieh, Jan Rivkin, Vicki Good, Al Warren, James Zeitler, Bharat Anand, David Ager,

David Garvin, Stephen Greenblatt, Tom Nicholas, Clayton Rose, Willy Shih, Lauren Cohen, Walter Friedman, Laura Linard, Scott Westfahl, Louis Menand, Kristin Mugford, Felix Oberholzer-Gee, and Erik Stafford deserve special mention. Dean Nitin Nohria has long been extremely supportive of my efforts and was particularly generous with his time and enthusiasm for this book. The Division of Research at HBS has helped me write this book in incalculable ways.

My colleagues in the Finance Unit at HBS have influenced my thinking in many ways, from seminars to teaching groups, and I am grateful to all of them. I was fortunate to be introduced to finance by a remarkable set of teachers, including Michael Edelson, Scott Mason, Dwight Crane, Andre Perold, Peter Tufano, John Campbell, Oliver Hart, and Andrei Shleifer. My academic mentors — Marty Feldstein, Michael Graetz, James R. Hines Jr., and Andrei Shleifer — have provided me with lasting models of scholarly integrity and ambition.

I've been afforded incredible opportunities to interact with many thoughtful undergraduate, MBA, JD, doctoral, and executive education students. This book is a direct result of what they have taught me about these ideas and about teaching. The students who first received this work prompted me to turn this into a book, so I'm particularly grateful to the class of 2015 Harvard MBA students (particularly Parasvil Patel) and the executive education students of General Management Program 18. Many different student populations heard early versions of this talk, and I'm very grateful for all the feedback they provided. Two former students — Lea Carpenter and Gayle Tzemach Lemmon — were particularly generous with their time for this particular effort. Helpful conversations with Laura Amelio, Dan McGinn, Karen Dillon, Rachel Sherman, Sid Shenai, Richard Tedlow, Stephen Turban, Sujoy Jaswa, Paul Cooke, Adi Ignatius, Vikram Gandhi, Alan Jones, Elyse Cheney, James Dubela, Robert Pinsky, Gretchen Rubin, Brian Misamore,

Mark Veblen, Rimjhim Dey, Cassie Wang, David Reading, Hirsh Jain, Jonathan Slifkin, Geoffrey Kristof, Evan Hahn, Christian Liu, Adrienne Propp, and Henry Cousins show up in big and small ways in this book.

Reuben Silvers, Alan Lui, and Joshua Margolis have been wonderful friends as I wavered more than once during this effort. My mother and my late father remain, as always, inspiring paragons of intellect, curiosity, hard work, and loving affection. My brother Hemen and my sister Deepa have always been there for me in countless ways, and their support means the world to me. My brother's family, my sister's family, my wife's family, and my extended family have all provided tremendous support. Vikram Desai, Haresh Desai, and Hemal Shroff were particularly encouraging.

Mia Desai, Ila Desai, and Parvati Desai (my terminal values) were understanding beyond any reasonable expectations, and their cheerful energy and endless affection fueled my efforts. Teena Shetty provided the support and encouragement that have enabled me to undertake this effort — and so much more. Her love and affection provide me with all the assurance I could ever hope for.

In writing this book, I've suppressed a number of scholarly instincts. Most importantly, I've sacrificed precise attribution and sourcing in the text at the altar of readability.

In these references, I attempt to make amends. For each chapter, I have combined a discussion of specific sources for sections of the book, recommendations for further reading, and specific citations for any direct quotes. The sources for each chapter are organized in the order in which they contributed to the chapter. The suggestions for further reading are either an effort to point interested readers to original sources or to accessible treatments of these ideas. I hope these recommendations will also serve to acknowledge the many scholars whose work I have tried to summarize.

A textbook treatment of the ideas of finance is an excellent next step for those interested in learning more. I recommend Bodie, Zvi, Alex Kane, and Alan J. Marcus. *Investments.* Boston: McGraw-Hill Irwin, 2013; and Berk, Jonathan B., and Peter M. DeMarzo. *Corporate Finance.* Boston: Pearson Addison Wesley, 2013. A more accessible treatment of these ideas for practitioners is provided in Higgins, Robert C. *Analysis for Financial Management.* 11th ed. New York: McGraw-Hill Education, 2016. Robert Shiller's *Finance and the Good Society.* Princeton, NJ: Princeton University Press, 2012, is another excellent general source. My own effort at making finance accessible is the HBX online course "Leading with Finance." MOV. Boston: President & Fellows of Harvard College, 2016.

## Author's Note

PAGE

xiii   *"My object in living"*: The Frost quote is an excerpt of the last stanza of "Two Tramps in Mud Time." From *The Poetry of Robert Frost*. Edited by Edward Connery Lathem. New York: Henry Holt and Company, 1969.

## Introduction: Finance and the Good Life

The introduction draws on de la Vega, Joseph. *Confusion de Confusiones*. Eastford, CT: Martino Fine Books, 2013; Newman, John Henry. *The Idea of a University*. Edited by Frank M. Turner. New Haven, CT: Yale University Press, 1996; Nietzsche, Friedrich Wilhelm. "Guilt, Bad Conscience and Related Matters." In *On the Genealogy of Morals: A Polemical Tract*. Leipzig: Verlag Von C.G., 1887. I briefly reference the Lucas island model, which dates back to, at least, Lucas, Robert E., Jr. "Expectations and the Neutrality of Money." *Journal of Economic Theory* 4, no. 2 (1972): 103–24.

2   *"the general principles"*: Newman, "The Idea of a University." https://sourcebooks.fordham.edu/mod/newman/newman-university.html.

5   *"I really must say"*: de la Vega, *Confusion de Confusiones*, 2.

6   *"the oldest and most"*: Nietzsche, "Guilt, Bad Conscience and Related Matters," part 8 of the second essay.

## Chapter 1: The Wheel of Fortune

The primary literary sources for this chapter are Hammett, Dashiell. *The Maltese Falcon*. New York: Alfred A. Knopf, 1930; Stevens, Wallace. *Ideas of Order*. New York: Alfred A. Knopf, 1936; and Stevens, Wallace. *The Necessary Angel: Essays on Reality and the Imagination*. New York: Knopf, 1951. I also reference Byrne, David, Brian Eno, Chris Frantz, Jerry Harrison, and Tina Weymouth, writers. "Once in a Lifetime." The Talking Heads. Brian Eno, 1980. CD.

My discussion of the Flitcraft parable draws on Marcus, Steven. "Dashiell Hammett and the Continental Op." *Partisan Review* 41 (1974): 362–77; Jones, R. Mac. "Spade's Pallor and the Flitcraft Parable in Dashiell Hammett's *The Maltese Falcon.*" *Explicator* 71, no. 4 (2013): 313–15; and Irwin, J. T. "Unless the Threat of Death Is Behind Them: Hammett's *The Maltese Falcon.*" *Literary Imagination* 2, no. 3 (2000): 341–74.

My discussion of Peirce draws on Peirce, Charles S. *Chance, Love, and Logic; Philosophical Essays.* New York: Barnes & Noble, 1968; Peirce, Charles S. *Pragmatism as a Principle and Method of Right Thinking: The 1903 Harvard Lectures on Pragmatism.* Albany: State University of New York Press, 1996; Peirce, Charles S. "Reply to the Necessitarians: Rejoinder to Dr Carus." *Monist* 3–4 (July 1893): 526–70; and Peirce, Charles S. "Grounds of Validity of the Laws of Logic." *Journal of Speculative Philosophy* 2, no. 4 (1869): 193–208. Three excellent biographical sources are Brent, Joseph. *Charles Sanders Peirce: A Life.* Bloomington: Indiana University Press, 1993; Menand, Louis. *The Metaphysical Club: A Story of Ideas in America.* New York: Farrar, Straus and Giroux, 2002; and Menand, Louis. "An American Prodigy." *New York Review of Books*, December 2, 1993. Other sources include Russell, Bertrand. *Wisdom of the West.* Garden City, NY: Doubleday, 1959; Popper, Karl R. *Objective Knowledge: An Evolutionary Approach.* Oxford: Clarendon Press, 1972; Percy, Walker. "The Fateful Rift: The San Andreas Fault in the Modern Mind." *Design for Arts in Education* 91, no. 3 (1990): 2–53; and Wible, James R. "The Economic Mind of Charles Sanders Peirce." *Contemporary Pragmatism* 5, no. 2 (December 2008): 39–67.

For the intellectual history of statistical thinking, I draw primarily on Hacking, Ian. *The Taming of Chance*. Cambridge: Cambridge University Press, 1990; Porter, Theodore M. *The Rise of Statistical Thinking: 1820–1900*. Princeton, NJ: Princeton University Press, 1986; Stigler, Stephen M. *The History of Statistics*. Cambridge, MA: Harvard University Press, 1990; Mellor, D. H., ed. *Science, Belief, and Behaviour: Essays in Honour of R. B. Braithwaite*. Cambridge: Cambridge University Press, 1980; Simon, Pierre, Marquis de Laplace. *A Philosophical Essay on Probabilities*. New York: Dover Publications, 2005; and Galton, Francis. *Natural Inheritance*. London: Macmillan, 1889.

For very accessible and shorter treatments of this intellectual history, see Devlin, Keith J. *The Unfinished Game: Pascal, Fermat, and the Seventeenth-Century Letter That Made the World Modern*. New York: Basic Books, 2008; Kaplan, Michael, and Ellen Kaplan. *Chances Are—: Adventures in Probability*. New York: Viking, 2006; and Stigler, Stephen M. *The Seven Pillars of Statistical Wisdom*. Cambridge, MA: Harvard University Press, 2016. An excellent discussion of the Monty Hall problem can be found at https://www. khanacademy.org/math/precalculus/prob-comb/dependent-events-precalc/v/monty-hall-problem.

On Buffett, see Frazzini, Andrea, David Kabiller, and Lasse H. Pedersen. *Buffett's Alpha*. NBER Working Paper no. 19681, December 16, 2013. National Bureau of Economic Research. http://www. nber.org/papers/w19681.pdf; and Ng, Serena, and Erik Holm. "Buffett's Berkshire Hathaway Buoyed by Insurance 'Float.'" *Wall Street Journal*, February 24, 2011.

Insurance is central to economics and finance, and an excellent treatment of the fundamentals can be found in many places; my preferred treatment is Eeckhoudt, Louis, Christian Gollier, and Harris Schlesinger. *Economic and Financial Decisions Under Risk*. Princeton, NJ: Princeton University Press, 2006. For an accessible history of statistics and insurance, see Bernstein, Peter L. *Against the Gods: The Remarkable Story of Risk.* New York: John Wiley & Sons, 1996.

A selection of the most important fundamental work for the ideas of adverse selection and moral hazard includes Arrow, Kenneth J. "Uncertainty and the Welfare Economics of Medical Care." *American Economic Review* 53, no. 5 (June 1963): 941–73; Pauly, Mark V. "The Economics of Moral Hazard: Comment." *American Economic Review*, part 1, 58, no. 3 (June 1968): 531–37; Arrow, Kenneth J. "The Economics of Moral Hazard: Further Comment." *American Economic Review*, part 1, 58, no. 3 (June 1968): 537–39; Akerlof, George A. "The Market for Lemons: Quality Uncertainty and the Market Mechanism." *Quarterly Journal of Economics* 84, no. 3 (August 1970): 488–500; Holmstrom, Bengt. "Moral Hazard and Observability." *Bell Journal of Economics* 10, no. 1 (Spring 1979): 74–91; and Grossman, Sanford J., and Oliver D. Hart. "An Analysis of the Principal-Agent Problem." *Econometrica* 51, no. 1 (January 1983): 7–46. Much of this work is covered very well in Laffont, Jean Jacques, and David Martimort. *The Theory of Incentives,* Princeton, NJ: Princeton University Press, 2002.

For the history of insurance, I have relied on Trenerry, Charles Farley. *The Origin and Early History of Insurance, Including the Contract of Bottomry.* Edited by Ethel Louise Gover and Agnes Stoddart Paul. London: P. S. King & Son, 1926; Hudson, N. Geoffrey, and Michael D. Harvey. *The York-Antwerp Rules: The Principles and Practice of General Average Adjustment.* 3rd ed. New York: Informal Law from Routledge, 2010; and Clark, Geoffrey Wilson. *Betting on Lives: Life Insurance in English Society and Culture, 1695–1775.* New York: Manchester University Press, 1993.

On insurance and witchcraft, see Macfarlane, Alan. *Witchcraft in Tudor and Stuart England: A Regional and Comparative Study.* New York: Harper & Row, 1970; Davies, Owen. *Witchcraft, Magic and Culture: 1736–1951.* Manchester: Manchester University Press, 1999; Knights, D., and T. Vurdubakis. "Calculations of Risk: Towards an Understanding of Insurance as a Moral and Political Technology." *Accounting, Organizations and Society* 18, no. 7–8 (1993): 729–64; and Thomas, Keith. *Religion and the Decline of Magic.* New York: Scribner, 1971.

The discussion of the IOOF draws on Emery, George Neil, and John Charles Herbert Emery. *A Young Man's Benefit: The Independent Order of Odd Fellows and Sickness Insurance in the United States and Canada, 1860–1929.* Montreal: McGill-Queen's University Press, 1999. Evidence of adverse selection in the British annuities markets is from Finkelstein, Amy, and James Poterba. "Adverse Selection in Insurance Markets: Policyholder Evidence from the U.K. Annuity Market." *Journal of Political Economy* 112, no. 1 (2004): 183–208. Evidence on the effects of pensions on household formation is from Costa, Dora L. "Displacing the Family: Union Army Pensions and Elderly Living Arrangements." *Journal of Political Economy* 105, no. 6 (1997): 1269–92. More on trends in household formation can be found in Furlong, Fred. "Household Formation Among Young Adults." *FRBSF Economic Letter,* May 23, 2016. The Frost quote is from Frost, Robert. "The Death of a Hired Man." In *North of Boston,* pp. 14–18. New York: Henry Holt & Company, 1915.

The contrast between British and French public finance draws on Weir, David R. "Tontines, Public Finance, and Revolution in France and England, 1688–1789." *Journal of Economic History* 49, no. 1 (1989): 95–124; Kaiser, Thomas, and Dale Van Kley, eds. *From Deficit to Deluge: The Origins of the French Revolution.* Palo Alto, CA: Stanford University Press, 2010; and Hardman, John. *The Life of Louis XVI.* New Haven, CT: Yale University Press, 2016.

The evolution of tontines is covered well in McKeever, Kent. "A Short History of Tontines." *Fordham Journal of Corporate & Financial Law* 15, no. 2 (2009): 490–522; Milevsky, Moshe. *King William's Tontine: Why the Retirement Annuity of the Future Should*

*Resemble Its Past.* New York: Cambridge University Press, 2015; Ransom, Roger L., and Richard Sutch. "Tontine Insurance and the Armstrong Investigation: A Case of Stifled Innovation, 1868–1905." *Journal of Economic History* 47, no. 2 (1987): 379–90; Velde, Francois R. *The Case of the Undying Debt.* Federal Reserve Bank of Chicago. November 24, 2009; and Collier, Jonathan, writer. "Raging Abe Simpson and His Grumbling Grandson in 'The Curse of the Flying Hellfish.'" Directed by Jeffrey Lynch. *The Simpsons.* Fox Network, 1996.

The discussion of Stevens draws on Stevens, Wallace. *Ideas of Order.* New York: Alfred A. Knopf, 1936; Stevens, Wallace. *The Necessary Angel: Essays on Reality and the Imagination.* New York: Knopf, 1951; Bloom, Harold. *Wallace Stevens: The Poems of Our Climate.* Ithaca, NY: Cornell University Press, 1977; Schjeldahl, Peter. "Insurance Man: The Life and Art of Wallace Stevens." *New Yorker,* May 2, 2016; Mariani, Paul L. *The Whole Harmonium: The Life of Wallace Stevens.* 1st ed. New York: Simon & Schuster, 2016; Vendler, Helen. "The Hunting of Wallace Stevens." *New York Review of Books,* November 20, 1986; Dechand, Thomas. "'Like a New Knowledge of Reality': On Stevens and Peirce." *MLN* 121, no. 5 (2006): 1107–23; and Nichols, Lewis. "Talk with Mr. Stevens." *New York Times,* October 3, 1954.

11  *"most central moment":* Marcus, "Dashiell Hammett and the Continental Op," 367.

12  *"the appurtenances of":* quotes through "them not falling" all from Hammett, "G in the Air," in *The Maltese Falcon,* chapter 7.

13  *"how did I get here?":* Byrne, Eno, Frantz, Harrison, and Weymouth of the Talking Heads, "Once in a Lifetime."

14  *"certainly the greatest":* Russell, *Wisdom of the West,* 227.
    *"one of the greatest":* Popper, *Objective Knowledge,* 207.
    *"laid the groundwork":* Percy, "The Fateful Rift," 18.

15  *"each of us is an insurance":* Peirce, "Grounds of Validity of the Laws of Logic," 207.

*"monster of desultory intellect"*: James, quoted in Peirce, *Pragmatism as a Principle and Method of Right Thinking*, 11.

*"seedy, almost sordid"*: ibid.

20  *"all events, even"*: Simon, *A Philosophical Essay on Probabilities*, 3.

*"the wonderful form"*: Galton, *Natural Inheritance*, 66.

*"it reigns with"*: ibid.

21  *"chance itself pours"*: Peirce, "Reply to the Necessitarians," 560.

23  *"The Rhodian Law"*: Hudson and Harvey, *The York-Antwerp Rules*, 16.

24  *"punishment of witches"*: Macfarlane, *Witchcraft in Tudor and Stuart England*, 109.

25  *"not only was the"*: Davies, *Witchcraft, Magic and Culture*, 294.

30  *"chance itself pours"*: Peirce, "Reply to the Necessitarians," 560.

*"all human affairs"*: Peirce, *Chance, Love, and Logic*, 72–73.

32  *"Death makes"*: ibid.

*"that famous trio"*: ibid., 75.

*"the quintessential American poet"*: Schjeldahl, "Insurance Man." http://www.newyorker.com/magazine/2016/05/02/the-thrilling-mind-of-wallace-stevens.

*"most modern philosophers"*: Stevens, quoted in Dechand, " 'Like a New Knowledge of Reality,' " 1107.

33  *"funny money man"*: Berryman, "So Long? Stevens," quoted in Vendler, "The Hunting of Wallace Stevens." https://audiopoetry.wordpress.com/2007/08/24/so-long-stevens.

*"dependence of the individual"*: Stevens, preface to *Ideas of Order*, iv.

*"one weapon against"*: Mariani, *The Whole Harmonium*, 188.

34  *"imagination is the only genius"*: Stevens, *The Necessary Angel*, 139.

*"only clue to reality"*: ibid., 137.

*"imagination is the power"*: ibid., 136.

*"power that enables"*: ibid., 153.

*"the work of the poet"*: Stevens, quoted in Dechand, "'Like a New Knowledge of Reality,'" 1117.

*"poetry and surety claims"*: Stevens, quoted in Nichols, "Talk with Mr. Stevens." http://www.nytimes.com/books/97/12/21/home /stevens-talk.html.

## Chapter 2: Risky Business

The primary literary sources used in this chapter are Austen, Jane. *Pride and Prejudice.* 1st ed. London: T. Egerton, Whitehall, 1813; Trollope, Anthony. *Phineas Finn.* Leipzig: Tauchnitz, 1869; Melville, Herman. "Bartleby, the Scrivener: A Story of Wall Street." *Putnam's Magazine* 2, no. 11 (November 1853): 546–57; and Bellow, Saul. *Seize the Day.* New York: Viking Press, 1956.

For more on the role of government securities in English literature, see "Percents and Sensibility; Personal Finance in Jane Austen's Time." *Economist*, December 24, 2005.

On the contributions of Louis Bachelier, see Bachelier, Louis. *Louis Bachelier's Theory of Speculation: The Origins of Modern Finance.* Translated and with an introduction by Mark Davis and Alison Etheridge. Princeton, NJ: Princeton University Press, 2006; Bernstein, Jeremy. "Bachelier." *American Journal of Physics* 73, no. 5 (2005): 395; Pearle, Philip, Brian Collett, Kenneth Bart, David Bilderback, Dara Newman, and Scott Samuels. "What Brown Saw and You Can Too." *American Journal of Physics* 78, no. 12 (2010): 1278; and Holt, Jim. "Motion Sickness: A Random Walk from Paris to Wall Street." *Lingua Franca*, December 1997.

The discussion of options relies on Aristotle, *Politics*. Vol. 1. Translated by H. Rackham. Cambridge, MA: Harvard University Press, 1944; de la Vega, Joseph. *Confusion de Confusiones.* Edgeton, CT: Martino Fine Books, 2013; Frock, Roger. *Changing How the World Does Business: FedEx's Incredible Journey to Success: The Inside Story.* San Francisco, CA: Berrett-Koehler, 2006; and Emerson, Ralph Waldo. "The Transcendentalist." In *Nature: Addresses and*

*Lectures.* http://www.emersoncentral.com/transcendentalist.htm. My
discussion of Bartleby draws on Agamben, Giorgio. *Potentialities.*
Palo Alto, CA: Stanford University Press, 1999.

The discussion of diversification draws on Price, Richard, writer.
"Moral Midgetry." *The Wire.* Directed by Agnieszka Holland. HBO.
November 14, 2004; McCloskey, Donald N. "English Open Fields
as Behavior Towards Risk." *Research in Economic History* 1 (Fall
1976): 124–70; Cohen, Ben. "The Stephen Curry Approach to
Youth Sports." *Wall Street Journal,* May 17, 2016; and Moggridge,
Donald. *Maynard Keynes: An Economist's Biography.* London: Rout-
ledge, 1992. Aristotle's discussion of friendships is from Aristotle.
*Nicomachean Ethics.* Translated by W. D. Ross. http://classics.mit.
edu/Aristotle/nicomachaen.8.viii.html.

A rich intellectual history, and explanation, of the original capi-
tal asset pricing model is provided in Bernstein, Peter L. *Capital
Ideas: The Improbable Origins of Modern Wall Street.* 1st ed. New
York: Free Press, 1992; Perold, André F. "The Capital Asset Pric-
ing Model." *Journal of Economic Perspectives* 18, no. 3 (2004):
3–24; Sharpe, William F. "Capital Asset Prices with and Without
Negative Holdings." Nobel Lecture, Stanford University Graduate
School of Business, Stanford, CA, December 7, 1990; and Black,
Fischer. "Beta and Return." *Journal of Portfolio Management* 20,
no. 1 (1993): 8–18.

The original works on diversification are Markowitz, Harry. "Portfolio Selection." *Journal of Finance* 7, no. 1 (March 1952): 77–91;
and Roy, Andrew D. "Safety First and the Holding of Assets." *Econometrica* 20, no. 3 (July 1952): 431–39. In addition to these papers,
other critical papers include Tobin, James. "Liquidity Preference
as Behavior Towards Risk." *Review of Economic Studies* 25, no. 2
(February 1958): 68–85; Lintner, John. "The Valuation of Risk Assets and the Selection of Risky Investments in Stock Portfolios and
Capital Budgets: A Reply." *Review of Economics and Statistics* 47
(1965): 13–37; Sharpe, William F. "Capital Asset Prices: A Theory

of Market Equilibrium Under Conditions of Risk." *Journal of Finance* 19, no. 3 (September 1964): 425–42; Treynor, J. L. "Toward a Theory of Market Value of Risky Assets." MS, 1962. Final version in *Asset Pricing and Portfolio Performance*, 15–22. Edited by Robert A. Korajczyk. London: Risk Books, 1999; and Roll, Richard. "A Critique of the Asset Pricing Theory's Tests Part I: On Past and Potential Testability of the Theory." *Journal of Financial Economics* 4, no. 2 (1977): 129–76; Merton, Robert C. "An Intertemporal Capital Asset Pricing Model." *Econometrica* 41 (September 1973): 867–87.

Two particularly good textbooks on options are McDonald, Robert L. *Derivatives Markets*. Boston: Addison-Wesley, 2006; and Hull, John, Sirimon Treepongkaruna, David Colwell, Richard Heaney, and David Pitt. *Fundamentals of Futures and Options Markets*. New York: Pearson, 2013. Critical important early papers on options include Black, Fischer, and Myron Scholes. "The Pricing of Options and Corporate Liabilities." *Journal of Political Economy* 81, no. 3 (May/June 1973): 637–54; and Merton, Robert C. "Theory of Rational Option Pricing." *Bell Journal of Economics and Management Science* 4, no. 1 (Spring 1973): 141–83. An elegant treatment of these topics is provided in Merton, Robert C. *Continuous-Time Finance*. Cambridge: B. Blackwell, 1990.

35  *"It is a truth"*: Austen, *Pride and Prejudice*, chapter 1.
36  *"You should take"*: ibid., chapter 19.
    *"If you take it"*: ibid., chapter 20.
37  *"one false step"*: ibid., chapter 46.
    *"happiness in marriage is"*: ibid., chapter 6.
    *"I am not"*: ibid., chapter 22.
39  *"Here, then, is the correct"*: Holt, "Motion Sickness." http://lingua franca.mirror.theinfo.org/9712/9712hyp.html.
40  *"A child and a man"*: Trollope, *Phineas Finn*, 154–55.
41  *"It does not seem"*: ibid., 148.
    *"I shall take the first"*: ibid., 150.

42 *"taunted with the uselessness"*: Aristotle, *Politics*, vol. 1, book I, part 11.http://www.perseus.tufts.edu/hopper/text?doc=Perseus%3Atext%3A1999.01.0058%3Abook%3D1%3Asection%3D1259a.

*"He raised a small sum"*: ibid.

*"it is easy"*: ibid.

43 *"lend me money"*: de la Vega, *Confusion de Confusiones*, 16–22.

*"will be only limited"*: ibid.

*"sails for a happy"*: ibid.

*"a happy voyage"*: ibid.

*"an anchor of"*: ibid.

45 *"What difference does"*: Frock, *Changing How the World Does Business*, 135.

47 *"I prefer not to"*: Melville, "Bartleby, the Scrivener," 550.

48 *"After a long"*: Bellow, *Seize the Day*, part IV.

*"ten such decisions"*: ibid., part I.

*"Let me out of"*: ibid.

49 *"The great knot"*: ibid., part VII.

*"ten men may"*: Trollope, *Phineas Finn*, 130.

51 *"the right method in"*: Keynes, quoted in Moggridge, *Maynard Keynes*, 585.

55 *"love each other"*: Aristotle, *Nicomachean Ethics*, book VIII. http://classics.mit.edu/Aristotle/nicomachaen.8.viii.html.

56 *"most people seem"*: ibid.

## Chapter 3: On Value

On the parable of the talents, see Blomberg, Craig. *Interpreting the Parables*. Downers Grove, IL: InterVarsity Press, 2012; Chenoweth, Ben. "Identifying the Talents: Contextual Clues for the Meaning of the Parable of the Talents." *Tyndale Bulletin* 58, no. 1 (2005): 61–72; and Carpenter, John. "The Parable of the Talents in Missionary Perspective: A Call for an Economic Spirituality." *Missiology* 25, no. 2 (1997): 165–81. I am quoting the English Standard Version of the parable of the talents found at Matthew 25:14–30. https://www.biblegateway.com/passage/?search=Matthew+25%3A14-30&version=ESV. The parable of the workers in the vineyard is at Matthew 20:1–16. https://www.biblegateway.com/passage/?search=Matthew+20%3A1-16.

The other primary sources for this chapter include Johnson, Samuel. "On the Death of Dr. Robert Levet." In *The Oxford Book of English Verse*. Oxford: Clarendon, 1901; Milton, John. "When I Consider How My Light Is Spent." In *Poems (1673)*. London: Thomas Dring, 1673; Wesley, John. "The Use of Money." In *John Wesley*. Edited by Albert Outler. Oxford: Oxford University Press, 1980; and Furnivall, F. J., ed. *The Tale of Beryn*. London: Forgotten Books, 2015.

The importance of the parable for Milton and Johnson is examined by Fussell, Paul. *Samuel Johnson and the Life of Writing*. New York: Harcourt, Brace, Jovanovich, 1971; Hackenbracht, Ryan. "Milton and the Parable of the Talents: Nationalism and the Prelacy Controversy in Revolutionary England." *Philological Quarterly* 94, no. 1 (Winter 2015): 71–93; and Hunter, William B., ed. *A Milton Encyclopedia*. Vol. 8. Lewisburg, PA: Bucknell University Press, 1978. I was introduced to the importance of the parable for Milton through this excellent online lecture: Rogers, John. "Credible Employment." Lecture, English 220 Class: Milton. Yale University, New Haven, CT. http://oyc.yale.edu/english/engl-220/lecture-3. Robert Pinsky's essay on the Levet poem provided the impetus for including it in this book: Pinsky, Robert. "Symmetrical Lines and Social Comforts." *Slate*, February 18, 2015. http://www.slate.com/articles/arts/classic_poems/2015/02/robert_pinsky_discusses_samuel_johnson_s_classic_poem_on_the_death_of_dr.html.

The underlying ideas behind valuation have various sources, but three particularly important ones, to my eye, are Fisher, Irving. *The Theory of Interest: As Determined by Impatience to Spend Income and Opportunity to Invest It.* New York: Macmillan, 1930; Dean, Joel. *Capital Budgeting: Top-Management Policy on Plant, Equipment, and Product Development.* New York: Columbia University Press, 1951; and Williams, John Burr. *The Theory of Investment Value.* Cambridge, MA: Harvard University Press, Fraser Publishing Reprint (1977).

For an accessible discussion of the practice of valuation, see McKinsey & Company, Tim Koller, Marc Goedhart, and David Wessels. *Valuation: Measuring and Managing the Value of Companies.* Hoboken, NJ: John Wiley & Sons, 1990. For a view of what practitioners actually do, see Graham, John, and Campbell Harvey. "How Do CFOs Make Capital Budgeting and Capital Structure Decisions?" *Journal of Applied Corporate Finance* 15, no. 1 (2002): 8–23. A particularly compelling set of profiles of value creation can be found in Thorndike, William N. *The Outsiders.* Boston: Harvard Business Press, 2013.

For the value of college education, see Black, Sandra, and Jason Furman. "The Economic Record of the Obama Administration: Investing in Higher Education." Council of Economic Advisers, White House, 2016. https://www.whitehouse.gov/sites/default/files/page/files/20160929_record_higher_education_cea.pdf. For an excellent interactive feature on price-rent ratios around the world and historically, see http://www.economist.com/blogs/graphicdetail/2016/08/daily-chart-20.

The discussion of efficient markets draws on an extensive literature, the development of which is well reviewed in Bernstein, Peter L. *Capital Ideas: The Improbable Origins of Modern Wall Street.* 1st ed. New York: Free Press, 1992. The original works in this stream of research are well discussed in this pioneering paper: Fama, Eugene. "Efficient Capital Markets: A Review of Theory and Empirical Work." *Journal of Finance* 25, no. 2 (May 1970): 383–417. In particular, Fama is generous with his referencing of earlier work, including that of Paul Samuelson, Bill Sharpe, Benoit Mandelbrot, Paul Cootner,

Jack Treynor, and others. This lecture is an excellent source on the ideas of efficient markets: Fama, Eugene. "A Brief History of the Efficient Market Hypothesis." Lecture, Masters of Finance. February 12, 2014. https://www.youtube.com/watch?v=NUkkRdEknjI. An alternative stream of important research on this topic was triggered by Grossman, Sanford J., and Joseph E. Stiglitz. "On the Impossibility of Informationally Efficient Markets." *American Economic Review* 70, no. 3 (June 1980): 393–408.

Efficient markets continue to be a subject of contentious debate, with particular emphasis on the profitability of various trading strategies and the ability to isolate managers with persistent skills. For those interested, a variety of views can be found at Ang, Andrew, William N. Goetzmann, and Stephen M. Schaefer. *Review of the Efficient Market Theory and Evidence.* Columbia University, April 27, 2011. https://www0.gsb.columbia.edu/faculty/aang/papers/EMH. pdf; Berk, Jonathan B. "Five Myths of Active Portfolio Management." *Journal of Portfolio Management* 31, no. 3 (2005): 27–31; and Harvey, Campbell, Yan Liu, and Heqing Zhu. ". . . and the Cross-Section of Expected Returns." *Review of Financial Studies* 29, no. 1 (January 2016): 5–68; Jones, Robert C., and Russ Wermers. "Active Management in Mostly Efficient Markets." *Financial Analysts Journal* 67, no. 6 (November/December 2011): 29–45; Jurek, Jakub W., and Erik Stafford. "The Cost of Capital for Alternative Investments." *Journal of Finance* 70, no. 5 (October 2015): 2185–226.

For an evaluation of the role of finance in growing income inequality, see Philippon, Thomas, and Ariell Reshef. "Wages and Human Capital in the U.S. Finance Industry, 1909–2006." *Quarterly Journal of Economics* 127, no. 4 (November 2012): 1551–611. For a discussion of the rise of the alternative asset industry and its effect on Wall Street, see Desai, Mihir A. "The Incentive Bubble." *Harvard Business Review* 90, no. 3 (March 2012): 123–29.

For an excellent but rigorous overview of the state of play in asset pricing generally, see Campbell, John Y. "Empirical Asset Pricing: Eugene Fama, Lars Peter Hansen, and Robert Shiller." *Scandinavian Journal of Economics* 116, no. 3 (2014): 593–634; and Cochrane, John H. *Asset Pricing*. Princeton, NJ: Princeton University Press, 2001. A slightly more accessible version of these ideas is provided in Cochrane, John H., and Christopher L. Culp. "Equilibrium Asset Pricing and Discount Factors: Overview and Implications for Derivatives Valuation and Risk Management." In *Modern Risk Management: A History*, 57–92. London: Risk Books, 2003. A particularly provocative and accessible discussion of the state of play of research in efficient markets can be found at Cochrane, John H. *Efficient Markets Today*. https://faculty.chicagobooth.edu/john. cochrane/research/papers/Cochrane_efficient_markets.doc.

> 63 *"Having, First, gained":* Wesley, "The Use of Money."
> 68 *"He that neglects":* Johnson, quoted in Fussell, *Samuel Johnson and the Life of Writing*, 100.

## Chapter 4: Becoming a Producer

The discussion of Mel Brooks's *The Producers* draws on Brooks, Mel, and Thomas Meehan. *The Producers*. Directed by Mel Brooks. By Mel Brooks. Performed by Zero Mostel, Gene Wilder, and Estelle Winwood. United States: Embassy Pictures, 1968. Film; Kashner, Sam. "The Making of *The Producers*." *Vanity Fair*, January 2004, 108–40; Tynan, Kenneth. "Frolics and Detours of a Short Hebrew Man." *New Yorker*, October 30, 1978, 46–131.

An excellent source for the corporate governance literature is Shleifer, Andrei, and Robert Vishny. "A Survey of Corporate Governance." *Journal of Finance* 52, no. 2 (June 1997): 737–83. Some of the primary work on the agency problem includes Fama, Eugene F. "Agency Problems and the Theory of the Firm." *Journal of Political Economy* 88, no. 2 (1980): 288–307; Jensen, Michael C., and William H. Meckling. "Theory of the Firm: Managerial Behavior, Agency Costs, and Ownership Structure." *Economic Analysis of the*

*Law* 3, no. 4 (1976): 162–76; Jensen, Michael C. "Agency Costs of Free Cash Flow, Corporate Finance, and Takeovers." *American Economic Review* 76, no. 2 (1986): 323–27; Jensen, Michael C. "Value Maximization, Stakeholder Theory, and the Corporate Objective Function." *Journal of Applied Corporate Finance* 14, no. 3 (Fall 2001): 8–21. For my take on recent developments in the capital markets and on corporate governance, see Desai, Mihir A. "The Incentive Bubble." *Harvard Business Review* 90, no. 3 (March 2012): 123–29. Other sources cited in chapter 1 on moral hazard are excellent sources for corporate governance issues as well.

An excellent textbook treatment of these issues is provided in Tirole, Jean. *The Theory of Corporate Finance*. Princeton, NJ: Princeton University Press, 2006. For an international perspective, see La Porta, Rafael, Florencio Lopez-De-Silanes, and Andrei Shleifer. "Corporate Ownership Around the World." *Journal of Finance* 54, no. 2 (April 1999): 471–517. An exposition of venture capital securities is provided by Gompers, Paul A., and Joshua Lerner. *The Venture Capital Cycle*. Cambridge, MA: MIT Press, 1999.

On the developments at Tootsie Roll, I draw on several journalistic accounts: Kesling, Ben. "Tootsie Roll CEO Melvin Gordon Dies at 95: Shares Rise as Investors Eye Candy Company as Potential Takeover Target." *Wall Street Journal*, January 21, 2015; Kesling, Ben. "Tootsie's Secret Empire: A CEO in His 90s Helms an Attractive Takeover Target. So What's Next? No One Really Knows." *Wall Street Journal*, August 22, 2012; and Best, Dean. "Tootsie Roll CEO Melvin Gordon Dies at 95." Just-Food Global News (Bromsgrove), January 22, 2015.

On the developments at Apple, see Desai, Mihir A., and Elizabeth A. Meyer. "Financial Policy at Apple, 2013 (A)." Harvard Business School Case 214-085, June 2014.

On the literature on stock price reactions to CEO deaths, see Johnson, Bruce W., Robert Magee, Nandu Nagarajan, and Harry

Newman. "An Analysis of the Stock Price Reaction to Sudden Executive Deaths: Implications for the Management Labor Market." *Journal of Accounting and Economics* 7 (1985): 151–74; and Quigley, Timothy J., Craig Crossland, and Robert J. Campbell. "Shareholder Perceptions of the Changing Impact of CEOs: Market Reactions to Unexpected CEO Deaths, 1950–2009." *Strategic Management Journal*, March 2016.

In exploring the parallels of the principal-agent framework to our lives, I employ Luna, Elle. *The Crossroads of Should and Must: Find and Follow Your Passion.* New York: Workman Publishing, 2015; Miller, Alice. *The Drama of the Gifted Child.* New York: Basic Books, 1996; Joyce, James. *Ulysses.* Paris: Sylvia Beach, 1922; Grosz, Stephen. *The Examined Life: How We Lose and Find Ourselves.* New York: W. W. Norton & Company, 2013; and Forster, E. M. *A Room with a View.* Edited by Malcolm Bradbury. New York: Penguin Books, 2000.

77 *"suppliers of capital get":* Shleifer and Vishny, "A Survey of Corporate Governance," 738.

90 *"My dear, I am":* Forster, *A Room with a View,* 165.

91 *"Should is how others":* Luna, *The Crossroads of Should and Must,* 51.

*"Must is who":* ibid., 31.

*"I don't know what":* Tynan, "Frolics and Detours of a Short Hebrew Man," 108.

*"in the course of":* ibid., 108–9.

92 *"What's in a name?":* Joyce, *Ulysses,* 201.

*"the greatest man":* Brooks and Meehan, *The Producers.* https://sfy.ru/?script=producers.

93 *"Max and Leo are":* Brooks, quoted in Kashner, "The Making of *The Producers,*" 113.

*"If I could go":* Tynan, "Frolics and Detours of a Short Hebrew Man," 65.

"*'You know, my'*": Brooks, quoted in Kashner, "The Making of *The Producers*," 113.

"*the loveliest and best escape*": Sidney Glazier, quoted in ibid.

"*a genius at charming*": Karen Shepard, quoted in ibid.

94  "*Karen Blixen*": Grosz, *The Examined Life*, 10.

96  "*One evening, I*": Tynan, "Frolics and Detours of a Short Hebrew Man," 131.

## Chapter 5: No Romance Without Finance

The introduction draws on one film and four songs: *Working Girl*. Directed by Mike Nichols. By Kevin Wade. Performed by Melanie Griffith, Harrison Ford, and Sigourney Weaver. United States: Twentieth Century Fox Film Corporation, 1988. Film; Grimes, Tiny, Charlie Parker, Clyde Hart, Jimmy Butts, and Harold Doc West, writers. *Romance Without Finance*. Savoy, 1976. CD; Clayton, Sam, Bill Payne, and Martin Kibbee. *Romance Without Finance*. Little Feat. Zoo/Volcano Records, 1995. CD; Charles, Ray, writer. *I Got a Woman*. Comet Records, 2004. CD; and West, Kanye. *Gold Digger*. By Kanye West, Ray Charles, and Renald Richard. Kanye West, Jon Brion, 2005. MP3.

The history of the dowry fund draws on Molho, Anthony. *Marriage Alliance in Late Medieval Florence*. Cambridge, MA: Harvard University Press, 1994; Kirshner, Julius. *Marriage, Dowry, and Citizenship in Late Medieval and Renaissance Italy*. Toronto: University of Toronto Press, 2015; and Kirshner, Julius, and Anthony Molho. "The Dowry Fund and the Marriage Market in Early Quattrocento Florence." *Journal of Modern History* 50, no. 3 (1978): 404–38.

There are many sources for the history of finance in Italy, but I was introduced to the centrality of the Medici Bank to Renaissance Florence by a particularly entertaining account: Parks, Tim. *Medici Money: Banking, Metaphysics and Art in Fifteenth Century Florence*. London: Profile Books, 2013. An excellent history is provided in de Roover, Raymond. *The Rise and Decline of the Medici Bank, 1397–1494*. London: Beard Books, 1999.

Two alternative views of the depiction of the dowry fund in *The Arnolfini Portrait* are provided by Seidel, Linda. *Jan Van Eyck's Arnolfini Portrait: Stories of an Icon.* Cambridge: Cambridge University Press, 1993; and Hall, Edwin. *The Arnolfini Betrothal: Medieval Marriage and the Enigma of Van Eyck's Double Portrait.* Berkeley: University of California Press, 1994. I was introduced to the phrase *choix du roi* by Gopnik, Adam. "Like a King." *New Yorker,* January 31, 2000, 40–51.

The account of the Rothschild marriages draws on Ferguson, Niall. *The House of Rothschild: Money's Prophets, 1798–1848.* New York: Viking, 1998; and Ferguson, Niall. *The House of Rothschild: The World's Banker, 1848–1999.* London: Penguin, 2000. The study of Thai family firms is Bunkanwanicha, Pramuan, Joseph P. H. Fan, and Yupana Wiwattanakantang. "The Value of Marriage to Family Firms." *Journal of Financial and Quantitative Analysis* 48, no. 2 (2013): 611–36.

There is now a rich literature on recent trends in assortative mating: Greenwood, Jeremy, Nezih Guner, Georgi Kocharkov, and Cezar Santos. *Marry Your Like: Assortative Mating and Income Inequality.* Working paper no. 19829. National Bureau of Economic Research, January 2014; and Eika, Lasse, Magne Mogstad, and Basit Zafar. *Educational Assortative Mating and Household Income Inequality.* Working paper no. 20271. National Bureau of Economic Research, July 2014. Journalistic summaries are provided in Bennhold, Katrin. "Equality and the End of Marrying Up." *New York Times,* June 12, 2012; Cowen, Tyler. "The Marriages of Power Couples Reinforce Income Inequality." *New York Times,* December 24, 2015; Miller, Claire Cain, and Quoctrung Bui. "Equality in Marriages Grows, and So Does Class Divide." *New York Times,* February 27, 2016.

The account of the AOL–Time Warner merger is based on Okrent, Daniel. "AOL–Time Warner Merger: Happily Ever After?" *Time,* January 24, 2000; Klein, Alec. *Stealing Time: Steve Case, Jerry Levin, and the Collapse of AOL Time Warner.* New York: Simon

& Schuster, 2003; Munk, Nina. *Fools Rush In: Steve Case, Jerry Levin, and the Unmaking of AOL Time Warner.* New York: Harper-Business, 2004; Arango, Tim. "How the AOL–Time Warner Merger Went So Wrong." *New York Times*, January 10, 2010; *Marriage from Hell: The Breakup of AOL Time Warner.* United States: CNBC, January 6, 2010. News Documentary; Barnett, Emma, and Amanda Andrews. "AOL Merger Was the Biggest Mistake in Corporate History, Believes Time Warner Chief Jeff Bewkes." *Telegraph*, September 28, 2010; and Perez-Pena, Richard. "Time Warner Board Backs AOL Spinoff." *New York Times*, May 28, 2009.

For excellent, practitioner-oriented overviews of mergers and acquisitions, see Bruner, Robert F. *Applied Mergers and Acquisitions.* Hoboken, NJ: J. Wiley, 2004; Bruner, Robert F. *Deals from Hell: M&A Lessons That Rise Above the Ashes.* Hoboken, NJ: John Wiley & Sons, 2005; and Weston, J. Fred, Mark L. Mitchell, and J. Harold Mullherin. *Takeovers, Restructuring and Corporate Governance.* Upper Saddle River, NJ: Pearson Prentice Hall, 2004.

The account of the relationship between GM and Fisher Body draws on Klein, Benjamin, Robert Crawford, and Armen Alchian. "Vertical Integration, Appropriable Rents, and the Competitive Contracting Process." *Journal of Law and Economics* 21, no. 2 (1978): 297–326; Klein, Benjamin. "Vertical Integration as Organizational Ownership: The Fisher Body–General Motors Relationship Revisited." *Journal of Law, Economics and Organization* 4, no. 1 (March/April 1998): 199–213; Klein, Benjamin. "Fisher–General Motors and the Nature of the Firm." *Journal of Law and Economics* 43, no. 1 (2000): 105–42; Freeland, Robert F. "Creating Holdup Through Vertical Integration: Fisher Body Revisited." *Journal of Law and Economics* 43, no. 1 (2000): 33–66; Coase, R. H. "The Acquisition of Fisher Body by General Motors." *Journal of Law and Economics* 43, no. 1 (2000): 15–32; and Casadesus-Masanell, Ramon, and Daniel F. Spulber. "The Fable of Fisher Body." *Journal of Law and Economics* 43, no. 1 (2000): 67–104; and

Sloan, Alfred P. *My Years with General Motors.* Garden City, NY: Doubleday, 1964.

The less romantic interpretation of the GM–Fisher Body story is a version of the work pioneered in Coase, Ronald H. "The Nature of the Firm." *Economica* 4, no. 16 (1937): 386–405. The more romantic version of the story is a version of the work summarized in Hart, Oliver D. *Firms, Contracts, and Financial Structure.* Oxford: Clarendon Press, 1995. A middle ground of sorts is provided by Williamson, Oliver E. *Markets and Hierarchies: Analysis and Antitrust Implications: A Study in the Economics of Internal Organization.* New York: Free Press, 1983.

The account of the Ford-Firestone partnership and breakup is based on Newton, James. *Uncommon Friends: Life with Thomas Edison, Henry Ford, Harvey Firestone, Alexis Carrel, and Charles Lindbergh.* New York: Mariner Books, 1989; Aeppel, Timothy, Joseph B. White, and Stephen Power. "Bridgestone's Firestone Quits Relationship of 95 Years as Supplier of Tires to Ford." *Wall Street Journal,* May 21, 2001; "Firestone Ends Ties with Ford." *Digital Journal,* May 22, 2001. http://www.digitaljournal.com/article/32720; Lampe, John T. John T. Lampe to Jacques Nasser. "The Firestone-Ford Break-up Letter." *USA Today,* May 21, 2001; and Mackinnon, Jim, and Katie Byard. "William Clay Ford's Death Brings Back Memories of Grand Akron Wedding in 1947." *Akron Beacon Journal,* March 12, 2014.

103   *"the heart of this body":* from a 1470 law that restructured the fund, quoted in Kirshner and Molho, "The Dowry Fund and the Marriage Market in Early Quattrocento Florence," 438.

*"deflowered":* observation of Franciscan observant Angelo Carletti da Chivass, quoted in ibid., 434.

*"the dowry fund":* ibid.

104   *"In addition to the benefits":* Ferguson, *The House of Rothschild: Money's Prophets, 1798–1848,* 43.

105  *"only a Rothschild":* Ferguson, *The House of Rothschild: The World's Banker, 1848–1999,* xxvi.

  *"I and the rest of the family":* Ferguson, *The House of Rothschild: Money's Prophets, 1798–1848,* 322.

108  *"Let's be clear":* Munk, *Fools Rush In,* 180.

  *"I did it as":* Klein, *Stealing Time,* 102.

  *"the Time Warner–AOL merger should":* Arango, "How the AOL–Time Warner Merger Went So Wrong." http://www.nytimes.com/2010/01/11/business/media/11merger.html.

  *"It was the biggest mistake":* Barnett and Andrews, "AOL Merger Was the Biggest Mistake in Corporate History, Believes Time Warner Chief Jeff Bewkes." http://www.telegraph.co.uk/finance/news bysector/mediatechnologyandtelecoms/media/8031227/AOL-merger-was-the-biggest-mistake-in-corporate-history-believes-Time-Warner-chief-Jeff-Bewkes.html.

110  *"we need to":* Munk, *Fools Rush In,* 264.

111  *"like different species":* in Arango, "How the AOL–Time Warner Merger Went So Wrong."

  *"Thomas Edison":* Perez-Pena, "Time Warner Board Backs AOL Spinoff." http://www.nytimes.com/2009/05/29/business/media/29 warner.html.

118  *"Business relationships, like":* Lampe to Nasser, "The Firestone-Ford Break-up Letter." http://usatoday30.usatoday.com/money/autos /2001-05-21-firestone-letter.htm.

## Chapter 6: Living the Dream

The traditions surrounding Jeremy Bentham's "auto-icon" can be found at "Auto-Icon." UCL Bentham Project. https://www.ucl. ac.uk/Bentham-Project/who/autoicon. Details of the actual meeting are at "Jeremy Bentham Makes Surprise Visit to UCL Council." UCL. July 10, 2013. https://www.ucl.ac.uk/silva/news/news-articles/0713/10072013-Jeremy-Bentham-UCL-Council-visit. The discussion of the feud draws on Smith, Adam. *The Wealth of Na-*

*tions.* New York: Bantam Classics, 2003. Bentham, Jeremy. *Defence of Usury.* London: Routledge/Thoemmes, 1992; and Hollander, Samuel. "Jeremy Bentham and Adam Smith on the Usury Laws: A 'Smithian' Reply to Bentham and a New Problem." *European Journal of the History of Economic Thought* 6, no. 4 (1999): 523–51.

The discussion of the role of debt in *The Merchant of Venice* draws on Shakespeare, William. *The Merchant of Venice.* Edited by Barbara A. Mowat and Paul Werstine. New York: Washington Square Press, 1992; Sharp, Ronald A. "Gift Exchange and the Economies of Spirit in *The Merchant of Venice.*" *Modern Philology* 83, no. 3 (February 1986): 250–65; Draper, John W. "Usury in *The Merchant of Venice.*" *Modern Philology* 33, no. 1 (August 1935): 37–47; Auden, W. H. "A Merchant in Venice." In *The Merchant of Venice (Bloom's Shakespeare Through the Ages).* New York: Bloom's Literary Criticism, 2008; Bailey, Amanda. "Shylock and the Slaves: Owing and Owning in *The Merchant of Venice.*" *Shakespeare Quarterly* 62, no. 1 (Spring 2011): 1–24; Wills, Garry. "Shylock Without Usury." *New York Review of Books,* January 18, 1990; and Berger, Harry. "Marriage and Mercifixion in *The Merchant of Venice:* The Casket Scene Revisited." *Shakespeare Quarterly* 32, no. 2 (July 1, 1981): 155–62.

The discussion of Orwell and Bellow draws on McCrum, Robert. "The Masterpiece That Killed George Orwell." *Guardian,* May 9, 2009; Massie, Alex. "Jura Days." *Spectator,* August 2, 2013; Bowker, Gordon. *George Orwell.* London: Abacus, 2004; and Bellow, Saul. *There Is Simply Too Much to Think About: Collected Nonfiction.* Edited by Benjamin Taylor. New York: Penguin Books, 2015.

The discussion of Jeff Koons draws on Croak, James. "The Closer: Memories of Jeff Koons." Hamptons Art Hub. August 11, 2014.   http://hamptonsarthub.com/2014/08/11/the-closer-memories-of-jeff-koons; Haden-Guest, Anthony. "Jeff Koons: Art or Commerce?" *Vanity Fair,* November 1991; "Jeff Koons." Interview by Klaus Ottmann. *Journal of Contemporary Art,* 1995. http://www

.jca-online.com/koons.html. "Jeff Koons." Interview by Naomi Campbell. *Interview Magazine*, December 12, 2012. http://www.interviewmagazine.com/art/jeff-koons-naomi-campbell. "Jeff Koons: Diary of a Seducer." In *Imagine . . .* BBC One, June 30, 2015; Salmon, Felix. "Jeff Koons: A Master Innovator Turning Money into Art." *Guardian*, July 3, 2014; and Schjeldahl, Peter. "Selling Points: A Jeff Koons Retrospective." *New Yorker*, July 7, 2014.

For more on the dynamics of debt choices that I describe, there are many helpful and important sources, including Bhattacharya, Sudipto. "Corporate Finance and the Legacy of Miller and Modigliani." *Journal of Economic Perspectives* 2, no. 4 (Fall 1988): 135–47; Harris, Milton, and Artur Raviv. "The Theory of Capital Structure." *Journal of Finance* 46, no. 1 (March 1991): 297–355; Hart, Oliver, and John Moore. "Default and Renegotiation: A Dynamic Model of Debt." *Quarterly Journal of Economics* 113, no. 1 (1998): 1–41; Modigliani, Franco, and Merton H. Miller. "Corporate Income Taxes and the Cost of Capital: A Correction." *American Economic Review* 53, no. 3 (June 1963): 433–43; Modigliani, Franco, and Merton H. Miller. "The Cost of Capital, Corporation Finance, and the Theory of Investment." *American Economic Review* 48, no. 3 (June 1958): 261–97; and Myers, Stewart C., and Nicholas S. Majluf. "Corporate Financing and Investment Decisions When Firms Have Information that Investors Do Not Have." *Journal of Financial Economics* 13, no. 2 (1984): 187–221.

For debt overhang, in particular, see Ishiguro, Kazuo. *The Remains of the Day*. New York: Knopf, 1989; Myers, Stewart. "Determinants of Corporate Borrowing." *Journal of Financial Economics* 5, no. 2 (1977): 147–75. For an application of these ideas to sovereign debt, see Bulow, Jeremy, and Kenneth Rogoff. "Cleaning Up Third-World Debt Without Getting Taken to the Cleaners." *Journal of Economic Perspectives* 4 (1990): 31–42.

On the importance of regret, see Roese, Neal J., and Amy Summerville. "What We Regret Most . . . and Why." *Personality and*

*Social Psychology Bulletin* 31, no. 9 (September 2005): 1273–85; and Parker-Pope, Tara. "What's Your Biggest Regret?" *New York Times* (blog), March 23, 2011. http://well.blogs.nytimes.com/2011/03 /23/whats-your-biggest-regret/?_r=0. On commitment devices, see Bryan, Gharan, Dean Karlan, and Scott Nelson. "Commitment Devices." *Annual Review of Economics* 2 (September 2010): 671–98.

On the leverage "bonus," see Jensen, Michael C. "Agency Cost of Free Cash Flow, Corporate Finance, and Takeovers." *American Economic Review* 76, no. 2 (May 1986): 323–29; Watson, Thomas J., and Peter Petre. *Father, Son & Co.: My Life at IBM and Beyond.* New York: Bantam Books, 1990; Shenk, Joshua Wolf. "What Makes Us Happy?" *Atlantic*, June 2009; Vaillant, George E. *Triumphs of Experience: The Men of the Harvard Grant Study.* Cambridge, MA: Belknap Press of Harvard University Press, 2012; and Jefferson, Thomas. Thomas Jefferson to José Corrêa da Serra. December 27, 1814. Monticello, Charlottesville, Virginia. http://founders.archives.gov/documents/Jefferson/03-08-02-0143.

121   *"prodigals and projectors"*: Smith, *The Wealth of Nations,* book II, chapter 4.

122   *"there are, in this case"*: Bentham, *Defence of Usury,* 174.
       *"it is the highest impertinence"*: ibid., 157.
       *"stamp of indiscriminate"*: ibid., 135.
       *"He lends out"*: Shakespeare, *The Merchant of Venice,* act I, scene 3.

123   *"infinite obligation that"*: Auden, "A Merchant in Venice," 147.
       *"sink hooks of gratitude"*: Berger, "Marriage and Mercifixion in *The Merchant of Venice*," 160.
       *"there are few plays"*: Auden, "A Merchant in Venice," 140.
       *"in The Merchant of Venice"*: ibid.

128   *"smothered under journalism"*: McCrum, "The Masterpiece That Killed George Orwell." https://www.theguardian.com/books/2009 /may/10/1984-george-orwell.
       *"Everyone keeps coming"*: ibid.

"*extremely ungetatable*": Massie, "Jura Days." http://blogs.specta
tor.co.uk/2013/08/jura-days-2.

"*Alone with his page*": Bellow, *There Is Simply Too Much to Think About*, 201.

"*a large team must*": ibid., 135.

129 "*signal artist*": Schjeldahl, "Selling Points." http://www.new
yorker.com/magazine/2014/07/07/selling-points.

"*the idea person*": Koons, interview by Klaus Ottmann. http://www
.jca-online.com/koons.html.

"*to constantly escalate*": Schjeldahl, "Selling Points."

"*a system to control*": Koons, interview by Naomi Campbell. http:
//www.interviewmagazine.com/art/jeff-koons-naomi-campbell.

130 "*the Koons model*": Salmon, "Jeff Koons: A Master Innovator Turning Money into Art." https://www.theguardian.com/artanddesign
/2014/jul/03/jeff-koons-master-innovator-whitney-money-art.

"*Koons does something*": ibid.

133 "*marrying amongst more*": Ishiguro, *The Remains of the Day*,
51.

"*It occurs to me*": ibid., 173.

"*As far as I'm*": ibid.

134 "*sense of triumph*": ibid., 110, 227.

"*I gave [Darlington] the*": ibid., 242.

137 "*the threat caused*": Jensen, "Agency Cost of Free Cash Flow,
Corporate Finance, and Takeovers," 323.

138 "*Don't make friends*": Watson and Petre, *Father, Son & Co.*, 67.

139 "*Vaillant's other main*": Shenk, "What Makes Us Happy?" http
://www.theatlantic.com/magazine/archive/2009/06/what-makes-
us-happy/307439.

140 "*I have ever*": Jefferson to José Corrêa da Serra. http://founders.
archives.gov/documents/Jefferson/03-08-02-0143.

141 "*You have a sense*": Koons, "Jeff Koons: Diary of a Seducer."
https://vimeo.com/121220005.

## Chapter 7: Failing Forward

The account of Robert Morris's life draws on Smith, Ryan K. *Robert Morris's Folly: The Architectural and Financial Failures of an American Founder.* New Haven, CT: Yale University Press, 2014; Rappleye, Charles. *Robert Morris: Financier of the American Revolution.* New York: Simon & Schuster, 2010; and McCraw, Thomas K. *The Founders and Finance: How Hamilton, Gallatin, and Other Immigrants Forged a New Economy.* Cambridge, MA: Belknap Press of Harvard University Press, 2012.

The early evolution of the law around bankruptcy, and Robert Morris's role in it, are best captured by Mann, Bruce H. *Republic of Debtors: Bankruptcy in the Age of American Independence.* Cambridge, MA: Harvard University Press, 2002. Another excellent account is Skeel, David A. *Debt's Dominion: A History of Bankruptcy Law in America.* Princeton, NJ: Princeton University Press, 2001. The discussion of learning from failure is from Edmondson, Amy. "Strategies for Learning from Failure." *Harvard Business Review* (April 2011 reprint): 1–9. Bessemer Venture Partners' anti-portfolio can be found at https://www.bvp.com/portfolio/anti-portfolio.

For the Lehman bankruptcy, see McCracken, Jeffrey. "Lehman's Chaotic Bankruptcy Filing Destroyed Billions in Value." *Wall Street Journal,* December 29, 2008.

The most complete accounts of the American Airlines bankruptcy can be found in Shih, Willy. "American Airlines in 2011." Harvard Business School Case 615-009, July 2014 (revised November 2015); and Lynagh, Connor, Darryl Pinkus, Andrew Ralph, and Michael Sutcliffe. "The American Airlines Bankruptcy." Turnaround Management Association. https://turnaround.org/cmaextras /Carl-Marks-Competition-American-Airlines.pdf. There are several journalistic accounts that I also have drawn on: Bailey, Jeff. "Anger Management at American Airlines." *New York Times,* July 23,

2006; Mouawad, Jad. "A Waning Star of Air Travel Struggles as a Solo Act." *New York Times,* May 19, 2010; Lindsay, D. Michael. "A C.E.O.'s Moral Stand." *New York Times,* November 30, 2011; Maxon, Terry. "Former AMR Board Member Credits Ex-CEO Gerard Arpey for Keeping Company Going." *Dallas News,* November 30, 2011; Brown, Nick. "AMR Labor Needs Shifted After Bankruptcy." Reuters, April 26, 2012; "AMR All Shook Up." *Bloomberg News,* November 30, 2011; Gandel, Stephen. "American Airlines: Bankrupt Companies Are Healthier than They Used to Be." *Time,* November 30, 2011. The employment data is from "Overview of BLS Statistics by Industry." U.S. Bureau of Labor Statistics. 2016. http://www.bls.gov/bls/industry.htm. For a current review of bankruptcy practice, see Gilson, Stuart C. *Creating Value Through Corporate Restructuring: Case Studies in Bankruptcies, Buyouts, and Breakups.* New York: Wiley, 2001.

The discussion of Greek tragedy and Martha Nussbaum draws on Eliot, T. S. *Four Quartets.* London: Faber & Faber, 1944; Euripides. *Iphigenia in Aulis.* Translated by Nicholas Rudall. Chicago: Ivan R. Dee, 1997; Euripides. *Hecuba.* Translated by Janet Lembke, and Kenneth J. Reckford. New York: Oxford University Press, 1991; and Eknath, Easwaran. *The Bhagavad Gita.* Petaluma, CA: Nilgiri Press, 1985; Nussbaum, Martha C. *The Fragility of Goodness: Luck and Ethics in Greek Tragedy and Philosophy.* Cambridge: Cambridge University Press, 1986; Knull, Katie Roth, and Jack Sameth, producers. "Martha Nussbaum." Transcript. In *Bill Moyers's World of Ideas.* PBS, November 16, 1988; and Nussbaum, Martha C. "The Costs of Tragedy: Some Limits of Cost Benefit Analysis." *Journal of Legal Studies* 29, no. 2 (June 2000): 1005–36. An excellent discussion linking the Bhagavad Gita and T. S. Eliot (and of Bentham and Smith) can be found in Sen, Amartya K. "Money and Value: On the Ethics and Economics of Finance." Bank of Italy Baffi Lecture, 1991.

143   "the American economy": Mann, *Republic of Debtors*, 262.
144   *"like a little earthquake"*: Fisher, quoted in Smith, *Robert Morris's Folly*, 207.
145   *"That Morris could"*: Mann, *Republic of Debtors*, 207.
      *"a milestone in the law"*: ibid., 229.
146   *"the inevitability of failure"*: Edmondson, "Strategies for Learning from Failure," 9.
147   *"The fundamental dilemma"*: Mann, *Republic of Debtors*, 255.
151   *"Call me old-fashioned"*: Bailey, "Anger Management at American Airlines." http://www.nytimes.com/2006/07/23/business/your money/23arpey.html.
      *"I still believe"*: Arpey, quoted in Mouawad, "A Waning Star of Air Travel Struggles as a Solo Act." http://dealbook.nytimes.com /2010/05/20/waning-star-of-the-air-struggles-as-solo-act/?_r=0.
      *"he's a very rare"*: Boren, quoted in Maxon, "Former AMR Board Member Credits Ex-CEO Gerard Arpey for Keeping Company Going." http://www.dallasnews.com/business/airlines/2011/11/30/ former-amr-board-member-credits-ex-ceo-gerard-arpey-for- keeping-company-going.
152   *"We are talking"*: American Airlines press release, quoted in "AMR All Shook Up," and Gandel, "American Airlines."
155   *"A heavy doom"*: Agamemnon, quoted in Nussbaum, "The Costs of Tragedy," 1005–36. This line is translated in various ways in different texts. I am using the version cited in footnote 7 of Nussbaum's article. An alternative version can be found at lines 215–18 of http://www.poetryintranslation.com/PITBR/Greek/Agamemnon .htm.
      *"Not fare well"*: Eliot, *Four Quartets*, 31.
156   *"the richer my"*: Nussbaum, *The Fragility of Goodness*, 7.
157   *"the art of what"*: Brown, "AMR Labor Needs Shifted After Bankruptcy." http://www.reuters.com/article/us-amr-hearing-idUS BRE83P1L220120426.

158 *"A lot has been":* James Dubela, email to author, July 15, 2016.

159 *"I think it's pretty":* Nussbaum, interview in *Bill Moyers's World of Ideas.* http://www.pbs.org/moyers/journal/archives/nussbaumwoi _flash.html.

160 *"I must constantly choose":* Nussbaum, *The Fragility of Goodness,* 5.

## Chapter 8: Why Everyone Hates Finance

The primary pieces of literature for this chapter are Tolstoy, Leo. "How Much Land Does a Man Need?" Translated by Ronald Wilks. New York: Penguin Books, 2015; Dreiser, Theodore. *The Financier.* Cleveland, OH: World Pub., 1940; Ellis, Bret Easton. *American Psycho.* New York: Vintage Books, 1991. DeLillo, Don. *Cosmopolis.* New York: Scribner, 2003; Cather, Willa. *O Pioneers!* In *Willa Cather: Novels and Stories 1905–1918.* New York: Library of America, 1999.

The Joyce quote is from Orwin, Donna Tussing. *The Cambridge Companion to Tolstoy.* Cambridge: Cambridge University Press, 2002.

For Martin Shkreli, I drew on Goldman, David. "Who Is Martin Shkreli? A Timeline." CNN Money, December 18, 2015. http://money.cnn.com/2015/12/18/news/companies/martin-shkreli/; McLean, Bethany. "Everything You Know About Martin Shkreli Is Wrong—or Is It?" *Vanity Fair,* February 2016; and Sanneh, Kelefa. "Everyone Hates Martin Shkreli. Everyone Is Missing the Point." *New Yorker,* February 5, 2016. Public opinion about finance is summarized in Owens, L. A. "The Polls—Trends: Confidence in Banks, Financial Institutions, and Wall Street, 1971–2011." *Public Opinion Quarterly* 76, no. 1 (2012): 142–62.

The Dreiser interview is from Rusch, Frederic E., and Donald Pizer, eds. *Theodore Dreiser: Interviews.* Urbana: University of Illinois Press, 2004.

The background on attribution errors can be found in Heider, Fritz. *The Psychology of Interpersonal Relations.* New York: Wiley, 1958; Larson, James R. "Evidence for a Self-Serving Bias in the

Attribution of Causality." *Journal of Personality* 45, no. 3 (1977): 430–41; and Miller, Dale T., and Michael Ross. "Self-Serving Biases in the Attribution of Causality: Fact or Fiction?" *Psychological Bulletin* 82, no. 2 (1975): 213.

I was alerted to the relevance of the work of Willa Cather by Cox, Stephen. "The Panic of '93: The Literary Response." In *Capitalism and Commerce in Imaginative Literature*. Edited by Edward Younkis. Lanham, MD: Lexington Books, 2016.

161  *"the greatest story that"*: Joyce, quoted in Orwin, *The Cambridge Companion to Tolstoy*, 209.

162  *"landowner, in"*: Tolstoy, "How Much Land Does a Man Need?," 4.
      *"filled with joy"*: ibid., 5.
      *"everything seemed wonderful"*: ibid., 8.

163  *"We have a set price"*: ibid., 13.
      *"Pakhom's workman picked"*: ibid., 21.
      *"If I had plenty"*: ibid., 2.

164  *"I'll give you land enough"*: ibid.
      *"The incident made"*: Dreiser, *The Financier*, 11.

165  *"the strange, forceful"*: Dreiser, quoted in Rusch and Pizer, *Theodore Dreiser*, 35.

171  *"raise every dollar"*: Cather, *O Pioneers!*, 171.
      *"talked to the men"*: ibid., 170.
      *"Down there they have"*: ibid.
      *"But how do you"*: ibid., 171.
      *"I know, that's"*: ibid.
      *"I would never have"*: ibid., 190.

172  *"Lou and I"*: ibid., 181.
      *"Everything you've made"*: ibid., 220.
      *"If you had any"*: ibid., 192.
      *"That would be a"*: ibid.
      *"We hadn't any"*: ibid., 194.

173  *"curiously unfinished"*: ibid., 178.

*"I don't need money"*: ibid., 287.
*"that was what"*: ibid., 220.
*"He was in a"*: ibid., 280.
*"I am never"*: ibid., 283.
*"Suppose I do"*: ibid., 289.

174   *"There are only"*: ibid., 196.

## Afterword

The debate on two cultures runs through Snow, C. P. *The Two Cultures and the Scientific Revolution.* 1st ed. New York: Cambridge University Press, 1959; Wilson, Edward O. *Consilience: The Unity of Knowledge.* New York: Vintage Books, 1999; and Gould, Stephen Jay. *The Hedgehog, the Fox, and the Magister's Pox: Mending the Gap Between Science and the Humanities.* New York: Harmony Books, 2003.

175   *"the whole literature"*: Snow, *The Two Cultures and the Scientific Revolution,* 15.
*"this polarization is"*: ibid., 12.
*"at the heart of"*: ibid., 17.

176   *"for the sake"*: ibid., 53.
*"when these two"*: ibid.

177   *"Ionian Enchantment"*: Wilson, *Consilience,* 5.
*"There is only"*: ibid., 137.
*"of the elegance"*: ibid., 71.

# ILLUSTRATION CREDITS

*page 1:* Old Stock Exchange, Amsterdam, Netherlands. Photo by Ann Ronan Pictures/Print Collector/Getty Images.

*page 11: Fortuna,* by Behaim. Eighteenth-century German engraving. Bettmann Collection/Getty Images.

*page 35:* The English writer Jane Austen (1775–1817). 1873 engraving. Photo by traveler1116/Getty Images.

*page 58: The Parable of the Talents,* by Lucas van Doetechum (c. 1530– c. 1584). From a private collection. Photo by Fine Art Images/Heritage Images/Getty Images.

*page 75:* Zero Mostel and Gene Wilder in *The Producers.* © The Al Hirschfeld Foundation. www.AlHirschfeldFoundation.org.

*page 97: The Arnolfini Portrait,* by Jan van Eyck (1395–1441). Photo by Universal History Archive/Universal Images Group/Getty Images.

*page 120:* Salanio and Salarino encounter Shylock on a street in Venice, in Act III, Scene I, of Shakespeare's *The Merchant of Venice,* circa 1596. A watercolor by Sir John Gilbert. Photo by Rischgitz/ Hulton Archive/Getty Images.

*page 125:* Chart illustrating assets and liabilities/net worth, courtesy of the author.

*page 142:* Daniel Defoe in the pillory. 1868 engraving. Photo by Duncan Walker/Getty Images.

*page 161:* Sundown at the old Dane Church attended by Willa Cather. Photo by Farrell Grehan/National Geographic/Getty Images.

adverse selection, 27–29
Aeschylus, 155
*Agamemnon* (Aeschylus), 155, 158
agency theory. *See* principal-agent
    problem
alpha, 71–73
alternative assets industry, 73–74
American Airlines, bankruptcy, 9,
    151–52, 156–60
*American Psycho* (Ellis), 165
annuities, 25–29
AOL–Time Warner merger,
    107–112
Apple, 77–78, 83
Archimedes, 124
Aristotle, 42, 55–56
*Arnolfini Portrait, The* (van Eyck),
    97 (illus.), 103
Arpey, Gerard, 151–52, 154–59
    David Boren on, 151
Art Tatum Trio, 98
asset pricing, 7–9
asshole theory of finance, 168–70
assortative mating, 106
attribution errors, 168–70
Auden, W. H., 123
Austen, Jane, 7, 35, 35 (illus.)

Bachelier, Louis, 39–40
Bancroft, Anne, 95–96

bankruptcy, 8–9
    automatic stay, 148
    "discharge" of debt, 146
    history of American law on,
        145–46
    moral questions, 150–52, 154,
        160
    opportunity for rebirth, 147
    orderly bankruptcy, 148–49
"Bartleby, the Scrivener" (Melville),
    46–48
Bellow, Saul, 48–49, 128, 137
Bentham, Jeremy, 121–23, 140
Berger, Harry, Jr., 123
Berryman, John, 33
Bessemer Venture Partners, 147
beta. *See* capital asset pricing
    model
Bewkes, Jeff, 108
Bhagavad Gita, 155
*Big Short, The* (film), 97
Book of Matthew, 60
Brooks, Mel, 8, 75, 91–96
    *Critic, The* (film), 93
    relationship with Anne
        Bancroft, 95–96
    relationship with Gene Wilder,
        94
    relationship with mother, 93
    relationship with Sid Caesar, 94

Brown, Robert, Brownian motion, 38–40
*Buck v. Bell* (1927), 21
Buffett, Warren, 22
Burroughs, John, 117
Byrne, David, 13–14

capital asset pricing model, xi, 53–56
    advertising company betas, 53–54
    gold, 54–55
    high-beta and low-beta assets, 53–56
    insurance, 54–55
    LinkedIn relationships vs. friendship vs. unconditional love, 55–56
    negative betas, 54–55
Case, Steve, 108, 109, 112
Cather, Willa, 9, 170, 172, 174
Charles, Ray, 99
Chaucer, Geoffrey, 18, 74
*choix du roi*, 104
Coase, Ronald, 115
Code of Justinian, Lex Rhodia, 23
commitments, 6, 154–56, 159–60
*Confusion de Confusiones* (de la Vega), 5, 43–44
*Consilience* (Wilson), 177
Cook, Tim, 77, 79, 80, 83
corporate finance, 7–9
corporate governance
    misaligned incentives, 80, 81
    stock-based compensation, 81
Corrêa da Serra, José, 140
*Cosmopolis* (DeLillo), 165
Costa, Dora, 30
Crews, Frederick, 94

*Crossroads of Should and Must, The* (Luna), 90–92
Curry, Stephen, 51

Davies, Owen, 25
*Dead Poets Society* (film), 17
debt overhang, 132–35
"Defence of Usury" (Bentham), 121
de la Vega, Joseph. *See* Vega, Joseph de la
DeLillo, Don, 165
diminishing marginal utility of wealth, 166
disability insurance, 24
diversification
    human capital, 50–52
    open-field agriculture, 50
    risk management, 51–53
*Double Indemnity* (film), 22, 29
Dowry Fund, 101–103
*Drama of the Gifted Child, The* (Miller), 95
Dreiser, Theodore, 9, 164–65
Dubela, Jim, 158
Dutch East India Company, 5, 43
Dylan, Bob, 62

Ecclesiastes, 51
Edison, Thomas, 117
Edmondson, Amy, 146
efficient markets hypothesis, 72–74
Einhorn, David, 83
Einstein, Albert, 38–39
Eliot, Charles William, 15
Eliot, T. S., 155
Ellis, Bret Easton, 165
Emerson, Ralph Waldo, 44
England, 26
    annuity market, 28
    Glorious Revolution, 26

England (*cont.*)
    public finance, 35–36
    Seven Years' War, 26
Enron, 80–81
eugenics, 21
Euripides, 158
*Examined Life, The* (Grosz), 94–95

failure, reaction to, 146–47
Federal Express, 44–45
Ferguson, Niall, 104–5
Fermat, Pierre de, 19
finance
    chasm with humanities, 176–77
    comparison to biology, 7
    etymological origin, 74
    greed, 167–68
    humanity of, 6
    model financier, 170–74
    reputation of, 161–66, 168
financial instruments, 43–45, 129
*Financier, The* (Dreiser), 164–65
Finkelstein, Amy, 27
Firestone, Harvey, 117
Firestone, Martha Parke, 118
Firestone Tire, 117–18
Fisher, Joshua Francis, 144
Fisher Body, 113–17
529 plans, 102
Flitcraft parable, 11–14, 34
Florence, origins of modern
    banking, xi, 8, 100, 101–2
Ford, Harrison, 97–98
Ford, Henry, 117
Ford, William Clay, Sr., 118
Ford Motor, 117–18
Forster, E. M., 8, 89–90
Fortuna, Roman Goddess, and *rota
    fortunae*, 11 (illus.), 18
*Fragility of Goodness, The*
    (Nussbaum), 154, 156

France, 25
    Linotte rente, 27
    public finance, 26–29, 35
    Revolution of 1789, fiscal crisis
        of, 25–27
Franklin, Benjamin, 22
Freud, Sigmund, 92–95
Frost, Robert, xiii, 30
futures contracts, 129

Galton, Francis, 7, 19–21
General Motors, 113–17
Glazier, Sidney, 93
Goldman Sachs, 40
Gordon, Melvin, 84
"Gotta Serve Somebody" (Dylan),
    62
Gow, Andrew, 128
*Graduate, The* (film), 95
Grant Study of Harvard
    undergraduates, 138–39
Greenlight Capital, 83
Griffin, Merv, 18
Griffith, Melanie, 97–98
Grimes, Tiny, 98–99
Grosz, Stephen, 94
*Groundhog Day* (film), 22

Hacking, Ian, 17
*Hamilton* (musical), 75, 143
Hamilton, Alexander, 142–43
Hammett, Dashiell, 7, 11–14, 16,
    34
Hart, Oliver, 115
Hartford Accident and Indemnity
    Company, 33
Harvard Business School, 2, 176
    attendance policy and
        commitment, 153–54
    "last lecture": The Wisdom of
        Finance, 2–4

*Hecuba* (Euripides), 158–59
hedge funds, 22, 73, 81
Heisenberg uncertainty principle,
    40
Holmes, Oliver Wendell, 21
Holmström, Bengt, 115
Holt, Jim, 39
Horton, Tom, 151–52, 157–58, 160
"How Much Land Does a Man
    Need?" (Tolstoy), 162–64
Huston, John, 11

"I Got a Woman" (Charles), 99
Icahn, Carl, 84
*Ideas of Order* (Stevens), 33
incomplete contracts, 115–17
insurance and insurance
    companies, 7, 14–16, 166.
    *See also* annuities
aggregate outcomes, 21, 25,
    30–31
chance and randomness, 21–22
contract of bottomry, 23
deductibles, 29
disorder and chaos, 34
families and, 29–30
history of, 22–24
Independent Order of Odd
    Fellows, 24
mandate, 29
modern image of, 22
risk aversion and diminishing
    marginal utility of wealth,
    166–67
Roman burial societies, 23–24
"rules of jettison" or law of
    general average, 23
witchcraft and, 24–25
investors
CEO deaths, reaction to, 78, 80
diffuse ownership, 78, 81, 82

informational asymmetry, 79
pension and endowment funds,
    82
Ishiguro, Kazuo, 9, 133

James, William 15
Jefferson, Thomas, 139–40
Jensen, Michael, 137–38
Johnson, Samuel, 7, 59, 74
    "On the Death of Dr. Robert
    Levet," 68–69
*Journal of Law and Economics*, 115
Joyce, James, 91–92, 161
Jura, 128

Kafka, Franz, 47
Kant, Immanuel, 154–55
Keynes, John Maynard, 51
Kirshner, Julius, 103
Klein, Francesca, 101
Koestler, Arthur, 128
Koons, Jeff, xi, 8, 127, 129–31,
    137, 140–41
    *Celebration* series, 140
    effective use of leverage, 140–41
    *Play-Doh*, 129
    *Popeye*, 141

Laplace, Pierre-Simon, 20
LeFevre, Gregg, 174
Lehman Brothers insolvency,
    147–48
*Let's Make a Deal* (TV show), 16
leverage, 8
    benefits and drawbacks, 123–26,
    135
    Bentham and Smith conflict on,
    121–22
    "bonus" of leverage, 137–38
    debt overhang, 132–35
    definition, 123–24

leverage (*cont.*)
   leveraged buyout, 127
   risk and return, 125–27
   static trade-off theory, 126
leverage, personal and artistic,
      127–30
   commitment device, 131, 137–40
   connection to debt overhang,
      132–35
   degree of leverage, 130–32
   effective use, 138–39
   failure and rebirth, 149–50
   life-cycle hypothesis, 135–36
   role of reputation, 139–40
Levin, Jerry, 108–11
Levine, Joseph, 93–94
Little Feat, 99
Luna, Elle, 90–91

Macfarlane, Alan, 24
*Mad Max* (film), 54–55
*Maltese Falcon, The* (Hammett), 11
Mann, Bruce, 143, 145, 147
Mao Zedong, 67
Marcus, Steven, 11
Mars, Kenneth, 93
Mariani, Paul, 33
McNamee, Roger, 108
Melville, Herman, 46–49
*Merchant of Venice, The*
      (Shakespeare), 8, 120
      (illus.), 122–23
mergers, 8
   AOL–Time Warner merger
      mistakes, 109–12
   asymmetric mergers (bolt-on
      acquisitions), 111
   Ford Motor and Firestone Tire
      partnership, 117–18
   General Motors and Fisher Body
      merger, 113–17

Hewlett Packard and Autonomy
      acquisition, 109
   integration planning, 110
   mergers of equals, 111
   serial acquirers, 111
   synergies, 109–10
Merton, Robert, 40
Miller, Alice, 95
Milton, John, xi, 7, 59, 68–69, 74
   "When I Consider How My Light
      Is Spent," 70–71
*Miracle Worker, The* (film, play),
      96
Miranda, Lin-Manuel, 75
Molho, Anthony, 103
Monte Dei Paschi di Siena, 100
*Monte delle doti*, 101–4
"Monty Hall" problem, 16
moral hazard, 28–30
Morris, Robert, 142
   career, 143–45
   financier of the revolution, 143
   relative to J. P. Morgan and John
      D. Rockefeller, 143
Mostel, Zero, 75
Moyers, Bill, 155, 158

Newman, John Henry, 2
Newton, Isaac, 40
Nichols, Mike, 97
*Nicomachean Ethics* (Aristotle), 55
Nietzsche, Friedrich, 6
*1984* (Orwell), 127
normal distribution, 19–20, 39
Nussbaum, Martha, 154–56,
      158–60

*O Pioneers!* (Cather), 170–74
"Once in a Lifetime" (Talking
      Heads), 13–14
*Oxford English Dictionary*, 68

options, 40–49
  personal setting, 45–49
  risk management, 42–44
  risk-taking, 44–45
Orwell, George, 127–28, 130

pachinko, 19–20
Paltrow, Gwyneth, 13
parable of the talents, 7, 58–60, 62
  interpretation of, 67–72, 74
  *Parable of the Talents, The*
    (van Doetechum), 58 (illus.),
    59
  "Use of Money, The" (Wesley), 63
parable of workers in vineyard,
  70–71
Parker, Charlie, 98
Parsons, Dick, 110–12
Pascal, Blaise, 19, 24
  Pascal's Wager, 24
Peirce, Charles Sanders, xi, 7, 14,
  159
  chance and randomness, 21,
    30–32, 34
  Harvard lectures on probabilities
    and insurance, 15–16, 25
  randomized trials, 30–31
Percy, Walker, 14
*Phineas Finn* (Trollope), xi, 38,
  40–41, 49
Plowman, Dorothy, 128
Popper, Karl, 14
Poterba, James, 27–28
pragmatism, 14–15, 31
*Pride and Prejudice* (Austen), xi,
  35–37, 56–57
Priestley, Joseph, 121
principal-agent problem, 8, 77–85
  agency theory, 81, 83
  alternative solutions, 81–85
  daisy chain of problems, 83–85

MBA leadership case,
  86–87
  personal/family application,
    87–89, 95–96
private equity, 73, 82, 127
probabilities. *See also* insurance
    and insurance companies
  fatalism, 19–20
  martingale strategy, 18, 31
  Pascal's Wager, 24
  probabilistic intuition, 16–17, 19
  problem of points, 17
*Producers, The* (film), 8, 75 (illus.),
  75–76, 91–93

quincunx and normal distribution,
  19–20, 39, 72

Reiner, Carl, 93
*Remains of the Day, The*
    (Ishiguro), xi, 9, 133–35
risk and risk management, 7,
  166–67
  diversification, 49–52
  diversification of personal
    relationships, 52–53
  marriage and death of optionality,
    46
  "open field" agricultural system,
    49–50
  options, 41–46
  options and diversification, 38,
    40, 41–43
  romance and finance. *See also*
    mergers
  continuum of commitment,
    112–13
  Ford, William Clay, Sr., and
    Martha Parke Firestone,
    118–19
  marriages as mergers, 104–6

romance and finance (*cont.*)
    in modern America, 105–6
    in Renaissance Florence,
        100–101
    in Thailand, 105
"Romance Without Finance"
    (Grimes, Little Feat), 98–99
*Room with a View, A* (Forster), 8,
    89–91
Rothschild family, 8, 100, 104–5
    Hannah Mayer and marriage, 105
    James and marriage to Nicky
        Hilton, 106
    Mayer Amschel and marriage,
        104
Royal Coat of Arms of the United
    Kingdom, 40
Russell, Bertrand, 14

Salmon, Felix, 130
Schjeldahl, Peter, 32, 129
Scholes, Myron, 40
*Seize the Day* (Bellow), 48–49
Shakespeare, William, 8, 122
Sheldon, Sidney, 96
Shenk, Joshua Wolf, 139
Shkreli, Martin, 166
Shleifer, Andrei, 77
*Simpsons, The* (TV show), 28
*Sliding Doors* (film), 13
Sloan, Alfred P., 117
Smith, Adam, 121–22
Smith, Fred, 44–45
Snow, C. P., 175–77
Socrates, 168
Stevens, Wallace, xi, 7, 32–34, 170
    disorder and chaos, 33–34
    insurance executive, 32–33

talent, etymology of, 58–59, 74
"Tale of Beryn" (Chaucer), 74

Talmud, 52
Thales of Miletus, 7, 42–43, 162,
    177
Tiger Moms, 95
Tolstoy, Leo, 9, 162–64
tontines, 28–30
    Tontine Coffee House, 28
Tootsie Roll Industries, 78–80,
    83–85
transaction cost approach to
    mergers, 115
*Trilogy of Desire* (Dreiser), 165
Trollope, Anthony, 7, 38, 175
Trump, Donald, 127, 152
Turner, Ted, 108
"Two Cultures" (Snow), 175
"Two Tramps in Mud Time" (Frost),
    xiii
Tynan, Kenneth, 96

*Ulysses* (Joyce), 91–92

Vaillant, George, 138–39
value creation and valuation, 7,
    59
    accounting vs. finance, 64
    alpha generation or getting paid
        for beta, 71–73
    destruction of value, 63
    discounted cash flows, 65
    measuring value creation,
        64–67
    stewardship and, 61–63, 74
    terminal values, 66–67
    weighted average cost of capital,
        65
value of education, 65–66
value of housing, 66
van Doetechum, Lucas, 58 (illus.),
    59
van Eyck, Jan, 97 (illus.), 103

Vega, Joseph de la, 5–6, 43–44
venture capital, 73, 82
Vishny, Robert, 77

*Wall Street* (film), 165, 166
Warhol, Andy, 129
Washington, George, 142–43, 145
Watson, Thomas, 138
*Wealth of Nations, The* (Smith),
    121
Weaver, Sigourney, 97–98
Wells Fargo, 80
Wesley, John, 63

West, Kanye, 99
*Wheel of Fortune* (TV show),
    17–18
White, Vanna, 18
Whitney Museum of Modern Art,
    140
Wilder, Gene, 94
Wilson, E. O., 177
*Wire, The* (TV show), 50
*Wolf of Wall Street, The* (film), 97
*Working Girl* (film), xi, 97–98
WorldCom, 80
Wynn, Steve, 141